PRAISE FOR *DEMOCRACY IN ONE BOOK OR LESS*

"Wry, quickly readable, yet informed and edgy . . . whimsy and pop culture, enlisted toward the end of knowledge."
—*The Atlantic*

"Brings Dave Barry–style humor to an illuminating book on what is wrong with American democracy—and how to put it right."
—*The Washington Post*

"It's rare to feel good about the way things are going, but Litt's book will get you there."
—*Elle*

"Litt's book laces his signature humor into his exploration of American Democracy and how it has transformed over the years."
—*Time*, "**45 New Books You Need to Read This Summer**"

"Casts a welcome, cleansing beam of light on a subject that has become increasingly murky and frustratingly confusing."
—*Booklist* (starred review)

"[A] snappy and well-informed dissection of the current state of American democracy . . . Both optimistic and clear-eyed, this quip-filled call to action will resonate strongly with young progressives."
—*Publishers Weekly*

The author's brother-in-law

The author

It's Only Drowning

*A True Story of Learning
to Surf and the Search
for Common Ground*

David Litt

Gallery Books

New York Amsterdam/Antwerp London Toronto
Sydney/Melbourne New Delhi

G

Gallery Books
An Imprint of Simon & Schuster, LLC
1230 Avenue of the Americas
New York, NY 10020

First Gallery Books hardcover edition June 2025

GALLERY BOOKS and colophon are registered trademarks of Simon & Schuster, LLC

Simon & Schuster strongly believes in freedom of expression and stands against censorship in all its forms. For more information, visit BooksBelong.com.

For information about special discounts for bulk purchases, please contact Simon & Schuster Special Sales at 1-866-506-1949 or business@simonandschuster.com.

The Simon & Schuster Speakers Bureau can bring authors to your live event. For more information or to book an event, contact the Simon & Schuster Speakers Bureau at 1-866-248-3049 or visit our website at www.simonspeakers.com.

Interior design by Jason Snyder

Manufactured in the United States of America

10 9 8 7 6 5 4 3 2 1

Library of Congress Control Number: 2024037109

ISBN 978-1-6680-3535-1
ISBN 978-1-6680-3537-5 (ebook)

To Jacqui, who amazes me more each year with her toughness, intelligence, sense of adventure, and taste in husbands

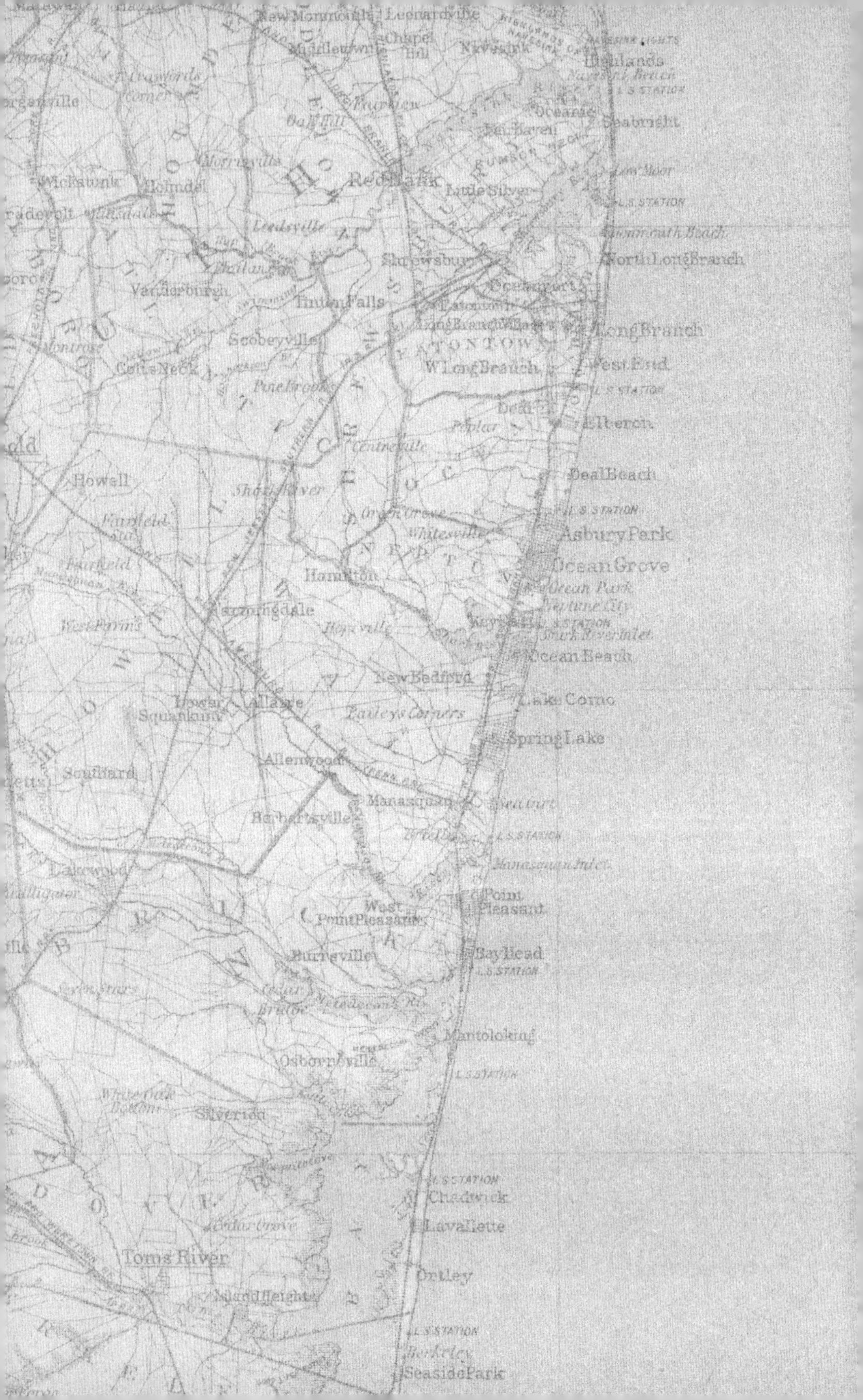
New Monmouth
Leonardville
Chapel Hill
Middletown
Navesink
Highlands
Navesink Beach
L.S. STATION
Seabright
Fair Haven
Oceanic
Red Bank
Little Silver
Holmdel
Wickatunk
Morrisville
Leedsville
Shrewsbury
Monmouth Beach
North Long Branch
Vanderburgh
Tinton Falls
Long Branch
Scobeyville
Colts Neck
W. Long Beach
West End
Deal
Elberon
Poplar
Centreville
Deal Beach
Howell
Shark River
Whitesville
Asbury Park
Ocean Grove
Ocean Park
Neptune City
Hamilton
Farmingdale
Hopeville
Shark River Inlet
Ocean Beach
New Bedford
Lake Como
Allaire
Squankum
Bayley's Corners
Spring Lake
Allenwood
Manasquan
Scullard
Herbertsville
Manasquan Inlet
Lakewood
Point Pleasant
West Point Pleasant
Burrsville
Bay Head
Mantoloking
Osbornville
Silverton
Chadwick
Lavallette
Cedar Grove
Toms River
Ortley
Island Heights
Berkeley
Seaside Park

CONTENTS

CHAPTER ONE: *Surfing Is for Lunatics*   1

CHAPTER TWO: *Woochee*   13

CHAPTER THREE: *Pain and Sorrow Before They Quit*   27

CHAPTER FOUR: *Free Speech!*   45

CHAPTER FIVE: *It's Only Drowning*   57

CHAPTER SIX: *The New Jersey Rubicon*   75

CHAPTER SEVEN: *If You Ever Get into Fights*   93

CHAPTER EIGHT: *I Just Don't Want to Be the Guy Who Dies of Hypothermia in His Parking Space*   113

CHAPTER NINE: *Water Wizards*   131

CHAPTER TEN: *Shrimply Irresistible*   143

CHAPTER ELEVEN: *Beanbag*   161

CHAPTER TWELVE: *The Honda Odyssey*   175

CHAPTER THIRTEEN: *Try That in a Small Town*   195

CHAPTER FOURTEEN: *Sparring with Hurricanes*   211

CHAPTER FIFTEEN: *Le Snake*   231

CHAPTER SIXTEEN: *Nothing's Worse Than Knowing Too Much*   255

CHAPTER SEVENTEEN: *Between Us*   271

ACKNOWLEDGMENTS   287

It's Only Drowning

CHAPTER ONE

Surfing Is for Lunatics

MATTHEW KAPPLER IS MY BROTHER-IN-LAW, and we're very different, and one of the biggest differences between us is that if I lived like him I would die.

Matt owns two motorcycles. The first is a Kawasaki for racing, the second a Harley for roaring down the Garden State Parkway at speeds he once described as "only" a hundred miles per hour. He's an electrician, and a good one, in part because of how seriously he takes his work, and in part because of how casually he takes the prospect of violent shocks. Matt once threw out his back training to be a mixed martial arts fighter. I once threw out my back lifting a bag of cat litter.

We met in the summer of 2012. I'd been dating his older sister, Jacqui, for about a year, and she and I had driven up from Washington, DC, to visit her parents in New Jersey. At the time I was a twenty-five-year-old speechwriter for Barack Obama, with sensibly parted hair, an ergonomic keyboard, and a strong preference for the half-Windsor tie knot over the more conventional four-in-hand. Matt was living at home. He was twenty-two years old, on the tail end of a rebel-without-a-cause phase that had begun, as far as I could tell, at birth.

Because I was busy trying to impress Jacqui's parents during that initial visit, I didn't pay much attention to her brother. Matt first appears in my memory not as a person but as a muscle shirt–wearing specter, floating silently to the kitchen to blend a protein shake before disappearing into the garage to jam on his electric guitar. But more trips followed; my future in-laws lived minutes from the Jersey Shore, so Jacqui and I started coming up for beach weekends each summer.

Matt and I thus got to know each other a little better, and the better we got to know each other, the clearer it became that we had absolutely nothing in common. My professional life revolved around politics; he had never registered to vote. Matt played in a locally famous ska band; I played in a co-ed recreational Ultimate Frisbee league. My idea of a perfect meal was a bowl of homemade knife-cut noodles, studded with bits of pork and drenched in chili oil, from a hole-in-the-wall restaurant near the university where I studied on a summer fellowship that sent Ivy League undergraduates to Beijing. His was chicken tenders.

I didn't dislike Matt. I found him quite interesting, in the way all men who need two computer monitors for work find all men who need a pickup truck for work quite interesting. But we never became anything like friends.

The closest we got to bonding were the times when, in a spirit of anthropological curiosity, I asked him about small details of his life. The tattoo covering his left shoulder, for instance. It depicted a giant robotic claw reaching across his collarbone, slicing his flesh with metal talons, and ripping back his skin to reveal a bloody mess of muscle and machine parts.

"So, Matt," I once asked, in my best NPR voice, "what made you decide to get that tattoo?"

He thought for a second, then shrugged contentedly.

"I dunno."

I tried conjuring a follow-up and couldn't. I've been told that one of my first words was *ambivalent*. To permanently brand oneself with any image, of any size, struck me as an inconceivably risky invitation to regret. And to pick an image that was huge, gruesome, and highly visible, for basically no reason? I was left gasping in confusion like a goldfish plucked from its bowl.

Which is all to say that when, five years after we met, Matt bought a beat-up used surfboard, I did not think, *At last, a healthful pastime that might bring me closer to my future brother-in-law!* I thought, *Surfing is for lunatics.*

Nothing in the years that followed changed my view. On one occasion, Matt arrived at a family gathering wild-eyed, his light-brown hair not so much tousled as beaten. He'd woken at dawn, he explained as though this were normal, and spent his morning being pummeled against rocks and slammed into the seabed. I would have found this alarming at any time of year, even summer, when the Jersey Shore is packed with beachgoers. But this was Christmas Day.

"Aren't you worried about, you know, drowning?"

"Neh," he replied, in his slightly pinched Jersey accent. I waited for him to elaborate. He didn't.

"Okay. What about freezing to death?"

"The best waves are in winter," he said, in what I could not help but notice was not an answer to my question. "You should try it."

I declined his offer, not so much verbally as through my very existence. It was true that once, on a family trip to Mexico, I'd taken something described as a "surf lesson," during which I knelt on a plank for an hour while a teenager rolled his eyes and pushed me toward a beach. But surfing—really surfing—was clearly different. Along with absurd levels of fitness and dexterity, it required a near-total lack of common sense.

It also seemed like a waste of time. My adult life had been defined by a line from Barack Obama's first presidential campaign: "In the face of impossible odds, people who love this country can change it." Even after leaving the White House, I'd remained a proudly earnest workaholic. I filled my days, along with most nights and weekends, with productivity. Writing books and TV pilots. Working on speeches for private clients. Volunteering for campaigns. While each project was different, when you zoomed out far enough the goal was always the same: to change the world.

Matt seemed to surf for no higher purpose whatsoever. He did it simply because he enjoyed it. That made no sense to me.

In 2018, Jacqui and I got married in Asbury Park, a Jersey Shore town best known as the spot where Bruce Springsteen got his start. The following year we bought a small vacation house there. It was listed, optimistically, as a "Victorian cottage," and located a half mile from the beach. Sometimes while strolling the boardwalk, I'd see a gaggle of wetsuit-clad figures bobbing like apples in the sea. Every so often, one would turn, stand, and cruise toward shore.

It was noteworthy: these individuals were not my brother-in-law, yet they surfed. Still, nothing could change what was, in my opinion, the most relevant fact about Matt's favorite hobby. If it was for people like him, it wasn't for people like me.

Besides, I was an adult now, with a wife and a mortgage and two cats and intermittent back pain and a determination to make the most of my limited time on earth. To the extent I looked toward the ocean and thought, *I wish I'd tried it*, surfing was just another scribble on the map of roads not taken that people in their early thirties can't help but draw. I should have seen Tom Petty in concert. I should have made out with Leah Franklin at that party freshman year. I should have learned to surf. Who cares?

The answer, as it turned out, was me. Enormously.

And all it took to realize it was the worst year of my life.

~~~~~~~~~~

When I was four years old, I was terrified—absolutely terrified—that Saddam Hussein would emerge from my toilet and strangle me.

This was during the first Gulf War, so my fear was rational, assuming you knew, as I did, the rules governing Saddam's behavior. First, he lurked in the pipes. Second, he could travel instantly between rooms and even buildings, so long as he remained submerged. Third, while Saddam could overpower any child whose bathroom he invaded, he couldn't escape the plumbing on his own. Only the emptying of a toilet bowl would release him.

I never told an adult about the danger. Even at age four, I understood grown-ups were unlikely to believe me. Nor did I stop flushing; I gathered adults would frown upon that, too. Instead, for the duration of the war, and (to be on the safe side) for several months after it ended, I did what any reasonable person would do. I flushed and ran.

This all took place decades ago, but I bring it up now for context: I have always taken current events a bit personally.

For most of my childhood, that was a good thing. Born halfway through the 1980s, I formed my first memories as the Berlin Wall fell and spent my youth as a fortunate son of the world's sole superpower. Growing up, I knew—and everyone I knew knew—that America was good and getting better and everywhere else was getting more like America. Demographers call us the millennials. In truth, I belong to the greatest-expectations generation. We flew closest to the sun.

And then? September 11th; the Great Recession; the Trump era; a million smaller yet previously unimaginable crises in between. A towering lasagna of calamity. As people my age entered our thirties, the problems we were supposed to be on our way to solving—mass shootings, income inequality, racial prejudice, climate change—all seemed to be getting worse instead of better. Rather than staying vanquished, the villains of the twentieth century, Nazis and white supremacists and Russian tyrants, returned with a vengeance.

As if this weren't brutal enough, for us, young adulthood did not recede gradually, like a hairline. It was snatched away by the worst pandemic in one hundred years.

By the standards of people living through a global catastrophe, Jacqui and I were lucky when Covid hit. Health intact. Family safe. Jobs that could be done remotely. No children to enroll in Zoom school. We even had a refuge from the heat and humidity of DC, where we were living at the time. The first summer after buying our Asbury Park cottage, we'd rented it to vacationers from New York City for a small profit, but by the second summer the world was on fire and we rented it to ourselves for free. Jacqui gardened. I grilled. At first, I kind of liked it.

Then I fell apart. Despite my good fortune—and despite being from a generation accustomed to pinballing between crises—Covid felt different. Maybe it was the scale. Maybe it was the isolation, or the fact that the pandemic arrived as I approached my thirty-fifth birthday. Maybe it was the variants that pulled the rug of normalcy out from under us, even after the release of a vaccine.

It is said that Shakespeare wrote *King Lear* during a pandemic. Good for him. I bought a PlayStation and drank lots of wine. Every so often, in increasingly urgent tones, Jacqui would suggest I pick up a hobby. But I already had a hobby: reading the news and worrying. By the fall of 2021, a perfect storm of growing certainties—that Covid was not an event but an era, that Trumpism was not a blip but a spreading stain, that a world on fire was not a challenge to be overcome but a permanent condition to be endured for the rest of our lives—began howling in my head.

Psychologists call this "situational depression," meaning that it was brought on by events, rather than purely by brain chemistry. But that was hardly comforting when the world had become one big situation. Night after night I lay awake, mind whirring like a washing machine on the fritz. *Am I wasting my life? Is humanity hurtling toward extinction? Are Jacqui and I waiting too long to have kids? Am I doomed, if we do have kids, to be a sad dad who mopes around worrying he's wasted his life and humanity is hurtling toward extinction?*

I would say it was like running on a treadmill, but that would imply health and fitness. It was more like *being* a treadmill, spinning in circles while getting repeatedly stomped on. Regardless of the subject of my panic—the planet, the country, my life—I arrived at the same conclusion: The best was over. There was nowhere to go but down.

My spiral was privileged and high-functioning. Few of my friends knew what was happening below the surface, and I never stopped working weekends. But the faith that had lifted me out of previous low moments—that what I did mattered—now seemed totally naïve.

As far as I could tell, only three categories of people made it through Covid without succumbing to despair: happy warriors, pathological narcissists, and Taylor Swift. Many of my friends in DC fell into the first group. So did my wife. Jacqui was working as a legislative director for a congressman, and I admired her ability to fight the good fight. But the attitude displayed by her and my DC friends no longer made sense to me. The courage of the happy warriors struck me as a form of denial.

So did the narcissism of the narcissists. They seemed to experience the same crushing realization I did, that the world was full of chaos and time was running out. But instead of responding rationally, with depression, they tried to overturn elections or committed cryptocurrency fraud or purchased entire social networks just to maintain the illusion of control. They were hardly role models. Yet I was impressed by their relentlessness.

Why is it, I wondered, *that so many of the world's worst people have no trouble getting off the couch?*

This was the kind of question I pondered while lying on my couch. It would be easy to say I was stuck in a rut. But that doesn't capture the gravitational pull of hopelessness, the twisted comfort that comes from wrapping oneself in a blanket of bleakness. I felt stuck in a tar pit, at once static and frantic, sinking deeper into gloom.

I remained lucky in one crucial respect: I never seriously considered harming myself. But I came frighteningly close. One morning in early 2022, I left our Victorian cottage, stepped onto the tracks running through town, and saw, in the distance, an oncoming NJ Transit locomotive. For a moment, I paused and faced the train.

It's not for me, I thought. *But I get the appeal.*

My brother-in-law, meanwhile, was thriving. I couldn't understand it. He was neither a warrior, a narcissist, nor Taylor Swift. Yet the second year of the pandemic—the same year I slid deeper into depression— was the most successful of Matt's life. As New Yorkers fled the city for the Shore, he made a killing fixing lights in their guest bedrooms and installing charging stations for their Teslas. Before long, he'd started his own company and bought a house in Brick, a blue-collar exurb in New Jersey's small but passionate Trump Country.

Matt referred to his new hometown, affectionately, as "Bricktucky." This was one of many things I might not have even noticed before the pandemic, and that now felt like an example of everything wrong with him and also the entire world. As recently as 2019, our differences in taste hadn't meant much. He drove a Dodge Ram; I drove a Subaru. He lifted weights to death metal; I jogged to Lizzo. He was a Joe Rogan superfan; I was a Stephen Sondheim aficionado. So what? Now, though, our preferences were more than preferences. They were identifiers, declaring not just what we liked but who we were. Matt still wasn't registered to vote, so the divide between us wasn't technically partisan. But we'd been drafted into opposite sides of a cultural civil war.

The deepest fault line was, of course, vaccination. Had Matt been a friend rather than my wife's younger brother, I probably would have cut off contact after learning he'd refused the Covid shot. As it was, Jacqui and I came up with excuses ("He's an introvert"; "He works in empty houses"; "He doesn't eat in restaurants anyway") to justify not taking a stand. Afraid of the blow-up that would result, I never confronted him about his decision, and because failing to confront him felt like a betrayal of principles, I stopped speaking much to him at all. On the increasingly rare and always outdoor occasions when I saw him, we exchanged clipped, awkward snippets.

"Work's been good?"

"Meh."

"Mrmm."

Yet the fact remained: at the moment I judged Matt more harshly than ever, he was doing better than ever. I wasn't sure where his inner strength came from. But I couldn't help wondering if what I'd dismissed as recklessness—the loose screw that compelled him to zoom down the Parkway on his Harley or handle live wires for a living or float on a fiberglass plank in a freezing wintry ocean—was in fact fearlessness, driving him forward when I was stuck.

The days got longer, which helped. I began seeing a therapist over Zoom. That helped, too. Still, as spring drew to a close and summer beckoned, Matt remained on track while I stayed stuck in my tar pit.

And then, on June 14, 2022, I opened the door to Glide, a surf shop in Asbury Park.

Looking back, it seems impossible that this was a coincidence. At a moment when Matt was blooming and I was wilting, was it really random chance that I decided to try his favorite hobby? Did it not occur to me, even subconsciously, that surfing was the one thing he enjoyed that I could, in the far reaches of my imagination, picture myself enjoying, too?

I dunno.

All I know is that it felt pretty random to me. I didn't walk into Glide planning to one day surf with Matt. How could I have? We were barely speaking. I just wanted to do something new at a time when it took enormous effort to do anything at all. So I bought a wetsuit. I asked the young woman behind the counter, a curly-haired brunette named Katie, if she knew someone who could teach me to surf. And when she said, "I could?" I ignored the uncertainty in her voice and scheduled a lesson for later that week.

At the time, I imagined learning to surf would be a fun but manageable challenge, like learning a language. It was only later—after being stung by jellyfish and run over by ill-tempered youth; after being flung through the air by waves the size of shipping crates and paddling out in near-freezing winter swells; after, with my brother-in-law watching from the beach, executing what can only be described as a bellyflop but for testicles—that I revised my view.

Learning to surf is like learning a language that wants to kill you. With the sole exception of being a person in the world in the late-early twenty-first century, it's the hardest thing I've ever tried to do.

CHAPTER TWO

Woochee

AT A DIFFERENT TIME—one in which asking my brother-in-law for help wouldn't have meant fraternizing with the unvaccinated enemy—I would have told him I'd signed up for surf lessons. Then I would have asked him a series of questions, ending with "Is this likely to kill me?"

Instead, I sat in my home office and googled "surfing deaths."

I was no stranger to doomscrolling. For at least half a decade, bingeing the world's most dispiriting information had felt like a combination of civic responsibility, religious practice, and drug habit. It was only natural that after finishing one article about a surfing tragedy, I moved immediately to the next. And the news wasn't all bad. The number of people who die while surfing was encouragingly small.

The number of *ways* to die while surfing, however, was discouragingly enormous. Here were just a few of the possibilities I imagined with increasing vividness as my lesson with Katie neared:

• I could get sucked out to sea by a rip current and find myself unable to paddle back to shore.

• My leash—the cord connecting my board to my ankle—could wrap around rocks on the ocean floor, trapping me underwater. Or it could wrap around my neck, cutting off the flow of oxygen to my brain. Or it could snap, sending my board flying out of reach and leaving me adrift.

• I could be pinned below the surface by a monster wave, or by a whole series, or "set," of monster waves. According to the articles I read on the subject, the key to surviving one of these brutal "hold-downs" was to relax. This was a roundabout way of saying I would not survive.

• I could swan dive off a wave and plow my brittle cranium against a jetty or reef. Once unconscious, my lungs, ordinarily as buoyant as beach balls, would fill with water and send me on a one-way plummet to the seabed.

• If I surfed in winter—which I never would, but if I *did*—I could find myself swept out to sea in ice-cold water. Actually, colder than ice-cold, since salt water freezes at about twenty-eight degrees. At such temperatures, humans generally lose consciousness in under thirty minutes, and their lives soon after. (A proper wetsuit, it should be noted, can double or even triple these survival times—good news for those who wish to add a bonus hour of misery to their inevitable demise.)

• If I was enticed by climates warmer than that of New Jersey, I could be violently chomped by a saltwater crocodile. Or bull-rushed by a sex-crazed elephant seal. Or nipped by a sea snake, whose dainty fangs, as tiny as the prongs on a strip of Velcro, dispatch enough venom to kill six human adults.

- Sharks.

- I could be ensnared by a box jellyfish, a creature almost certainly underrepresented in your nightmares. Its body is unimposing, just an upside-down Ziploc bag with googly eyes. But it is armed, so to speak, with up to sixty tentacles, each ten feet long and primed with half a million microscopic harpoon guns that launch cell-sized poison darts into anything they touch. Box jellyfish toxin is among the most agonizing substances to which a human body can be exposed. According to WebMD, symptoms of a sting include severe burning, nausea, changes in breathing, skin tissue death, cardiac arrest, and—this last one hardly seems necessary—"unusual behavior due to pain." Also, while box jellies have historically confined themselves to the tropics, thanks to warming oceans, they're moving north. Not too long ago, one washed up on a beach in New Jersey.

Even if I didn't fall prey to toothy or poisonous marine life, and even if I managed to keep my head above water long enough to maintain my precious stores of oxygen, I could clonk myself in the head with my surfboard, or be clonked in the head by someone else's surfboard, or have an artery sliced by a razor-sharp fin, or be run over by an intoxicated boater, or all of the above.

Then there was the list of not-quite-fatal hazards—sea urchins, stingrays, violent macho locals, blown-out knees—which was even longer than the list of deadly ones. Matt had encountered plenty of these dangers firsthand. Once, in pre-pandemic days, he'd told me about the February morning when the lip of a monster wave, powered by a nor'easter roaring toward Canada, snapped his surfboard in half and sent shards of fiberglass slicing like chef's knives through his torso.

"I made it back to the beach, but I was *pouring* blood," he said.

"And that's when you . . . decided to give up surfing?"

"Nah, it wasn't too bad. Anyone can handle stuff like that. You just have to be a strong swimmer."

"Oh," I said. "I see."

I was not a strong swimmer.

~~~~~~~

Every night for a year, I'd been jolted awake by existential terror, so I was accustomed to sleeping poorly. The night before my first surf lesson, however, a hit parade of new anxieties joined the classics. Sure, the death rate from surfing was low—but the death rate from not surfing was lower by a factor of infinity. No one, to my knowledge, had ever been stung by a box jellyfish while rewatching *Schitt's Creek*.

Then there was the deeper fear keeping me awake, less googleable but no less real. What if I wasn't tough enough? I wasn't sure what it meant to succeed at a beginner surf lesson. But if I failed—if I tried something difficult and quit in the face of adversity—it would confirm my gnawing suspicion that I lacked resilience, that my past year was not a one-off but the defining episode of my life.

Better to quit without trying at all. At 6 a.m., when I should have been driving to my lesson, I texted Katie and told her I had an early-morning work emergency. *I paid her for her time, so I'm not a total jerk,*

I reassured myself. *I'm merely a pathetic coward.* This didn't make it easier to fall back asleep.

What drove me to reschedule for the next morning, and to actually show up for my lesson, was not an inner reserve of courage but the fear of my brother-in-law's judgment. I knew what would happen if I chickened out again. Sooner or later, Jacqui would let the news slip to her mother. My mother-in-law, whose ability to share embarrassing information about her relations borders on the telepathic, would alert her son. Matt would know how weak I'd been. Ever after, for a lifetime of family cookouts and holiday parties, he would greet me with a smirk.

I couldn't let him judge me like that—especially not now, when the vaccine debate still raged and I was supposed to be judging him.

For our lesson, Katie chose the beach at Avon-by-the-Sea. Despite being as tightly packed as Legos, Jersey Shore towns each have their own distinct character, and Avon, just ten minutes south of bustling Asbury Park, is a cozy, expensive Pleasantville. By 9 a.m., its half-mile stretch of sand would be teeming with families out of Norman Rockwell paintings laying patterned towels beside colorful umbrellas. But when I arrived an hour after sunrise, the beachfront parking spaces were deserted.

I was grateful for that. It meant no one would see me change into my wetsuit.

For most of my life, I'd been a slightly above-average athlete who prided himself on staying in shape. In high school I wrestled. At the White House I batted leadoff on STOTUS, the Softball Team of the United States. Jacqui was on her college cross-country team, so when we started dating, I started running. Then Covid hit. Slim-cut jeans were replaced by polyester khakis from Walmart, which were replaced by whatever was on top of the laundry pile and had an elastic waist. I began showing up for Zoom meetings with uncombed hair. I shaved at random.

It wasn't just my appearance that deteriorated. Shortly before the pandemic, I decided to purchase life insurance and was offered a surprisingly good deal. But I procrastinated, and by the time a nurse showed up in our kitchen for the mandatory at-home physical, eighteen months of Covid-era sloth had passed. When I received the final paperwork a few weeks later, I was startled to discover my monthly rate had tripled.

"Oh," said the woman on the customer service line. "You're a Category Four."

"A what?"

"Your original quote was for someone in Category One. Because of your increased weight and elevated cholesterol, you're no longer in that category. You're a Category Four."

There was a long silence.

"There are fourteen categories," she offered encouragingly.

It was nice to know that ten groups of people were unlikely to outlive me. Still, I had always considered myself a healthy person, and now, according to an organization that makes money by guessing who dies first, that was no longer true.

In the year since my three-category downgrade, I'd taken a few steps to reverse my physical decline. Slightly less takeout. Slightly more exercise. Even so, the moment I slipped an ankle into my wetsuit, all glimmers of body positivity vanished into rubbery shame. Perhaps you've seen one of those viral videos where a snake, through sheer perseverance, swallows something far too big for it, like a goat. I was that goat. Panting from exertion, I yanked each leg through a constricting tube of neoprene until it reached my hip. Then I repeated the process with hands and sleeves, an act that somehow required lots of jumping. By the time I snapped a fastener across the chest zip, I was red-faced and covered in a second skin of sweat.

It was only as I slumped against my car to recover that I realized: a silver Honda Fit had pulled into a spot a few yards away. Beside it, with wide eyes and a forced smile, stood Katie. In her own wetsuit she resembled a stick figure, with lanky limbs that seemed borrowed from someone else's torso. Slowly, as though trying not to startle a caged animal, she gave me a thumbs-up.

"You okay?"

"All good," I panted. Then I opened the trunk, removed a surfboard, and dropped it on my foot.

Just as someone who's never ridden a horse can recognize the power coursing through each muscle of a Kentucky thoroughbred, the sight of a well-crafted board can send waves of excitement down the spines of surfers and non-surfers alike. This wasn't that. Chunky in profile, toothpaste green, with a white stripe running down the center and a patch of rash-like bumps on the tail, my board was manufactured by a large global company called Wavestorm.

In the surf world, that's like saying my tuxedo was designed by Kmart. Unlike traditional surf craft, whose foam cores are wrapped in rock-hard shells of fiberglass or resin, Wavestorms resemble large packing peanuts. A notable benefit of these foamboards, or "foamies," is that on impact, they're unlikely to hurt you or anyone foolish enough to come near you. A downside is their complete lack of aerodynamism. Katie watched with growing concern as I stooped over the asphalt, struggling to lift the sofa-sized, Tylenol-shaped lump.

"Try carrying it like this," she said, miming an agile, fit person cradling a board beneath an arm. I gave it a shot, but the effort was doomed. Hoisting the Wavestorm above my head, I puffed my way across the boardwalk toward the sand, each gust of wind turning my foamie into a giant sail. Right before I stumbled into the water, Katie stopped me.

"Not yet. Let's practice on land."

In the rare moments when I hadn't been googling sea snake fang lengths or symptoms of box jellyfish stings, I'd watched a few instructional videos. From these I knew that "popping up" is essential to all surfers and second nature for experts. Katie lay belly-down to demonstrate. After confirming I was paying close attention, she planted her hands as though preparing to do a push-up. Then she teleported into an athletic stance. To make sure I hadn't missed anything, she did it again.

"Don't worry," she said, resuming her position on the sand. "I'll break it down step by step. First you put your hands on the deck of the board. Then you straighten your arms and lift your chest up. Then you step up with your back foot. Then you swing your front foot so it lands between your hands. Then you stand up. Watch." She rose to her feet in a single motion.

"Now you try."

Joints creaking, left eyebrow arched in skepticism, I lay atop my board. Yet when I focused on Katie's advice—raise my chest, back foot forward, front foot next—everything snapped into place. In an instant, I was standing, my arms to my sides in imitation of surfers I'd seen in movies and on TV.

"Nice!" Katie said. "Want to give it another try?" I popped up again, even more fluidly than I had the first time. Then I did a few more pop-ups, just to lock the movement into my muscle memory. Holding my wave-riding pose, I looked over at Katie. She seemed genuinely impressed. I couldn't remember the last time an unreservedly optimistic thought had popped into my head, but now, like a seed bursting into bloom after years of drought, one did:

Maybe I'm a natural!

~~~~~~~~~

I was not a natural.

The problem, I realized, was twofold. The first was every aspect of my physical and mental life. The second was water. Forget springing to my feet—in the sloshing surf, even lying prone was impossible. My Wavestorm, which on land had been as hefty as a picnic table, upon contact with the ocean became a tightrope. The waves were no taller than daffodils, yet they turned me into a wobbling slice of Jell-O. Gripping the board's rails for balance only tensed my body and made balancing even harder. I soon lost purchase and plonked into the sea.

"Everything good?" yelled Katie, who had waded about a dozen yards away.

"Yep!" I lied.

"Want to try to paddle?"

"Sure!" I lied again.

Imagine deciding to take up golf, only to discover that walking from the clubhouse to the first tee—not swinging a club, not chipping or putting or blasting free from a sand trap, just walking—requires more physical strength than you've mustered in your entire adult life.

That's surfing. I would later learn that what makes paddling a board so torturous is not just the amount of muscle required, but the fact that the required muscles are pressed into service by surfers and essentially no one else. Take the *levator scapulae*. They connect the neck to the shoulders; if yours disappeared, you'd notice. But they're supposed to be the stage managers of the biomechanical world, not the stars. Dragging a hand and forearm through water while lying on a surfboard is one of the few activities that thrust them into the spotlight.

My scapulae were not ready for prime time. Neither were my scalene muscles (which connect my upper ribs and vertebrae) or *erector spinae* (running vertically down my back). I took ten strokes toward Katie, then tumbled into the sea. After remounting my board, I repeated the process with eight strokes, then six, then four. I wasn't sure I'd ever reach her. Judging from Katie's expression, neither was she. Finally, moments before my entire torso became a single quivering spasm, I arrived.

"Okay," she said cautiously. "Let's . . . try to catch a wave?"

Before I could ask what that might entail, Katie gripped the hull of my Wavestorm and pointed me toward the beach. For a minute, she kept hold of the board and made small talk—about surfing; about Jersey; about the kitten she'd adopted. Then, suddenly, she snapped to attention. I looked over my shoulder, following her gaze. A small, rolling hill of water had appeared behind us.

"Face the beach!" Katie said. Every muscle stiffened. I gritted my teeth. Just when I was certain the wave would crash directly on top of me, she gave my board a shove.

"Paddle paddle paddle!" she yelled. I paddled.

"Pop up pop up pop up!" she yelled. I leapt to my feet, pinwheeled my arms as though slipping on black ice, and toppled into the sea.

At first I kept track of my attempts. "It was really tough," I imagined telling Matt at the next family party. "It took me three tries." But three tries became five, and five became seven, and seven became no longer counting.

The reason getting to my feet on the beach had seemed easy, I now understood, is that it was easy. A toddler can stand up on land. On water the most fractional mistake—a hand placed an inch too far forward; arms extended a half second late; a foot planted slightly off center—sent me flying. If I was lucky, I kerplunked into the ocean. If I was unlucky, I bounced off my board onto my tailbone (or sometimes, just for variety's sake, my knee and then my tailbone), and kerplunked into the ocean.

"Quick question," I said. "Am I especially bad at this?"

Katie thought for a very long time.

"Well," she finally said. "Everybody's different."

I nodded weakly. It was exactly as I'd feared: I wasn't tough enough for this. I no longer hoped to discover I was a secret surfing prodigy, or even to catch a wave. All I wanted was to stop trying and go home. With fifteen minutes left in the lesson, I began stalling for time.

"So," I said, "you mentioned you had a kitten. What's her name?"

"Woochee," Katie replied. A wave sailed harmlessly past.

"What color is she?"

"Black."

"And what kind of name is 'Woochee'?"

"It comes from a Chinese word, actually. It means 'void.'" Another wave rolled underneath.

"How old is she? Did you adopt from a foster home or a shelter? Is this your first cat?"

Joggers had appeared along the boardwalk. Families were filling the beach. Our lesson would soon be over, and with the end in sight, I kept the questions flowing. "How long did it take you to learn to pop up?" (A few tries. This was inconceivable.) "My brother-in-law surfs in winter. He's crazy, right?" (She didn't think so. This was equally inconceivable.) "Do you need the name of a good local cat sitter?" (No, her sister would look after the kitten if she was out of town. This I understood.)

Then many things happened at once.

Katie's eyes got big. Not *is-David-going-to-have-a-heart-attack-dragging-his-board-to-the-beach?* big. Excited big. In a single movement she scooted to the back of my Wavestorm and gave its chunky tail a shove.

"Go go go go!"

I didn't hear her yell "Pop up!" All I knew was that I was lying on my board, then something happened, then I was on my feet. Head high. Eyes toward the beach.

To the joggers and sunbathers, it probably didn't look like much. Just a man in an unflattering garment teetering atop a bulky foam slab before collapsing into the sea.

But for me?

There were a few discrete sensations: wind against my face;

Katie hooting in encouragement; my toes pressing against the day-old-baguette texture of the deck. Yet what I felt most clearly was the absence of sensation. For a few timeless seconds, the chaos around me—the crash of waves and the world in perpetual crisis and the sense that time was not just passing me by but dragging me by the ankles as it passed—ceased to matter. I was part of the universe and propelled by the universe, floating high above a sea of troubles as I rocketed toward shore.

Later that morning, I lay in bed, replaying the moment again and again as I drifted toward deep, sound slumber.

I am Woochee the kitten, I thought, half dreaming. *I have become the void.*

CHAPTER THREE

Pain and Sorrow Before They Quit

THE MOTTO OF OCEARCH, a leading shark research organization, is "Facts Over Fear." It's a bad motto. If there's anything we've learned from recent history, it's that facts and fear are not mutually exclusive.

I demonstrated this myself when, a week before my second surf lesson, I logged on to the OCEARCH website and learned there was an 880-pound great white shark lurking off the New Jersey coast. Her name was Freya. Fifteen months earlier, a researcher had clipped a homing beacon to her fin the way you might slip a Bluetooth tracker into your luggage, adding her to a roster of several hundred tagged sharks cruising the world's oceans. Occasionally, a shark's beacon emits a ping, and scientists study these pings to learn more about shark movement. This is an indirect way of saying there's still an awful lot scientists don't know about sharks, including, in most cases, where they are.

When I first checked the site, Freya had most recently been located near Toms River, about twenty miles south of Asbury Park. But pings aren't frequent and sharks swim fast. She could be off the coast of Long Beach Island, traversing the invisible border that divides Yankees fans from Phillies fans. She could be patrolling

Seaside Park, where Hurricane Sandy swept an entire roller coaster off the boardwalk. Freya could even be stalking the shallow surf near Matt's house in Brick.

Not that he would care. While we hadn't really spoken in months, the culture wars made our reactions, even regarding something as apolitical as sharks, easy to predict. People like my brother-in-law—who knew the names of all the top MMA fighters and had never worn masks indoors—wouldn't allow themselves to be afraid of great whites. To the extent they acknowledged them, it would be to talk about punching them in the face.

My reaction to Freya was similarly preordained. Sharks are noble creatures. Reams of data show they rarely pose a threat to humans, and as apex predators, they're essential to healthy ocean ecosystems. Demonizing sharks is barbaric. Worrying about them is anti-science. As someone who cares about the planet, I believed these things wholeheartedly.

As someone who prefers his internal organs to remain on the inside, however, I found it harder to toe the party line. The odds of being bitten by a shark are almost zero. But for a few unlucky people, the crucial part of that sentence is "almost." In much the way my grandfather once ate several salmon-flavored dog biscuits thinking they were gourmet crackers, sharks occasionally—but very memorably—confuse people for seals. Surfers, with seal-shaped boards and dark wetsuits, are particularly susceptible to such mix-ups. The risk is especially great if a surfer thrashes against the water in the manner of a wounded seal.

I was new to paddling. All I did was thrash.

For a little while, Freya stayed put. Then, as though she, too, had booked a lesson with Katie, she began cruising up the coast. By the time I removed my Wavestorm from the car in Bradley Beach, two towns south of Asbury, Freya's most recent ping had come from an undersea canyon directly offshore.

"Everything okay?" asked Katie as we waded in. The waves were tiny, but I took careful steps, pushing my foamie ahead of me as a shield.

"All good," I replied. Then, trying to sound casual, I added, "Oh, by the way, did you know there's a great white shark in the area?"

"Yeah, Barry!"

The idea that Freya had a colleague—and that this second shark was not a fair-minded Nordic lady but a ruggedly individualistic American male—was a fact for which I was unprepared.

"If I see a shark," I asked, "or sharks, plural, what should I, you know, do?"

Katie cocked her head, as if the question had never before occurred to her.

"I wouldn't worry about it."

That's nice, I thought, *but* why *wouldn't you worry about it? Isn't worrying about sharks while standing in shark-infested waters exactly what a person should do?* I'd hoped to recapture my Woochee moment, but the ocean was alive with phantom fins and toothy shadows, and I was far too busy keeping watch to catch a wave. Even when exhaustion dulled my vigilance, my worries didn't disappear. They just moved on to something else.

"I've noticed a problem," I said to Katie just before our lesson ended. "It frequently feels like the wave is going to break on top of me, and, well, snap me in half. What do I do about that?"

I braced myself for another unhelpful *don't-worry-about-it* response. To my surprise, Katie beamed.

"The flower of fear!"

"Huh?"

She leaned over my board, catching my gaze the way my grandfather, when he wasn't eating dog biscuits, used to look at me before sharing a profound and hard-earned truth.

"When you paddle for a wave, and you feel the flower of fear opening, it's a good thing. That feeling is one of the most important parts of surfing. It's how you know you're in the right spot."

This was a notion I'd never encountered. I'd always thought of fear as something to be overcome or succumbed to, faced or ignored. But the way Katie saw it, fear, when harnessed correctly, was not just good but essential, a source of power and drive. In four simple words, she had described not just a different way to think about waves, but a different way to think about everything. I floated on my Wavestorm, doing my best to embrace this transformational new idea.

"Or," I said, unable to help myself, "the flower of fear means you're about to die."

~~~~~~~~

Thanks to the Kappler family grapevine, I knew Matt hadn't surfed all summer. The same waves I'd battled—the ones that had knocked me off my board like a parent brushing crumbs from a child's shirt sleeve—he'd dismissed as "flat."

Flatness wasn't the only thing Matt disliked about summertime surfing. For nine months of the year, most of New Jersey's coastline is a free-for-all. You can paddle out anywhere, and no one will stop you. But from Memorial Day to Labor Day, shore towns reserve almost all their beaches for swimming. The Asbury Park oceanfront, for example, stretches about one and a half miles. Its summer surfing beach—which doubles as its dog beach—is just four blocks long.

To Matt, who regarded government-designated surf breaks the way a wild orangutan might regard zoos, this was a personal attack. Even more galling, official surf spots were protected by beach patrol. Matt had once told me he only surfed at beaches without lifeguards.

"Why?" I asked.

"Less crowded."

"But that's because there are no lifeguards."

"Exactly."

Matt so disdained summer surfing that he sometimes waited until June or July to get new tattoos. That way, he could spend two recovery weeks out of the water without missing good waves. For me it was the opposite. The list of grievances that kept him from the ocean was the list of reasons I was willing to brave it. One June morning, after double-checking the lifeguard hours on the municipal website, I finally worked up the courage to surf without Katie by my side.

Like most stretches of Jersey seashore, the Asbury Park dog beach is flanked by a pair of jetties—narrow piers made of boulders that extend into the water like teeth from a comb. After tiptoeing across the blazing-hot sand, I waded into the sea between them. Pointing my board toward the lifeguard tower, I waited for the "whitewater," the churning foam that erupts from a breaking wave and surges to shore. As it neared, I psyched myself up with a mantra.

To the beach!

This proved aspirational rather than descriptive. By the time I planted my right foot, my Wavestorm and I were already moving in opposite directions, and I flew backward like a cartoon drunk slipping on a banana peel. After a brief dunking, I scrambled to my feet in the knee-deep water and gathered my board. As I stood there, catching my breath and marinating in my own ineptitude, an entire bachelorette party glided happily and competently toward shore.

An increment of surfing, like one of therapy, is known as a session. As in, "Epic session, bro!" or "You down for an afternoon session?" or "Shredding whatever paltry scraps of hope I'd brought with me to the dog beach, my inaugural solo surf session went from bad to worse." I wiped out approximately twenty times. My toes were pinched by crabs approximately thirty times. I got to my feet twice, and even those two rides were nothing like the one I'd experienced with Katie that first morning. They felt less like flying on a magic carpet than standing on a rusty conveyer belt. When I got home, every muscle twitched from exhaustion and overuse.

"Did you have fun?" asked Jacqui hopefully.

"Fun? Definitely not."

Part of the problem was my age. The best time to start surfing, I learned long after the knowledge might have helped me, is between five and seven years old. Fifteen is pushing it. Twenty is over the hill. Thirty is geriatric. To pick up a board at thirty-five, as I did, is the rough equivalent of signing up for guitar lessons on your deathbed.

You might think the hopelessness of the task would deter people from trying, but so far that hasn't been the case. I was one of millions of adults who grabbed a foamboard during the pandemic. The surf industry, which happily sells shorts and T-shirts to customers regardless of skill level, has welcomed the influx of beginners. So has the internet, where a pantheon of viral gurus caters to those picking up a board later in life.

Hardcore surfers have taken a slightly different approach to the newcomers. They hate them. Some use "VAL"—short for "vulnerable adult learner"—as a slur. Others direct their anger at the beginners' equipment. In surf-speak, "Dude, lots of foamies in the water" roughly translates to "There are novices here, and they are subhuman, and their mere presence fills me with loathing and rage."

A few surfers are more eloquent, but no less disdainful. At Glide, the surf shop where Katie worked, the Pulitzer Prize–winning *Barbarian Days: A Surfing Life* sat on a table between the sunscreen and wax. I bought a copy. One hundred twenty-three pages in, I read author William Finnegan—who by all accounts is an otherwise liberal and tolerant person—describe adult learners like me.

"People who tried to start at an advanced age, meaning over fourteen, had, in my experience, almost no chance of becoming proficient, and usually suffered pain and sorrow before they quit."

How dare he assume something like that? I thought. *Also, how dare he be right?* While my own surfing life spanned all of two weeks, I'd already compiled an encyclopedia of discomfort: the swollen knee from landing funny on the deck; the throbbing in my shoulders each time I thrashed out another paddle stroke; the bruised left butt cheek from falling backward in ankle-deep water.

Other setbacks, while less painful, were no less sorrowful. One morning at the dog beach, a wipeout tossed me over my heelside rail and deposited me a few yards from shore. Sighing with frustration, I got to my feet, and had just reeled in my leash when a knee-high wave plucked my Wavestorm from my hands and flung it into another rider's path. He catapulted over the nose of his board, splatted belly-down into the shallow surf, and emerged from the water dripping and ferocious, a beefy, balding sea monster.

"Fucking kook!" he said.

This, I knew, was a surf-specific putdown, one whose meaning sat at the pungent four-way intersection of *moron*, *newbie*, *dork*, and *asshole*. He stomped toward me.

"Fucking kook," he muttered again.

Living, as I do, in a nation choking on rage and firearms, the sensible reaction would have been to mumble an apology. But I didn't appreciate being insulted, and I could feel my blood boil.

"Hey," I snapped, "I have no idea what I'm doing!"

It took us both a second to realize I'd taken his side. Anger waylaid by confusion, the sea monster hopped back on his board (he was quite graceful, given his proportions and temperament) and paddled away. But my own words hung in the air, far more devastating than his insult. Even by the low standards of adult learners on foamies, I was terrible at this. I myself had said so. And I seemed destined to remain terrible forever.

Yet I didn't quit. I returned to the dog beach twice more the week of my first solo session, and four more times the week after that. I could count my total number of successful pop-ups on my fingers, so it wasn't the rush of riding waves that kept me coming back. It was something deeper. During each surf session I felt frustrated, exhausted, humiliated, terrified, depleted, confused, and sore—but never depressed. While flailing in pursuit of whitewater may not have been fun, it was something different to think about. It paused the spin cycle in my mind.

Surfing even made it easier to stop worrying about the news. At one time, I'd wanted to help save the world. Now I wanted to forget it needed saving, and my new hobby made that possible. Instead of asking, *Are we witnessing, in real time, the devastation of our planet, the rise of fascism, and the death of the American Dream?* I asked, *Is this wave about to shatter my spine?* I remained skeptical that fear was a flower. But I certainly preferred it to the cactus of existential dread.

~~~~~~~~~~

Given how he acted like he owned the place, I figured the guy who called me a kook was a dog beach regular. In fact I never saw him again, even as I became something of a regular myself.

Most surf breaks are like high school cafeterias, with cliques roughly corresponding to skill level, and I soon got to know the other kids at the VAL table. Troy was in his early thirties, with a banana-yellow foamboard, a mane of black hair, and an endless supply of bad advice from the internet. Neil was older—the far side of fifty—but he paddled for waves with such scrawny tenacity that you couldn't help but be impressed even when he failed to catch them, which was always. Eva was the youngest, and the only woman, a tall brunette with a double-wide foamie that made my Wavestorm look nimble by comparison.

We never hung out on land or referred to ourselves in a collective sense. When we spoke, it was mostly just Troy offering tips from whichever Instagram reels he'd watched recently. "Move all the way up on your board!" "Paddle with both arms at once!" "Move all the way back on your board!" But bound together by beginners' enthusiasm and novices' shame, we formed a crew. We even had our own spot-within-a-spot: off the very center of the beach, where the surf was smaller and less consistent, and therefore undesirable.

The cool kids posted up beside the rocky tips of the jetties jutting into the sea. There, at low tide, a pair of steep waves would appear—a left-breaking one by the north jetty, and a right-breaking one by the south. (In surfing, left and right are always from the perspective of a surfer facing the beach. The other two cardinal directions, *outside* and *inside*, mean "toward the horizon" and "toward land.") Most surfers stand with their left foot ahead of their right, and because it's easier to lean forward over one's toes than backward over one's heels, they prefer riding waves that break right. For this reason, the south jetty was the dog beach's most coveted spot.

I never introduced myself to the south-jetty clique. I didn't dare. Instead, studying its members intensely, I assigned each of them a nickname based on the fictional character or real-life celebrity they most resembled. Gaston had a fleshy chin and an arrogant smirk. Willie Nelson had stringy hair and a can-do attitude. Tilda Swinton had piercing eyes and a skeletal frame. Paul Rudd was handsome.

The undisputed king of the dog beach, though, was The Predator.

I noticed his board before I noticed him. Its turquoise tint was somehow eye-catching yet subtle, and I soon realized the person atop it was similarly in a category all his own. His eyes were steel blue. His back pulsed with muscles. His teeth, which flashed in the summer sun each time he took off on a wave, were pearly and menacing. His hair fell in long, tight braids across his shoulders.

This last feature was partly responsible for the nickname I assigned him: it called to mind the iconic extraterrestrial from the *Predator* film franchise. But what made the label stick was his attitude. Lurking far outside, he'd gobble up a wave before anyone else could get to it and start paddling back to the jetty the moment his ride ended. More often than not, by the time the next good one rolled through, he was already in position to grab it. I sometimes spent whole sessions drifting with my fellow VALs, watching The Predator gorge himself while we starved.

As someone who believes, as a policy matter, in leveling the playing field, I should have resented The Predator for hogging the surf. But the thought never occurred to me. His confidence, his athleticism, even the way he refused to acknowledge me as he cruised past: I found it all intoxicating. *What must it feel like*, I wondered, *to be able to surf like that?*

For somewhat obvious reasons, Jacqui found my growing obsession with a charismatic younger man disconcerting. Despite this, or perhaps because of it, she was the first to make the connection. There was, after all, another talented, fearless, occasionally antisocial surfer in my orbit; one who, unlike The Predator, might feel obligated to take me under his wing.

"You should try surfing with Matt sometime," she suggested.

"I don't think so," I replied. "We're on very different levels."

Perhaps if I'd started at a younger age, or been in better shape, or possessed even a hint of innate talent, I could have imagined myself riding big waves on a tiny, nimble board. As it was, I had no interest in becoming good enough to brave the kinds of conditions Matt apparently enjoyed. On waves thigh-high or smaller, my current ratio of pop-ups to wipeouts was about two in ten. If I worked hard for several summers, I might be able to bring that number up to three, or even five. At my advanced age, that was the best I could hope for.

Which was fine. People like Matt might look down on summertime surfers the way Thomas Paine once sneered at sunshine patriots. But what was so wrong about breaking out a foamie for three months a year, making marginal improvements, and not being depressed while doing it? To the extent surfing had taught me anything thus far, it was that part of being a grown-up is knowing when to settle.

~~~~~~

Katie, it seemed, was doing some settling of her own. Whatever hopes and dreams had inspired her to try surf coaching had collided with the harsh reality of me. For our fourth lesson, I suggested we go to the dog beach. I nose-dived on one wave and did a wounded-seal impression on another, but eventually I popped up, sliding toward shore for several seconds.

"Pretty good, right?" I said.

"Nice!" she agreed. But it was forced excitement, the kind you summon for a third-grader who correctly spells out "C-A-T." I didn't talk much during the rest of the lesson.

"Want to schedule another time?" I asked when it was over.

"Well," she replied, "I'm actually going on a surf trip to Nicaragua . . ."

I waited for the next part of the sentence, the one in which she'd tell me when she planned to return, but it never arrived.

"Why don't I text you when you're back?" I said, just to break the silence.

"Sure." She got in her Honda Fit and drove away.

For some people, Katie's disappearance would have confirmed that the idea of surf instruction is overrated. A lot of shredders and rippers would agree with that. They'll tell you the best way to learn is to grab a board and just figure it out. But that was not my style. When Covid hit, I listened to public health authorities; when Katie lost interest in teaching me, I found a surf school five beaches south of Asbury, in the country-clubbish borough of Spring Lake. While the new school's owner posted an unsettling number of right-wing memes about Nancy Pelosi, his name was promising. Sam Hammer. I wasn't sure how much potential I had, but if anyone could unlock it, it was him.

Then it turned out lessons with Sam Hammer himself were expensive and I ended up with a tan, wiry apprentice named Jamie.

"How long have you been surfing?" I asked, hauling my board across the beach.

"Since I was in middle school," Jamie replied confidently. "Eight years. No, seven." Only yesterday, I was the one distressing people with my youngness. Now I was being taught by someone who couldn't legally rent a car.

His youth made everything suspect. "When you paddle for the wave, you're splaying your legs out like this," he told me, making a *V* with his fingers.

"I know," I said, irritated. "That's because I can't balance otherwise."

"See what happens if you keep them together."

What happens if I keep my legs together, I thought, *is that in a desperate bid to remain on my board I throw out my back, something you know nothing about since you're too young to have any memory of Blockbuster Video, let alone 9/11.* But too tired to argue, I gave it a halfhearted try. Paddling on Jamie's cue, I kept my legs pressed tight, felt myself wobble, and . . .

I couldn't believe it. The tail of my board sank into the breaking water and stayed there. This is called *planing*, and while I'm sure physics is involved, it's magic. One moment, I was a rubber ducky in the world's largest bath. The next, I was as connected to the wave as my hair was to my head. Instead of chucking me into a nosedive, the water formed a giant, flat palm that gently lifted me to my feet. Standing up was easy. I was so full of adrenaline that paddling back was easy, too. I tried my new technique again and again, waiting for the magic to fade and grinning each time it didn't.

Finally, after a streak of at least a half dozen pop-ups, I nosedived. "I feel like when I take off late, I have trouble getting to the beach," I observed. "Any suggestions?"

"Don't worry about that," Jamie replied. "You're not supposed to go that way."

"I'm sorry, what?"

In the jaunty tone of a person to whom nothing really bad has happened yet, Jamie explained that my mantra—*To the beach!*—was useless.

"You want to ride down the line," he said, swooping his palm parallel to the shore. The next time a wave came toward us, I angled to the right. Instead of sticking out like a tongue over the lip, the board slipped onto the face. For the first time since my Woochee moment,

I wasn't fighting the ocean. *This* was the feeling I'd been trying to recapture for a month.

Near the end of our lesson, Jamie put a hand on my board, looked me in the eye, and spoke in a tone heavy with age and wisdom.

"I'm gonna leave you with this," he said. "There's gonna be sessions where you wipe out four times for every time you pop up, and it's gonna be *incredibly* discouraging. You just have to remember that every time you fall, you're a better surfer than you were before."

I drove straight to the dog beach after my lesson and found my crew between the jetties. After getting "out the back"—past the impact zone where the waves break—I kept my knees pressed together, paddled like my life depended on it, and angled down the line. The invisible hand sent me gliding.

"Awesome!" said Troy.

Where Jamie's advice really helped, though, wasn't during the rides. It was after the wipeouts. I was tired. My triceps ached with each paddle stroke, a sure sign that every larger, more powerful muscle had already abandoned ship. Trying to push my chest off the board felt like jacking up a car with a pair of pool noodles. But instead of snarling in self-recrimination, I thought to myself, *You're better than you were before.*

"Did you have fun?" Jacqui asked out of habit when I got home.

"Yeah! It was amazing!"

Before long, I was applying Jamie's words of wisdom to nearly every facet of my life. Charring a burger made me a better chef; trying and failing to stay off social media made me a better time manager. One afternoon I put Jacqui's workout leggings through the dryer on regular instead of tumble dry low. When they emerged several sizes smaller, I gave her a pensive look.

"This means I'm better at laundry," I explained. While she found that particular claim unconvincing, the broader point was undeniable: becoming a slightly better surfer had made me a slightly different person.

And if that was the case, what might becoming a much better surfer do?

As I followed this train of thought to its logical conclusion, my opinions about settling for a life of summertime surf didn't just shift. They reversed completely. I knew, on an intellectual level, that trading depression for mania might not be the wisest idea. But it was too late. A familiar, dormant ambition had flickered. I wasn't thinking about changing the world; that remained overwhelming. But for the first time in a long time, I was thinking about changing myself.

Everyone—from Pulitzer Prize winner William Finnegan to a balding guy who called me a kook to the voice in my head—keeps telling me I'm not tough enough. What would I have to do to prove them wrong?

Although I'd been surfing for less than two months, I knew the answer. Every bit of lore I'd consumed, not just *Barbarian Days*, but Matt Warshaw's *The History of Surfing* and the 2002 girl-power sports movie *Blue Crush* and the surf influencers I'd followed on Troy's recommendation, all pointed toward the same place. Surfing's mecca—its ultimate proving ground—was Hawaii's North Shore. There, on the island of Oahu, along a stretch of coast known as "the Seven-Mile Miracle," peaks of unrivaled steepness and power exploded onto dangerously shallow reef. Wild currents dragged the careless or unfit into open ocean. Monster swells could appear without warning, transforming placid seas into battlefields of snapped leashes and broken boards. People became legends there. People died there, too.

I knew that getting good enough to ride a legitimate, consequential wave on the North Shore was a long shot. But I also knew, even if I didn't yet know how, that pulling it off would mean more than just proficiency on a board. When I imagined taking on dangerous breaks spoken of in reverent tones, I was no longer hitting pause on depression. I was putting it behind me. I could feel myself running to instead of running from.

In a way it was all quite simple: the version of me who could surf an overhead wave on the North Shore was, by definition, very different than the version of me who could not.

Something else was obvious, too. Hawaii's most famous waves, like Pipeline or Rocky Point or Sunset, weren't like the dog beach, where paddling out solo was safe. Even on a crowded day, it would be an act of deadly lunacy to brave the North Shore alone. I needed a partner, a kindred spirit, a fellow surfer whose temperament mirrored my own and whose judgment I trusted completely.

There was just one problem: I didn't know anyone like that. In fact, with the exception of Katie, who was no longer returning my text messages, the list of fellow surfers whose contact information I possessed was exactly one name long.

I was going to have to surf with Matt.

CHAPTER FOUR

Free Speech!

I'D BEEN SURFING FOR A LITTLE over a month when one afternoon, while stepping into the shower, I glanced in the mirror and noticed a pair of comely dimples above my ass. My sense of satisfaction wasn't vain, at least not exclusively.

Do Category Fours have upper-butt dimples? I think not.

I was improving in other ways, too. Paddling out was still brutal, particularly if the waves were higher than my knees, but the anguish was now expected rather than shocking; it was the difference between filing your taxes and undergoing an audit. Also, I no longer assumed I would fall on every two-footer. Instead, I assumed I'd make it and was regularly disappointed when I didn't. That was progress. I was even getting closer to the popular crowd at the dog beach. Late one morning, I burst into the living room.

"We made eye contact!"

Jacqui, who had recently begun working as a legal counsel for the Democrats on the House Judiciary Committee, was drafting questions for lawmakers to ask at an upcoming hearing. She looked up from her laptop. "Who made eye contact?"

"Me and The Predator!"

"Okay . . ."

"You don't get it. I was paddling back after a ride, and he was paddling back after a ride, and he was like, 'Hey,' and I was like, 'Hey.'"

"I think I get it," she said. But she didn't really.

There was a lot about surfing that my wife didn't get. Why, for instance, had I begun arranging my work schedule around the tides? Or practicing my surf stance while waiting in line for a bagel? Or, when we strolled the Asbury Park boardwalk, looking toward the waves and saying "Ooh, nice one" every thirty seconds?

Jacqui appreciated the respite from doom and gloom that surfing provided me, and by extension provided her. Even so, her patience had limits. One late-July afternoon, as we drove to her parents' house for a family cookout, as I was explaining that a three-fin setup, also known as a thruster, has more control down the line, while a twin-fin, or "twinnie," has a looser feel, she interrupted.

"Maybe this is the kind of thing *my brother* would find interesting," she said.

"I know," I replied, "but first I have to tell him I've started surfing, and I'm waiting for the right moment. Anyway, the cool thing about a quad setup is—"

"Maybe you should tell him today."

I wasn't against the idea. Just the opposite. But the moment I realized I needed to surf with Matt, I became nervous he wouldn't want to surf with me. We were family, so I doubted he would reject me outright. Still, I could easily imagine the pursed lips and raised eyebrow informing me I wasn't worthy.

Jacqui and I always ran late to family parties, and Matt always left early, so that afternoon I wondered if I'd see him at all. But there he was, sitting on the steps leading from the back door into the yard, a cloud of cousins billowing around him. I grabbed a paper plate and strategized as I scooped potato salad.

Should I ask if he wants to paddle out together, or just bring up surfing in general? If he asks, "How good are you?" what do I say?

I joined the group just as the conversation turned to the social media platform Twitter, and in particular to its new owner, Elon Musk. "I think he's gone crazy," said Daniel, his mustache quivering in agitation. The youngest of the cousins, he'd recently graduated with a journalism degree. "He's become a total right-wing nut." There was a brief silence. Then Matt chimed in.

"I think he's a genius," he said. While I doubted anyone else noticed it, an impish grin flashed across his face, as though he'd just set off a stink bomb in the faculty lounge.

"But look at the stuff he's been saying," Daniel replied. "He wants to let racists back on, he wants to let neo-Nazis back on."

"Free speech!" Matt declared triumphantly.

Daniel looked at me for backup, assuming, correctly, that I was on his side. I felt strongly that the phrase "free speech," like "all lives matter" or "do your own research" before it, had been co-opted by the far right to undermine the very principle it claimed to express. But I wasn't about to say that out loud. The idea of a conversation with Matt on this topic, or any topic, suddenly seemed fraught with risk.

"Did you talk with him about surfing?" Jacqui asked me later.

"Not yet," I said. "I'm still waiting for the right moment."

Determined to reach a point where I could ask Matt to surf with me, I ditched the Wavestorm. My new board, a thruster setup, was still foam, still clunky, still cheap. But the consensus of Amazon reviewers was "Slightly better than a Wavestorm," and now it was mine.

I also signed up for another lesson with Sam Hammer's surf school. When I requested Jamie, however, it turned out he'd gone back to college. The instructor who met me at the Spring Lake boardwalk instead was a pale, lanky high-schooler named Dylan.

I don't want to be unfair. Maybe when discussing the finer points of Romance languages or the latest breakthrough in astrophysics, my new surf instructor was the sharpest knife in the drawer. When it came to surf instruction, though, the drawer was empty. You know how, when you get your password wrong on certain websites, the screen shimmies for a second and then wipes clean? That was Dylan upon hearing any information whatsoever.

"I think I've been missing waves because I pop up too quickly," I explained as we paddled out, "and I'm still struggling with nosedives, especially on late takeoffs."

"Cool!" he said. "Good to know."

I went for a small right, but popped up too quickly and it slid underneath my board. I looked expectantly at Dylan, who squinted as though doing an impression of someone deep in thought.

"You missed it," he finally said.

On the next wave I took off late and nosedived, pitching head-first into the sea. "Ooh," Dylan said. "You fell off." This happened several times until, finally, I got to my feet.

"You made it!" he announced.

"Is there anything you saw me do differently this time?" I asked. "Anything I might want to repeat?"

"Yeah!" he replied. "You didn't lose your balance."

For seventy minutes, Dylan cycled between "You missed it," "You fell off," and "You made it!" It was like taking instruction from a pull-string doll. As the summer sun rose, sweat beaded on my forehead, blended into a cocktail with the sunscreen on my skin, and dripped into my eyes where it pooled behind my contact lenses. I was blinking in agony when a final wave rolled through. For a moment, I thought it would break too far inside to be worth chasing. Then I changed my mind and paddled for it, yanking my exhausted arms through the water. It slid under me anyway.

"You missed it," Dylan announced. I glared at him.

"You know what your problem is," he added. "You spend too much time thinking. You're trying to figure out, 'Is the wave gonna break early or late? Is it going right or left?' I'd rather see you fully commit and wipe out than think too hard and miss it."

It is strange to have one's personality diagnosed by a teenager. That's especially true when the teenager in question has, until that moment, possessed all the insight of a fortune cookie. But he was right. It wasn't just my stumbling pop-up or feeble scapulae that stood between me and the North Shore. The more I thought about my new instructor's words, the more I realized the extent to which my life had been shadowed, and often shaped, by my chronic ambivalence.

I had mixed feelings about that. On one hand, a tendency to overanalyze can be useful for a writer. There's a reason Robert Frost never penned a poem about choosing paths quickly and moving on.

On the other hand, surfers have no time for contemplation at each fork in the road. You make a snap decision, you go all in, you don't look back. There is no other way.

While full commitment without full knowledge is scary under any circumstances, I learned over the next few solo sessions at the dog beach that it is uniquely terrifying at sea. My frontal cortex—the part of my brain responsible for maintaining my Wordle streak and composing devastating retorts to commenters on social media—knew that falling off a knee-high wave at the dog beach wasn't truly dangerous. But a different part of my brain, the part that snaps my hand back when I forget that the cast-iron skillet for which I am reaching was until quite recently in the oven, offered another opinion. *You are a very small animal in a very large ocean,* it said, at the approach of even the teensiest roller. *And you are about to die.*

Thanks to my earlier lessons with Katie, I knew what I was supposed to do in these moments. The flower of fear opened. I said to myself, *Go!* But I never went.

~~~~~~~~~~~

In the way some conservatives look at our nation's booming debt and conclude the solution is another tax cut, I decided the cure to my chronic overthinking was more knowledge. When I wasn't being pummeled by two-foot peaks, I sat at my desk, trying to figure out what waves are and where they come from.

Sometimes my research proved useful. For example: waves aren't water. They travel through water, in the same way sound waves travel through air, but the position of each piece of ocean in relation to every other is as fixed as each piece of leather in a whip as it cracks. This explained why sometimes, at the bottom of a wave, I'd feel a mysterious force launching me back up. It also explained why surfing, more than any other activity I'd tried, felt not just unfamiliar but alien. The wave energy surfers harness is a kind of horizontal gravity that can be experienced by humans in oceans, large lakes, and basically nowhere else.

More often, though, knowledge wasn't power. It was just knowledge. I could tell you, for instance, that a wave's intensity is proportional to the square of its height. This means that all else being equal, a wave twice as tall is four times more powerful, a wave three times as tall is nine times more powerful, and so on. But at the end of July, when, after weeks of thigh-high rollers, an unexpected tropical storm sent a waist-high swell to the dog beach, I became the living embodiment of the difference between "to know" and "to understand."

I'd figured that in larger surf, my Wordle-streak-maintaining frontal cortex would have to compete for my attention. I was unprepared, however, for the speed with which it left the conversation completely. Upon punching through the first line of breaking waves, I was flooded with a feeling not of accomplishment, but panic. *Small animal! Large ocean! About to die!* It was this sense of inescapable calamity, even more than the walls of whitewater, that made getting out the back difficult. By the time I made it, I was panting uncontrollably. My arms, tense from terror, felt as though I'd been paddling for hours, when just five minutes earlier they'd been bone-dry.

I could feel myself trembling when something caught my eye near the north jetty.

"Katie!" I shouted.

I'd resented her for ghosting me. Now, all was forgiven. I needed an adult. I paddled toward her as fast as I dared.

"Oh, hi," she said, with an appraising look. "It's a kinda big day."

"Totally," I replied, trying to sound nonchalant. "Do you surf here a lot?"

"I usually try one beach over, at Loch Arbour. It's less crowded."

"Nice. Maybe I'll try it next time."

But Katie had shifted her attention. Slowly, she paddled toward the jetty. *Don't leave me*, I pleaded silently. *I'm a small animal in a large ocean about to die.* Then, following her eyes, I saw what she'd seen.

In surfing, a "peak" is the wave's highest point, the part that breaks first. It can also, in the way a "head of cattle" refers to the whole animal, be used as shorthand for the entirety of the wave. By either definition, this peak was the scariest I'd ever seen. It was giant, easily stomach-high. Like most waves that afternoon, it started as a gentle hill, but as it drew closer it became a coil of imminent violence, a rattlesnake about to strike. Katie remained as nonchalant as I'd recently pretended to be. She looked back over her shoulder, then accelerated with four authoritative paddle strokes. It was as if she and the wave had been planning their rendezvous for ages. She stood casually as it broke, swooping left down the line. I looked around, expecting everyone else to be similarly wowed, but they hadn't even noticed her. Their eyes remained fixed on the horizon.

I glanced over my own shoulder in time to gain several pieces of knowledge-without-understanding simultaneously: this new wave was just as big as the one Katie had ridden; none of the north-jetty crowd was paddling for it; it was headed right for me. I turned my board. I could feel, the way you feel a bouncer headed in your direction at a bar, the water coiling behind me. I could hear nothing, even though waves were crashing all around.

I said to myself, *Don't go!*

I went. As pure terror blossomed behind me, I paddled harder than I'd ever paddled before. The ocean's gentle palm didn't open, and I didn't care. I forced my chest off the board, then fought to my feet until I stood triumphant, as full of life and vigor as the first creature ever to crawl from the sea.

There's a surfing term for what happened next. I went over the falls. Rather than cruising down the line, my board stuck to the breaking section of the wave like a mouse to a glue trap. The lip pitched forward and I went with it, smacking the surface of the ocean and bouncing about in the whitewater before emerging into the harsh afternoon light. My leash threatened to yank my right hip from its socket. My eyes burned from salt. The Atlantic Ocean—all eighty quintillion gallons of it—had gone up my nose.

I didn't care. For the first time ever, I'd felt the flower of fear and embraced it. I'd committed without hesitation. That feeling was every bit as magical as flying down the line.

Over the next few days, I replayed that tumble countless times in my head. And as I did, I realized there was another, no-less-daunting fear I had to stop thinking too much about. If I wanted to find out whether my North Shore plan could survive its first hurdle, it was time to fully commit.

David Litt

Cross the border between North Central Jersey and South Central Jersey, and the majority of special-occasion restaurants are either Italian or bad. The restaurant selected for Jacqui's aunt's birthday dinner was not Italian. I scanned the menu with concern. It was as if the chef at a country club had entered a coma in 1997 and only recently awoke. The entrees were dominated by chicken dishes, most doused in similar-sounding cream sauces, all accompanied by steamed vegetables and rice pilaf. An obligatory, misguided fish option sat above "Our Burger," which was a regular burger, but with mayonnaise.

I wasn't there for the food, though. I kept glancing left, down the long, rectangular table. At the far end, across from his longtime girlfriend Samantha, sat Matt.

"Are you still going to talk to him?" asked Jacqui.

"Yes."

"When?"

"I don't know."

"You know he always leaves early, right?"

"I'm aware."

As the ninety-minute mark approached, I could see Matt begin to make *if-we-don't-leave-soon-I-will-jump-out-of-my-skin* eyes across the table. The voice in my head told me not to go, and I went anyway.

"Hey," I said, as if I hadn't just made a beeline for him. "So . . ."

He wasn't obviously unhappy to see me. That was good. I carried on.

"Actually, um, I've, uh, started surfing."

"Yeah, I heard," he said. I couldn't read his tone. "How's it going?"

The question couldn't have been simpler, yet answering it felt like pulling on a thread of a sweater. *Painfully? Slowly? Humiliating yet somehow life-affirming at a time when I desperately need it, although I worry that, in both a literal and figurative sense, I'll be stuck battling tiny waves forever?*

"Not bad," I said.

We chatted equipment. As it turned out, Matt owned a foamboard. He only brought it out on the smallest days, when there was no point in surfing something more high-performance. Still, it was a patch of common ground and I jumped on it.

"I feel like it's helpful for working on my pop-ups."

"Yeah, those are tough," he said. "You've gotta practice on land. When I was starting out, I'd do two hundred pop-ups a day. Really helped build the muscle memory."

"Oh," I replied. When I'd tried practicing pop-ups, my arms gave out after ten. I felt our common ground crumbling like a cliff into the sea. He stood up, looking toward the parking lot.

"I've gotta get the bike back home before it's too dark."

"Yeah, of course," I said. "I get it."

I took a step backward, toward my side of the room. He headed for the door. Then, just before crossing the invisible line that would mean he'd left the table, Matt turned around as though a thought had suddenly struck him. He pursed his lips and raised an eyebrow.

"When the conditions are good, I'll call you," he said.

It was hard for me to remember a time—on land, anyway—when hope and dread had been so thoroughly conjoined. Just two months earlier, I'd felt a civic duty to distance myself from my brother-in-law. I still did, sort of. But I also felt bubbly, relieved, completely unaware of how much I'd wanted something until I knew I could have it, filled suddenly with a sense that life might have more possibility than I realized because maybe, just maybe, someone saw something in me I'd only just begun to see in myself.

I thought about all these feelings, and then I thought about how best to express them to my brother-in-law.

"Cool," I said. "Sounds good."

CHAPTER FIVE

It's Only Drowning

ONE AUGUST MORNING, after catching a wave the size of a garden gnome, I hopped off my board and saw The Predator striding into the ocean, eyes fixed and glassy, like Virginia Woolf. He had no surfboard with him. He waded in up to his waist. Then he stopped, dropped his hands to his sides, and pounded the water three times—*splash! splash! splash!*—in a kind of summoning ritual.

He was hoping, I knew, for hurricanes.

An uncomfortable fact about surfing is that great waves in one place often start with tragedy someplace else. Nowhere is this more true than along the East Coast during hurricane season. Here's just one example. On September 20, 2017, Hurricane Maria hit Puerto Rico. The storm killed more than two thousand people, knocked out the island's power grid, and caused more than ninety billion dollars in property damage. Eleven days later, a New Jersey–based news site posted a video of Maria's arrival in the Garden State. The caption read, "Surfers cash in on the great conditions."

Most surfers deal with the link between others' misery and their joy the same way they deal with the presence of sharks: by not worrying about it. Thanks to climate change, there is more to not worry about than ever. Warming oceans mean more evaporation, which means more water in the air, which means more fuel for storms as they track across the sea. In the coming years, we can expect hurricanes to deliver ever-larger amounts of death, damage, destruction—and waves.

Big storms are supposed to arrive earlier in the year, too, but in this respect 2022 defied prediction. On some late-August days it was so flat that The Predator only surfed for half an hour. On other days he didn't surf at all. It wasn't until the start of September, when Hurricane Danielle sprang into existence and was followed almost immediately by Earl, that The Predator finally got his wish. Over Labor Day weekend, as the twin storms rampaged through the Caribbean, I enjoyed a last hurrah on summer waves that broke with all the force of a hiccup. Once, just before taking off, I looked left to see a waterfall of minnows leaping down the face, shimmering in the evening light. It felt like a reward for months of effort. *A tiny slice of nature, a vision, just for me.*

On September 6, a Tuesday, I drove to the dog beach and black magic had taken place. Everything between the boardwalk and shore was familiar: same happy sunbathers, same Tommy Bahama chairs, same blazing hot sand. But the summertime sea to which I'd grown accustomed was gone. Overnight, it had been replaced by something menacing, something that believed in corporal punishment and bore a long-simmering grudge. Big swells converged from all angles, a pack of coyotes descending upon their prey.

You've done this a hundred times, I reminded myself. *Get a running start, wait for the first wall of water to reach you, then hop over it onto your board.*

What I failed to realize—and what I would soon come to realize all at once—is that surfing on a truly big day is a completely separate activity from surfing on a small one. It's like owning a cat and deciding to tame a lion; knowledge acquired from the former is transferable to the latter, but only to the tiniest degree. I counted down: "Three, two, one." Then I charged headlong into the sea, tried to clear a wall of water that reached eye level, and was swept away like a sapling in a flash flood. Before I had time to breathe, my head was under.

I felt the way an egg must feel when it's beaten. The ocean pushed and pulled from all angles, a million tiny waves embedded inside the big one, yanking each part of each of my limbs in its own direction. An enormous hand pressed me down, and then, with the flick of a massive finger, sent me pinwheeling toward the seabed. Surfers call this being "ragdolled," a term I assume was coined by someone abusive to their toys, and the worst part about it was that it wasn't the worst part. I had never before worried about getting my head above water. Now, I tried swimming upward only to find that the churning ocean formed a ceiling as solid as concrete. A silent scream built in my throat. I suppressed a gulp for air.

Just when there was no way I could fight it any longer, the wave released its grip. I shot my head to the surface, taking a deep, desperate breath. A second wall of whitewater rumbled toward me like an out-of-control bulldozer, and this time I didn't try leaping over it. Instead, I let the chaos deposit me near shore like the human flotsam I was.

I had now been surfing at least four days a week for more than two months. In that time, not once had I abandoned a session because paddling out was too scary. But I didn't know how to reach these waves, let alone ride them, and the thought of being trapped underwater a second time made my chest tighten. I gave up.

On Wednesday, I went to the dog beach but didn't go in the water. On Thursday I didn't go to the dog beach. Instead, I drove twenty minutes south to Belmar, where a surf shop called Eastern Lines was running a sale on shorts.

Belmar reminds me of a fully loaded pizza, and not just because it's home to Federico's, my favorite pizza place on the Shore. The town manages to sprinkle a little bit of everything—nightclubs, mansions, playgrounds, a ceviche restaurant, a manmade lake—onto less than two square miles, yet somehow each part is essential to the whole. Eastern Lines, across the street from the boardwalk, was home to a similar phenomenon: while almost all the gear sold there, from boards to fins to T-shirts, was a hodgepodge of big national brands, the place felt as shaped by personality as a walk-in closet.

The personality in question was lounging just outside the door in a beach chair as I approached, and while I'd never met him before, he was clearly the store's owner. Everyone else was either browsing merchandise or had a job. A small, round-faced man, he possessed wild gray hair and a belly that seemed designed for the contented resting of folded hands. Had he been a surfer at the dog beach, I would have called him Danny DeVito.

"Hi," he said, "I'm Crazy Michael."

"Hi, Crazy Michael," I replied. Then I added, without thinking, "I'm Regular David. I heard you guys are doing fifty-percent-off board shorts?"

"Sure are," he confirmed. But like most people in the surf industry,

Crazy Michael was more interested in surf than industry, and before long we were discussing the hurricane swell.

"I'm seventy-two," he said. "Strictly a gentleman surfer these days. But it's looking good!"

"I've never paddled out in waves like this. Any advice?"

"Nope!" he said cheerfully. "You've just got to go out and get your ass kicked. Everybody pays their dues."

From his tone, I could tell Crazy Michael expected me to leave his store eager to paddle out. Instead, after buying a half-price pair of shorts, I took a quick glance at the ocean, drove home, and put my surfboard in the shed. At first my decision felt cowardly, but as afternoon turned to evening, I grew increasingly confident in my choice. I'd taken stock of my skills and aspirations, and, after mature analysis, determined my weekend would be best spent catching up on email, buying mulch, and not dying. I was being a grown-up. Nothing unmanly about that.

Ting!

I looked down at my phone. It was a text. From Matt.

"You surfing on Saturday?"

In my head, I composed a reply: *Thanks for thinking of me, but I'm taking the weekend off. Maybe I'll try Monday.*

Then, regretting my actions even as I took them, I typed out, "Yeah!"

Later that evening, I called him to make a plan. "Let's aim for morning," he said. "Waves should be biggest then."

"Uh-huh."

"Should be best when the tide is falling, so we can sleep in. Let's meet at Hathaway Beach at eight."

"Matt," I asked, "if getting there at eight is 'sleeping in,' what time do you normally wake up?"

"Four thirty," he replied. "Sometimes five, if I'm skipping the gym."

I spent the next day pacing the floor of our house, nervously squeezing the thumb of one hand between the thumb and forefinger of the other. That evening, Jacqui informed me she'd made a phone call of her own.

"I told my brother that if he kills you, it's going to make family functions awkward."

"What did he say?"

"He laughed."

"After laughing, did he, by any chance, add something along the lines of 'Don't worry, I won't kill him'?"

She considered this.

"He did not."

~~~~~~~~

I grew up in New York City, so I don't know why this is, but in parts of Central Jersey people signal their wealth with columns. Style is unimportant. What matters is quantity. Homeowners accumulate decorative pillars the way rich men in biblical times hoarded camels. Deal, the town I drove to the next morning, jittery from lack of sleep and a surplus of adrenaline, has more columns than all the surrounding towns put together. Several of the houses I passed on Ocean Avenue were the size of airplane hangars. Every second car was a Porsche, every third a Tesla.

By some accident of history or oversight in class warfare, one of the best public surf breaks in New Jersey lies just east of these mega-mansions. The waves at Hathaway Avenue Beach are consistently good. Access is free to surfers year-round. There's plenty of street parking, and the break is located, crucially, a short drive from the middle-class neighborhood in Oakhurst where Matt was living with his parents when he learned to surf. While he had since moved south to Brick, whenever a really big swell hit he returned to Hathaway the way a sea turtle returns to the beach where it hatched.

Matt's truck—midnight blue, with a rack installed in the bed for transporting ladders and other heavy equipment—was easy to spot. I parked behind him. As I did, I noticed something on his rear window that I hadn't seen before: a decal of a skull with a lightning bolt running through it. The design wasn't identical to the Punisher logo used by right-wing militias. But it wasn't very different, either.

Should I ask him about it? I wondered.

The answer came so quickly as to make the question rhetorical. I couldn't imagine talking with Matt about reusable bags or paper straws, let alone domestic terrorism. As far as our surf session was concerned, I would follow his lead as best I could. If my leash snapped or Freya showed up hungry, he might, in the interest of making family functions less awkward, try to save me. But that was it. The rest I didn't know and didn't want to.

I walked to the bluff overlooking the sea, where I spotted Matt on the beach, going through a calisthenics routine. He seemed to be taking it seriously. The last time I'd done an unironic jumping jack was before a high school wrestling tournament, but when I reached him, I set down my foamboard and joined in.

"Looks big," I said.

"Looks good," he said.

Gazing out to sea, I saw for the first time what "good" meant to my brother-in-law. A swirling current pulled paddlers toward the jagged, Jeep-sized boulders of the jetty. Far outside, polished hills of water rose like giants awakening from slumber, rolled toward the beach, and exploded in fits of self-destruction. I was at least a football field from the impact zone. Even so, my legs became seismometers. Each time a wave crashed, the sand beneath my feet rumbled, and I could measure the power behind each peak by how far up my body its vibrations traveled. Sometimes they reached my shins.

Matt switched from jumping jacks to stretches. The water was warm enough that there was no need for wetsuits, and the tattooed metal claw on Matt's shoulder tugged at his skin as he bent to touch his toes. As the beach shuddered from the impact of another crashing wave, I tried to imagine Troy standing in my place, or Eva, or Neil. They didn't belong here. They'd get themselves killed. What did that mean for me? I turned toward Matt.

"So, I have to say . . . I'm a little scared."

I expected him to roll his eyes. Instead, he smiled reassuringly.

"It's always going to be intimidating at first," he said. "But hey, it's only water."

I immediately felt better. While I had no idea what I was getting myself into, Matt did, and he thought I'd be fine. Besides, he was right. It was only water. How bad could things get?

"Thanks," I said.

My brother-in-law nodded, then grinned.

"Hey," he repeated in the exact same tone. "It's only drowning."

Laughing, he jogged casually into the waves.

～～～～～～

Holy shit, I thought, two minutes later. *I'm keeping up with him!* My brother-in-law's technique was far superior to mine. He arched his back proudly as he paddled out, puffing his chest and driving his forearms through the water. But he was on a six-foot board, and the extra length and buoyancy of my foamie canceled out his skill. Halfway to the end of the jetty, we were moving briskly along parallel lines.

Then the whitewater rumbled toward us and our trajectories diverged. With powerful paddle strokes, Matt charged directly at the growling wall. Just before impact, he pushed the nose of his board below the surface, used his right foot to sink the tail, and swooped his body under with the casual grace of a matador dodging a bull. This is called duck-diving. It is very hard to do, and you pretty much need a shortboard to do it. Surfers on anything long and floaty must instead rely on something called the push-up technique. I'd practiced it often over the summer. I'd paddle toward the horizon, lift my chest off the deck, do a push-up while kicking my legs back, and let the water flow harmlessly between my body and the board.

The question raised by the push-up technique, however, is this: What does one do when the whitewater rushes so high and fast that one cannot push up and over it? And the answer is: nothing. One is fucked. The surge swept me off my board and tossed me like a frisbee back toward the beachside mansions.

When the water finally let me go, I was surprised and appreciative to see Matt waiting, paddling against the current and calmly ducking waves. It took a few minutes, but eventually I caught up to him.

"Hey," he said grimly. "You're gonna have to ditch your board."

To most people such an utterance might not seem weighty, but for surfers it's like telling an arctic explorer it's time to eat the sled dogs. "Don't ditch" is the first lesson of surf etiquette, and possibly the most important. In big waves, abandoning your board sends it rocketing toward the beach at a speed that can break your fellow surfers' noses and separate them from their teeth. Wearing a leash around your ankle tempers your irresponsibility, but only slightly, because leashes are usually the same length as the boards they're attached to, and they stretch. What Matt was suggesting— abandoning my eight-foot board—was the rough equivalent of closing my eyes and swinging a twenty-foot nunchuck over my shoulder. It's a desperate measure, a last gasp, an aquatic Hail Mary.

Also, compared to duck-diving, or even doing a push-up, ditching isn't a technique at all. Here's how it works: You paddle as hard as you can. Right as the wave is about to crash on top of you, you hop off, dive deep, and wait out the carnage above. If all goes well, the wave passes by and you keep going.

But all almost never goes well. Because when a head-high wave comes at you, it's not like being attacked by someone who is six feet tall. It's like being attacked by someone whose *fists* are six feet tall. Mistime your frantic leap and you will be pounded with a ferocity pointless to quantify and difficult to comprehend. And let's say you are fortunate enough to get below the surface, where the fists can't get you. They'll still get your board. You'll be dangling upside down in the water when your leash snaps tight, jerking you by your ankle so forcefully your leg reconsiders its longstanding association with your pelvis.

Eventually, the wave releases you. But your troubles have just begun. After fighting to the surface, you'll take a desperate gulp of air, which will be woefully insufficient even if you manage not to swallow seawater, which you won't. Coughing and choking, you'll tug on your leash until your board arrives. Finally, you'll scramble onto the deck, and for a moment you'll feel safe. Then you'll remember you have about ten seconds between waves, and you'll calculate (if you can call it calculating) that you've used up eight of them, and you'll look up to see another giant fist about to pound you. So you'll do the whole thing over again, only this time with muscles screaming and brain starved for oxygen and the current pushing you ever closer to the rocks. Eventually you'll look up, lock eyes with your brother-in-law, and realize that, for the first time you can remember, he appears genuinely concerned.

I didn't make it out the back. Utterly spent, I let the ocean wash my carcass toward shore.

I sat on the sand, shoulders slumped, heart pounding. *What am I doing here?* I thought. I imagined the other dog beach VALs sitting down to pleasant brunches, waiting for the waves to return to manageable size. And here I was, getting myself almost smashed into a jetty in an effort to show a possible right-wing militia member I belonged in a hurricane swell.

I was ready to pack it in when two guys carrying longboards passed me. Chatting eagerly, seemingly oblivious to the war zone they were about to enter, they ambled about thirty yards up the beach. I hadn't seen it before: a tiny gap in the surf, the faintest hint of a channel. The longboarders waited for the next lull between sets to arrive, then scooted briskly out the back, through the impact zone, into water deep enough that no waves were breaking.

I gathered my strength and walked to the spot they'd set out from. An incoming set pounded the ocean, and when the barrage was over, I hopped on my board and paddled like mad. My energy ebbed with each frantic motion. If I didn't make it out the back this time, there was no way I'd have the strength to try again. I counted off five paddle strokes. Ten. Twenty. A giant peak appeared in the distance, the first wave of a new set. I windmilled toward it, breath heavy, shoulders numb, triceps burning. I wasn't going to make it. I ditched my board, dove under, held my breath, waited for the water to fling me toward shore.

All went well.

I couldn't believe it. After surfacing, I recovered my foamie, paddled over one final monster—it was like falling up a mountain—and heard a thunderclap as the wave broke behind me. I was safe. And I'd never seen anything like it. While leviathans still rose, they passed harmlessly underneath my board, turning the seascape into a painting of rolling English countryside, only moving and made of water. I lay on my board in the morning sun, rising and falling with the waves, resting on God's ribcage. For a long time I stayed put. Then I realized that unless Matt saw me it wouldn't really count.

It was difficult to distinguish one surfer from another in the early-morning glare, but I finally spotted him about a hundred yards to the south. Slowly, careful to remain far outside the action, I paddled over. As he saw me approaching, he did the briefest of double-takes.

"You made it! Nice!" He was yelling, although this was due less to excitement than to practical concerns. I hadn't thought about it before, but on a big day, surfers' voices are drowned out by the ocean. While we were only five feet from each other, we might as well have been standing on opposite sides of a taxiing plane.

"You gonna paddle for one?" he shouted.

"I think I'm going to rest another minute!" I yelled back.

He gave me a shrug, the universal sign for "suit yourself." Like a cat stalking its prey, he maneuvered inside, toward the impact zone where the waves broke. Every few seconds he glanced backward. I studied his movements. He was putting himself in position for something. I didn't know what. He checked over his shoulder again.

Suddenly, electrified by mysterious instinct, his body became a loaded spring. A mountain of water formed behind him, surged toward him, and scooped him up to the peak. He waited until the last possible moment, but when he paddled, he paddled furiously, kicking his feet and scooping through the ocean with cupped hands.

The peak collapsed. Matt disappeared on the other side of it, into the impact zone. The blast from the wave sent droplets flying through the air, and the rising sun met the droplets and made a rainbow. For a moment that was all I could see: a rainbow and the absence of my brother-in-law.

Then he appeared.

I knew Matt was athletic. I'd assumed he had skill. What I didn't realize, until that moment, was that he had style. Most other good surfers I'd watched that morning slashed angrily through their waves, as though they were trying to win an argument. Not Matt. He surfed balletically, delicately, as though all six feet of his board were on tiptoe. Springing up the face, he stood for a moment atop the lip. Then the dancer became a painter as he dropped low, disappeared, and reappeared, tracing the rail of his board along the face like a brush along a canvas. When his ride ended, he paddled back to the lineup, ducking under waves as he went.

"That looked fun," I yelled, astonished.

"It was pretty good," he said. Then he did it again.

Watching him paint with movement, my thoughts turned back to the decal on his truck. There was still a lot about my brother-in-law I didn't want to know, let alone emulate. But his artistry, which I at once admired and didn't understand, had taken me by surprise.

In at least one way, I wanted to be more like Matt.

~~~~~~~~~~

Over the next twenty minutes Matt caught four more rights and a left. I considered going for a wave of my own, but realized that would mean getting close enough to the impact zone to be pummeled by a breaking lip. I stayed outside, happy to remain in the audience. When a longer-than-usual lull arrived, Matt paddled over, flipped onto his back, and stretched out on his board, his hands behind his head like Huck Finn lounging on a raft.

"How's your morning been?" he asked.

"Okay. It's nice just being out here."

I thought I saw him wince. He was not the participation-trophy type. I changed the subject to the current, then the wind, then to my father-in-law's cat, a female named Kitty who, after fifteen years spent largely beside him on the couch, had recently been put to sleep.

"I went over to your parents' place yesterday to check in," I told him as my board floated to the top of another rolling hill.

"How were they?" asked Matt from the valley. The wave rolled through and our positions reversed, as though we were at opposite ends of a seesaw.

"It was hard to say. I think they liked having the company."

"They must be pretty sad."

"I bet. Their house feels so empty without her."

It was the longest conversation we'd had in at least two years. It was also the most emotional, even if the emotions in question weren't ours. Just when I was wondering how much deeper we might go, and how deep we even wanted to, Matt's eyes darted toward the horizon.

"That's the one!"

I glanced backward and knew he was right. The roller coming toward us was among the more manageable waves of the day, no higher than a kitchen counter. And it was going to break just a few feet away. This was my wave.

I don't know where the strength came from, but I dug hard, and my foamie began moving. The palm opened and lifted me up.

What surprised me most was how much thinking I could get done in a such a short time. My first thought was: *I'm standing!* My second was: *I'm facing down the line.* My third was: *I've never been here before.* I was perched atop a high, steep, sliding shelf, the lip curled in front of me like a pitcher's wrist. Water flew up the face of the wave, struck the bottom of my board, and shot from the tail. It was extraordinary.

Then a fourth thought occurred to me: *I have no idea what to do next.* I was going to have to find a way down this near-vertical surface. If I fell—by far the most likely outcome—I would be rolled up in the wave and thrown toward the seabed for a ragdolling that would make my dog beach hold-down from earlier in the week seem gentle by comparison. The lip shot forward, daring me to go with it. Instead, I hopped primly off the tail of my board, landing safely back outside.

"You were up on it!" said Matt when I reached him.

"I started okay. But I chickened out."

Matt's face fell, and I immediately regretted telling him the truth. It was as though he'd realized for the first time what a surf-shop owner in Belmar already knew. I was Regular David. The two of us would never be cut from the same cloth.

"I'm starving," he said, voice flat with disappointment. "I'm gonna go in and eat my apple."

I stayed out for a bit, looking for a shot at redemption and failing to find it. Back on the beach, in the shadow of a faux-modern villa, Matt retrieved a blue Igloo cooler from the rocks. Eventually I paddled back in and joined him on the sand. For a moment we stood and watched the waves crash.

"How long after you started surfing did it take you to feel, you know, okay?" I asked him.

"I always did. But that's because I always went for it. Either miss the wave, make it, or wipe out hard."

It was as close as Matt had ever come to criticizing me. He must have realized he'd stretched a toe across the line, because he immediately gave me an encouraging look.

"You don't have anything to worry about," he said. "You can break your body and still do your job."

"Thank you," I replied, not exactly encouraged.

In the distance, a wetsuit-clad figure shot into a barrel—the tube between a powerful lip and the wave face—and my brother-in-law reacted like a dog spotting a squirrel.

"Let's get back out there," he said, already jogging toward the water. Without checking behind him, he raced into the ocean and began paddling out once more.

It took me five tries to get out the back, and when I finally made it, Matt and I were far apart. Neither of us tried to find the other. Earlier that morning, when we were talking ocean currents and beloved pets, it had felt like the gulf between us was narrowing. But his words on the beach—"I always went for it"—still stung. A massive dark-gray peak appeared. I paddled for it as hard as I could. At the last second, though, I leaned back on my board and bailed.

After another hour of not quite committing, I glanced toward shore. Matt was standing there; I hadn't noticed him go in. I could tell he was watching me. Wondering. Would I slink back in with my tail between my legs, crawling through the water in a paddle of shame? Or would I finally try to ride something?

I inhaled deeply, gathered all my remaining courage, and chose tail between legs. I was too tired. Too nervous. Too overwhelmed. Slowly, I dragged my arms shoreward, inching toward Hathaway Beach.

I was about a dozen yards in when I felt it behind me. I don't know how. Maybe there was a shift in the color of the water or a change in the light. Whatever the reason, I could tell something was coming. I looked over my shoulder to see a chest-high wave heading toward me. It was breaking left. I hadn't yet learned how to take off going left. I didn't care. I paddled hard.

Even as I yanked my forearms through the water, I braced myself for disaster, for the moment when the wave would seize control of my destiny and send me flying over the lip. Instead, I rose to my feet. The nose of my board swiveled down the line.

Then one of a million things happened—my front foot slipped, or my right arm trailed behind my hip, or I leaned back in a subconscious attempt to climb up and over the collapsing wall—and I lost my balance. The rail bit into the face of the wave, tentatively, then harder.

A few days earlier, when Crazy Michael had told me to go out there and get my ass kicked, I'd nodded politely. Now, I realized that I should have pressed for more detail. For example, I might have asked, "Excuse me, Crazy Michael, but does 'paying your dues' include pirouetting on the deck of your board so that you and the wave are facing each other, losing purchase right as the lip begins to break, and, in something that resembles (but is most certainly distinct from) a bellyflop, landing directly on your scrotum?"

If so, I paid my dues that afternoon in Deal.

A few minutes later, I dragged my foamboard onto the sand and limped up the beach. Matt was waiting.

"You looked good!" he said. "You went for it!"

I followed Matt up the bluff, still limping slightly. When we reached the street, he didn't ask me how I was feeling; I didn't ask him about the decal on his truck. But while my brother-in-law might still think of me as talentless, and I still had no idea what to think of him in general, he'd decided I wasn't a total disappointment.

For one session, that was victory enough.

~~~~~~~~~~

CHAPTER SIX

The New Jersey Rubicon

"SO, YOU LIKE SPENDING TIME with him?"

My therapist, Stewart, awaited my answer. Or at least the top half of his face did. Although he was quite professionally accomplished and his insights had helped me enormously, Stewart had never fully adjusted to working remote. He particularly struggled with camera placement. I'd grown accustomed to speaking with a pair of wire-rimmed glasses and white eyebrows, which peered above the bottom of his Zoom box like a frog keeping watch in a pond.

"I like that Matt's willing to surf with me," I said. "I like that there's someone in the water who will know if I drift away. It's helpful."

Stewart's eyebrows furrowed, as they often did when he felt I was being stingy with my subconscious. He tried another way in.

"When you're surfing, you're trying to get inside the hollow part of the wave, right?"

"It's called getting barreled, and I probably won't be able to do it for at least a few years. But yeah, eventually."

"So . . . the birth canal! Emerging into the light. You're looking for a kind of rebirth."

As always when things in therapy got anatomical, I changed the subject. Still, I had to admit that Stewart was not the only one flirting with cliché. For a certain type of thirtysomething male over-achiever who hits a speed bump, learning to surf is just what you do. Mark Zuckerberg picked up a board right around the time his public image went from "boy wonder" to "morally dubious oligarch." When the cryptocurrency hedge fund Three Arrows Capital collapsed amid fraud allegations, its founders, a pair of thirty-six-year-old men, hightailed it to Bali and took surf lessons.

The biggest difference between me and them—apart from many billions of dollars and a mountain of legal woe—was my newfound willingness to surf in winter. People for whom surfing is purely escapist do not escape to New Jersey between November and March.

When I told friends I planned to paddle out during the shortest days of the year, they were impressed by my toughness, and I felt no need to disillusion them. In truth, my decision to embrace the cold was practical and made reluctantly. Hawaii's North Shore usually goes flat all summer, picks up again in late fall, then turns psycho by Thanksgiving. Only during a brief window—the end of October and beginning of November—would I be likely to find waves that were overhead without being so overhead as to surely kill me. That gave me just twelve months to prepare.

"Out of curiosity," I asked Matt on the phone shortly after our Hurricane Earl session, "what's the lowest temperature you've ever surfed in?"

"Air or water?"

I didn't like where this was going.

"Water."

"I dunno," he said. "Probably thirty-four degrees."

"Not to be overly negative, but that sounds absolutely miserable."

"Don't worry," he replied. "In a thick wetsuit, you won't even notice the cold."

"If you say so."

"Trust me," he said. "What you'll notice is how heavy the waves are."

In surf lingo, *heavy* generally means "more violent." But when I looked it up later, I learned Matt was speaking literally. As liquid cools, the molecules within it pack together; a glass of water from your fridge weighs more than a glass from your sink. The difference is tiny. Fractions of an ounce. But imagine how many glasses of water can fit inside a single ocean wave and you begin to get a feel for winter. It is worth noting, in the interest of full disclosure, that scientists say this difference is imperceptible. It is also worth noting that hardcore Jersey surfers don't care what scientists say. The consensus, from those who had experienced it, was that getting hit by a breaking lip during a December swell was like being blasted by a firehose of wet cement. Not to be overly negative, but that sounded a good deal worse than absolutely miserable.

Also, I was pretty sure I'd notice the cold.

My plan was to wake up one morning and discover that overnight I'd become the kind of hardy outdoorsman who scoffs at the very idea of winter. Barring that, my plan was to acclimate. All I needed was time, which Jersey surfers measure not by the calendar, but by wetsuit thickness. I'd taken my first lesson with Katie at the tail end of 3/2 season, pronounced "three-two" for the three millimeters of neoprene padding the suit's torso and the two on the limbs. From roughly mid-July until mid-September you can surf in nothing but board shorts. A second 3/2 season lasts until mid-October, followed by 4/3 season until mid-November. After that, it's nearly six long months of 5/4 temperatures before the ocean warms again.

I doubted anything could make pleasant the experience of surfing in water colder than the inside of a fridge. But if I could add a millimeter of neoprene at a time, and surf regularly enough that the sea dropped only a few degrees each session, I might trick my body into finding winter bearable.

The acclimation plan would have been a sound one, if Congress hadn't ruined it. In September 2022, the House Judiciary Committee, where Jacqui still worked, summoned staff back to its Capitol Hill offices after more than two years spent largely remote. Living separate lives so I could remain a full-time novice surfer seemed a bit ridiculous, so I went with her. Suddenly, Surf World—or at least, what I'd come to think of as my corner of it—was three and a half hours away. One weekend in Washington became two weekends, then three. In what seemed like no time at all, 3/2 season had raced by.

And the real world was just getting started with me. A few weeks after returning to our nation's capital, I flushed the toilet and noticed rust-colored water emerging from our bathtub drain. It was one of those events that short-circuits the mind. *Curious. This smells like riding in my family's Volvo in the 1990s as we drove along the West Side Highway past the sewage treatment plant. What could explain it?* Then a clog of flushable wipes left by our home's previous owners ruptured a pipe above our kitchen, sending a noxious drip through the ceiling, and the truth became unavoidable. There was no hope of getting back to Jersey—my days were too packed with emergency plumbers and cabinet repair firms.

Before I knew it, 4/3 season was almost over. Each time I stepped into the shower I checked on my butt cheek dimples, worried they might fade.

~~~~~~~~~

Sometimes I asked Stewart if I needed to worry that depression would return now that I was no longer surfing regularly, and he never gave me a straight answer, and I paid him anyway, because that's therapy.

As it turned out, I didn't tumble all the way backward. Still, I could feel old patterns clawing to the surface. I began shooting bolt upright before dawn again, running through my existential-crisis checklist. On Election Day 2022, trying to summon my inner happy warrior, I volunteered at the headquarters of a Philadelphia voter protection hotline—but for an hour that afternoon, with a virtual queue of citizens eager to cast ballots, I abandoned my post to pace the block, check Twitter, and freak out.

Clearly, I needed to get back in the water. I had a work trip to Los Angeles scheduled for mid-November, and I made sure to book a surf lesson before my flight home.

It was the first time I'd ever surfed outside a five-mile stretch of Central Jersey, and even from the Santa Monica parking lot I could tell it would be a totally different experience. In the Garden State, riding waves remains parochial. The closest the Asbury dog beach gets to welcoming foreigners is when people drive there from

Pennsylvania or New York. In California, where surfing is a culture rather than a sub-culture, locals come from everywhere. Luis, my instructor that morning, learned to surf as a kid in Ecuador, moved to Florida as a teen, then switched coasts to LA in pursuit of better waves.

Beneath his trucker cap and Tom Selleck mustache, Luis sported a volleyball-sized gut. But if he shared my embarrassment about wearing a full-body neoprene condom, he didn't show it. He knifed into his wetsuit in a single motion and trotted confidently across the beach. His board was tiny—it made Matt's look like a foamie by comparison—but his balance while paddling was so impeccable that his stomach was practically cemented to the deck. He was strong, too. Zooming past the waist-high waves, he was out the back in seconds, hat and mustache completely dry.

I caught up with him, then took in my surroundings while my arms recovered. The Ferris wheel on the Santa Monica Pier was gleaming and metropolitan, nothing like the *I-got-a-permit-from-a-guy-who-knows-a-guy* attractions at Point Pleasant or Seaside Heights. On the East Coast, the sun comes up over the ocean; in California I watched it rise above towering beachside cliffs.

The waves were different, too. East Coast conditions are generally described as "pitchy," "punchy," "fast," and "steep." While these aren't necessarily bad things, they all mean that Jersey waves break quickly. Their California counterparts are typically slower and more gently sloped, and thus more forgiving. A Santa Monica peak breaks like a door being slowly closed by the hosts of a dinner party as they wave goodbye to their guests. A New Jersey peak breaks like a door being slammed in an argument. The first time I paddled for a California right, I leapt to my feet the moment my board began planing, lost my balance, and dove headfirst into the surf.

"You need to slow down," Luis said.

"Okay," I replied. "How long exactly should I wait?" He shrugged.

"Wait too long," he said. "See what works. When people start out, they think success is taking off and failure is falling. No. Success is knowing *why*. If you wipe out but you know the reason you wiped out, that's success. If you make the wave but you don't know why, you failed."

I tried following Luis's advice. Sometimes I was intentionally sluggish, sometimes I shot to my feet as though electrified. After each ride or wipeout, instead of asking *How did I do?* I asked *Why did that happen?* I became my own teacher. And I wasn't half bad. As the sun rose high above the cliffs, I felt my board glide atop each breaking peak for what seemed like hours. When I wanted to stand, I stood. Locked into the pocket—the churning, breaking section of wave face that is closest to the lip—I floated down the line.

If I'd been twenty-three years old, that's when I would have moved to Los Angeles. But I was now thirty-six, with a kitchen that needed mold remediation and a flight to catch.

"Before I leave, what's the biggest thing I need to focus on?" I asked Luis. "Keeping my elbows high when I paddle?"

"You have to stop looking ahead to the next thing," he told me. "When you're paddling, you have to think about paddling, not popping up. When you're popping up, you have to think about popping up, not getting down the line."

Like most people in the age of Instagram self-help, I was no stranger to "living in the moment." But in a subtle way, this was different.

Luis wasn't telling me to be passive—to become a stone around which flows the river of time. His relationship to the moment was not just present but active, aggressive, fighting to shape one set of circumstances before moving swiftly to the next.

I drove straight from the beach to the airport. That night in Washington, hours from the nearest surf break, I put a version of Luis's theory to the test. As usual, I shot upright long before dawn, my mind an out-of-control carousel. But this time, instead of telling myself to stop, I told myself to focus on one thing at a time. *Your job right now is to go to sleep. You have permission to fret in the morning.*

When morning came I awoke, well-rested, and discovered that fretting seemed less useful in the light.

~~~~~~~~~~

We finally got back to Asbury Park around Christmas. It was time for me to cross the Rubicon and become a winter surfer. I just wasn't sure if I wanted Matt with me when I did.

My decision was a tug-of-war between safety and pride. On one hand, the lifeguards were long gone. So were the crowds. If my board broke or leash snapped and I was swept away in the frozen Atlantic, no one would ever find me. On the other hand, just thinking about setting foot in an ice-cold ocean made me shudder in a way that, if anyone was watching, would leave little room for dignity. My brother-in-law already had enough doubts about my toughness.

I solved my problem by buying stuff. First, I ditched the foamie for a board that, while the same length, had a rock-hard shell that could stand up to heavy waves. Next, I bought a leash endorsed by pro surfers and virtually guaranteed not to break. Finally, I got a waterproof smartwatch with a built-in phone so I could call the Coast Guard from the ocean. Having neutralized the dangers of paddling out in winter solo, I waited for a day when Matt would have to work and wouldn't be surfing. Then I opened the closet door and took a long, hard look at my 5/4.

My winter wetsuit was only two millimeters thicker than my summer one, but it might as well have been a full set of plate armor. It stood stiffly at attention on its hanger, legs straight, arms to the sides, as though already occupied. With my lower body stuffed inside, I walked like a performer on stilts. The top half of the suit, meanwhile, was as restrictive as a corset while having the opposite of a slimming effect. Worst of all was the built-in hood. To keep it watertight, I had to cinch the face opening so securely the elastic cord bit into my lower jaw.

"You okay?" Jacqui yelled from downstairs.

"I'm fine!" I shouted back, in the way one does when being strangled while boiled alive.

And the suit was only the beginning. Next came a pair of neoprene boots as thick as skirt steaks and roughly as elastic. After that, I pulled a rubber mitten over my left wrist, where I'd already secured my smartwatch. That wasn't so bad, actually. But with the first mitten turning my hand into a claw, getting its partner over the right wrist was a nightmare, like trying to button a shirt sleeve with a monkey wrench.

My outfit finally complete, I clonked stiffly down the stairs, my face the color of steamed shrimp. Inviting Jacqui to laugh at me, I struck the closest thing I could to a runway pose. She gave me a look of deep concern.

"Are you *sure* you want to do this?"

"Matt says it's not even cold if you have the right gear."

"Yeah," she said, "but he's Matt."

I had no reply to that.

I drove toward Crazy Michael's shop in Belmar, where a camera livestreamed the beach and I knew there were at least a few other surfers out. While the afternoon was warm for January, the sun was already setting when I arrived at 4 p.m., with rays of silver-gray light peeking through slate-gray clouds and striking blue-gray sea. With my hood pressed tightly against both ears, even the sound of the waves seemed gray. I was used to surfing in the ocean. This was an abyss. I crossed the sand, clenched my teeth in anticipation, and lifted a booted toe. Then I dunked it into freezing water and gasped in shock:

Matt had been right! I didn't feel the cold at all. Wading in until the water reached my waist, I remained comfortable, even cozy. Shaking my head in disbelief, I paddled toward three similarly outfitted surfers who were already out the back.

The first wave that came my way was unquestionably an East Coaster, punchy and steep, but I made it to my feet. Time stopped atop the peak. Then someone pressed play on the world. I slid gently down the face, paddled back out, and did the whole thing again. As I floated on my board, a seabird popped its dripping head from the water, so close I could see the hook at the end of its orange beak. The two of us shared a secret: winter surfing was easy! I caught a third wave, then a fourth, and was paddling against the current to position myself for a fifth ride when I glanced toward the beach and realized I was totally alone.

Even the bird was gone. The wind had abruptly swung side-shore, sending the texture of the waves from clean to messy—from Lay's Classic to Ruffles—in seconds. Hundreds of yards away, near the boardwalk, I could see the last of my fellow surfers heading to his car. The only thing more frightening than the choppy surface was the light. I'd been too busy catching waves to notice that as the sun dipped, the sky had darkened to perfectly match the ocean. Looking toward the horizon, I struggled to figure out where water ended and air began.

The wave came out of nowhere, like a driver swerving into my lane. It was at least a foot taller than the ones I'd been riding, and steeper, and it broke further outside. *Take your time*, I told myself as I paddled, but Luis's advice no longer applied. Instead of staying open and inviting me to stand at my convenience, the peak guillotined shut. For a split second, I glimpsed my board's nose as it dove toward the sand.

My exposed face was first to feel the sting of heavy water. Then the ocean found a tiny gap between my hood and forehead, surged down my neck, and formed a freezing puddle against my spine. Held underwater, I soundlessly gasped. The cold put my temples in a vise, the mother of all ice-cream headaches. When at last I breached the surface, I had just enough time for one panicked breath before the next wave ragdolled me through the surf. Finally, after several more waves, a blissful lull arrived. Arms leaden from the weight of the waterlogged suit, chastened by the cold but grateful the pummeling was over, I reached toward my ankle to haul my board back in.

My leash was gone.

I pawed the water frantically, hoping to feel a familiar slight pressure as wrist bumped against cord. But there was nothing. The unbreakable leash had broken. Glancing inside, I watched my fancy new board rocket toward the beach. I wasn't a surfer anymore. I was a not-strong swimmer, alone in a freezing sea.

I glanced left and made a note of my position along the jetty. Then I took twenty big freestyle strokes toward shore and glanced left again. I was in the exact same spot. Of course I was. In my thick wetsuit, I might as well have been swimming in a sleeping bag. Or maybe I was trapped in a rip current. I knew rips were common on the Shore, and occasionally I'd paddled into them. But I hadn't yet learned how to spot one.

I looked at my left wrist, where my smartwatch was cinched tightly, and realized how stupid I'd been. Putting my emergency plan into action would mean tearing off my mittens and rolling up the tight sleeve of my wetsuit, then somehow, with dripping, freezing fingers, dialing 911. Even if I reached someone, they'd never hear me over the sound of the waves, or spot me from a distance in the ocean's gray expanse.

I tried taking another twenty freestyle strokes, but lifting my arms above the water had grown exhausting, and I gave up halfway through. I checked the jetty again, hoping against hope. No progress. A peak rolled through, and I treaded water, thinking it might push me to shore, but the wave welled up and passed beneath me, crashing a few yards inside.

A panicked lump had risen in my throat when I looked toward the horizon and saw, in the far distance, a slight variation in shadow. Slowly, then quickly, a mountain began to build. I knew what this meant. A "cleanup set"—an inexplicably giant group of waves—was coming. Ordinarily I lived in fear of these monsters. They break far enough outside to demolish entire lineups of surfers, hence the name. Now, though, a cleanup set was my last chance. I swam toward the beach with every remaining ounce of strength.

I came close enough to not making it to know, in a way I will never be able to unknow, what it feels like to be out of options. But at the last possible moment, just before moving on without me, the peak pitched forward. I spread my arms. The whitewater pinwheeled me toward shore. When the cold shot straight through my lower back into my lungs, the pain and shock went way beyond absolutely miserable, and I didn't care. All that mattered was that when I surfaced, I was slightly closer to the beach. I spread my arms and ragdolled again.

Halfway through the third ragdolling, my shoulder collided with something solid. My board! I clambered atop it and paddled toward shore. Twenty seconds later, a small inside roller washed me onto the beach, and I scrambled up the sand until I was sure the ocean couldn't get me. For a long time I sat there, overheating from exertion despite the cold, heart pounding against the neoprene wall of my wetsuit.

When I finally caught my breath, I looked down to check my ankle. The leash, as it turned out, wasn't faulty. I was. I'd been so busy worrying about what would happen when my toe first touched cold water that I'd forgotten to attach it.

Something vibrated against my wrist. I tried to ignore it. It vibrated again. I pulled off a mitten and unrolled my wetsuit's thick rubber sleeve.

"It looks," said my new watch, "like you're going for an open water swim."

~~~~~~~~~

Although the responsible choice was now obvious—banish my board to the shed and wait till summer—I never considered making it. The North Shore dream had its hooks in me too deep for that. I did, however, promise myself that the next time I surfed in winter, it would be with Matt.

The wait was longer than I'd expected. For three weeks I didn't hear from him. One afternoon toward the end of January, the waves were larger than usual, and the weather was harsher than it had been all month, with below-freezing temperatures, pelting rain, and sixteen-mile-per-hour gusts of wind. *Of course today's the day he'll want to surf*, I thought. And of course, he did.

"It's looking bad," Matt said. "Strong currents. Strong everything. Let's go to Deal."

I wondered, briefly, if I would ever get used to my brother-in-law's ability to state a set of predicates followed by the exact opposite conclusion.

"Shouldn't we wait until the rain eases up?" I asked. "It's pretty gross out."

"Yeah, it sucks. Really nasty. Let's go now."

Matt had grown out his beard for winter, and I was greeted in the Hathaway Avenue parking lot by a young, tattooed Rasputin. The skull-and-lightning decal, I noticed, was still affixed to his truck. It took me several minutes to suit up, and with every second he was forced to wait I could see the pressure building inside him like steam in a kettle. The moment my right mitten was on, he jogged straight for the surf.

The sets were huge, nearly as big as during Hurricane Earl, with even shorter lulls between them. Matt duck-dived his way out the back and disappeared from sight. I tried to follow him but couldn't. In addition to being restrictive, a fully saturated 5/4 wetsuit weighs about fifteen pounds, and paddling in one is like sprinting with a small dumbbell in each hand. I flogged my way toward the horizon, treadmilling against the sea.

Suddenly, a white streak shot right to left through my field of vision. It was my brother-in-law, wake trailing behind as he sped along the face. The lip reared up to bury him, but instead of flee-ing the breaking section, he pulled into it and entered the hollow part of the wave. It seemed like he was in there forever. Then he emerged into the light, reborn. I'd never actually seen him get bar-reled before. I'd never seen anyone get barreled from that angle. As the lip collapsed, it threw a rainbow into the gray winter sky.

My own situation was less transcendent. It took me several attempts to make it out the back, and the moment I did I was swept north by the current. By the time I was ready to try paddling for a wave, I'd floated past the jetty to an entirely different beach. I washed in, walked back to Hathaway, and tried again, but my strength was gone. Matt surfed for another hour. I watched from the shallows, practicing pop-ups in the whitewater and trying not to look as dispirited as I felt. After all the nerves, the planning, the les-sons, the abject terror as I drifted in the freezing sea, I had reached a catch-22. To improve, I needed to ride bigger waves in winter; to ride bigger waves in winter, I needed to improve. Doors were closing in Surf World.

Yet windows in the real world began opening. First, a speechwriting friend asked me if I might be interested in helping, in a confidential, behind-the-scenes way, on a big project involving climate change. While the work seemed interesting and meaningful, my instinct was to say no. After the last few years, I wasn't sure I could handle so much disheartening information.

That's the flower of fear! said a voice in my head. I signed up for the project.

The next open window came a few weeks later. Two friends of ours in DC, Sam and Lauren, had decided to foster a dog, and the agency they contacted offered them an extremely pregnant husky mix. To me, this seemed like driving home from the auto dealership in a clown car, but they gamely accepted. A few weeks after the litter tumbled forth, we arrived at their house bearing takeout. We were led to the basement, where six furry potatoes wriggled in a tarp-lined pen.

"Are you just here to see them?" Sam asked. "Or are you thinking about adopting one?"

"We've always wanted a dog," I replied, "but this is the worst possible time for a puppy. Jacqui's crazy busy at work. I've got the new climate change project. Plus in a few weeks I'm going on a six-day surf retreat to Costa Rica. The waves are supposed to be good for beginners, which might help me improve enough to surf more in Jersey this winter, plus the water's eighty degrees and . . ."

Sam was no longer paying attention to me. A tan, tail-waggling lump had climbed into Jacqui's lap.

That would be the moment when some couples know they're getting a puppy. For my wife and me, it was the moment when the discussions began. For three weeks, we talked about nothing else. Schedules were dissected. Training manuals consulted. We administered a doggy DNA test and called husky breeders in three states to ask them what forty-four percent of our future pet's personality might be. The debates were endless. Talmudic. The two of us took opposite sides, then switched in a kind of marital moot court. Finally, during what was supposed to be a date night at a ceviche restaurant, but which had devolved into yet more puppy analysis, I pushed my snapper with fermented jalapeño dramatically to the side and announced, "This reminds me of surfing."

Jacqui sighed, buckling in.

"Adopting a puppy is scary, because we don't know what will happen. But just because it's frightening doesn't mean it's bad for us. What if the fear is actually telling us this is the right decision? Have I ever told you when you take off on a wave, and you cross the point of no return, it's called 'going over the ledge'?"

Jacqui nodded. Of course I had.

"Well, I think we need to go over the ledge with the dog."

So we did, and I was right: it was the worst possible time for a puppy. We named her Emily, and when she was asleep, it was hard to imagine something so tiny, so innocent, so fluffy and perfect, could be such an unrepentant agent of chaos. When she was awake, it was hard to remember that blissful era known as "our lives until yesterday." Those first few nights, I dozed on the couch beside her tiny crate, my fingers dangling through the bars so she'd feel less alone. Every two hours, my alarm went off. I'd bolt to my feet, cradle

Emily in my arms, and sprint for the door. If I was lucky and quick, we'd make it outside in time to avoid an accident. Then, adrenaline pumping harder than it did after any wipeout, I'd carry her indoors to start the clock again.

Four days after bringing Emily home, I made what was quite possibly the only decision more foolish than getting a puppy because of a surfing analogy. I left my wife alone with said puppy and went to Costa Rica on my surf trip.

CHAPTER SEVEN

If You Ever Get into Fights

IT WAS NEIL, OF THE DOG BEACH VALs, who had first introduced the idea of a Costa Rican retreat.

"I did a week in Tamarindo," he'd told me one summer afternoon as we watched The Predator rocket past. "It was amazing. I learned a ton." He seemed eager to tell me more about the experience, but his reminiscence was cut short when he was swept off his board by a wave with all the power of a garden hose.

From this interaction I gained two insights: First, camps for beginners existed. Second, were I to attend one, I would be a better surfer than nearly all of my fellow campers.

Both of these features, already attractive in July and August, were positively alluring by mid-February, when I arrived in the dusty beach town of Nosara on the Pacific coast. My sole winter session with Matt had left me demoralized, less certain than ever that my Hawaii plan was possible. A tropical jump start was exactly what my surfing skills needed.

When it came to the fellow campers, my hope that I'd be better than everyone wasn't just about me wanting to win. I was too new to surfing to gauge my progress internally. I needed reference points, yardsticks to measure by. In Jersey's 5/4 season, I couldn't compare myself to other VALs because there weren't any. Most people at my level stayed out of the water. But if I was the best beginner at the beginners' retreat? That would prove I'd come a long way since summer, and would mean I could go much further by the fall.

Also, I wanted to win.

The retreat I'd chosen was called Barefoot Surf, and it operated out of the Hotel Guiones, a collection of white stucco bungalows linked by jungle walkways and clustered around a wooden main lodge. The night before our first session, all twelve campers gathered beneath the corrugated metal roof of the hotel's open-air restaurant for a get-to-know-you dinner. There, I quickly realized we fell into two groups: women picking up a hobby, and men trying to fill an unfillable void.

The first group was made up of Ellie, a sullen Chinese expat; Yasmin, a boisterous Bay Area native; and Melanie, a thoughtful twenty-something who worked for a social justice nonprofit. The remaining nine of us had, in one way or another, begun surfing after asking, "Is this all there is?" Prakash, a microchip designer from Northern California, had recently turned fifty. Ken, a jacked Texas grandpa, had retired. Jared and Ted had both survived heart surgery. Dennis had suffered a gruesome martial-arts accident.

Poor guy, I thought, as he described his months-long recovery. Followed by, *I bet I'm a way better paddler than he is.*

I awoke early the next morning to the thunder of howler monkeys and leapt into my board shorts, eager to get in the water. First, though, we were told to meet in the hotel's yoga hut, where two coaches would conduct a class on surf theory. Tabbi, a waifish

Tasmanian blonde who pronounced *no* as "noi" and *paddle* as "piddle," held the clicker that cycled through PowerPoint slides. Josh, a Brit with the center part and bowl cut popular among 1992's coolest first-graders, lectured in front of the screen.

Among the first words out of Josh's mouth were "I'm a big boy," and in terms of both height and thickness this was true. He was as solid and substantial as a bowling ball. Born in Cornwall, England, he'd traveled the world as a pro surfer in his twenties. Now in his early thirties, he spent half the year as an instructor in Costa Rica and the other half as an electrician in the UK.

"We'll get deeper into this later in the week," Josh said, as a slide on surf stance appeared onscreen, "but basically it's like if you ever boxed. Or had a fight, if you ever get into fights." As Tabbi made an *uh-oh* face, Josh raised the fists appended to his tree-trunk arms, crouched low, and flashed a roguish smile. One of his front teeth overlapped slightly with its neighbor. It wasn't hard to guess if he ever got into fights.

I'd hoped that at a surf camp for adult learners, I would find instructors who reminded me of me. Instead, I'd traveled over two thousand miles to find myself staring at a tattooed electrician with a rebellious past and an underdeveloped sense of danger. Nor was Josh the only presence I found familiar. It was remarkable how quickly everyone slid into well-worn roles—guy who shouts the answer before the teacher finishes the question; handsome dude who arrives late because rules don't apply to people with high cheekbones; girl looking so bored she could die. I, too, felt the stirrings of my toxic classroom trait.

"Excuse me," I asked from the front row, "but in the illustration on the slide behind you, you can only see two of the surfboard's three fins. Is that intentional, or unintentional?"

Josh shook his head sorrowfully, as though I'd been sent to the yoga hut to punish him for his sins.

"It's a drawing," he said. Class was dismissed soon after, and we plodded down a dusty road to collect our rental boards.

Given its macho culture, it's ironic that surfing is often a contest to see whose is smallest. The shorter the board you can ride, the better your wave-catching ability must be, so beginners are particularly size-obsessed. From what Neil had told me at the dog beach, I'd assumed most campers would ride giant foamies. But Ellie was given a sleek 7′2″ swallowtail, and Jared tucked a 7′4″ egg under his arm. Even Dennis, the martial-arts accident victim, grabbed an 8′0″.

I was handed a nine-foot longboard. I'd requested that length to be on the safe side, and figured others would do the same. Instead, in a sport where two inches is a meaningful difference, my board towered over the next-longest by at least half a foot. Their burdens light, eleven happy VALs traipsed along the dirt path that cut through a hundred yards of jungle to the beach. I hoisted my plank over my head and trudged behind.

Nosara's main break is called Playa Guiones, and I could hear its waves before I saw them. That was a bad sign. I'd chosen this location because it was supposed to be perfect for beginners, with gentle rollers on which to perfect my pop-up and extend my rides. But thigh-high waves don't boom. I stepped from the jungle path onto the beach and confirmed it: an unseasonably large swell had arrived. I couldn't yet tell how high the peaks were, because the break was far from shore. But the vibrations in the sand rumbled all the way up to my shins, just as they had when I surfed Hurricane Earl with Matt.

After setting up a camera with a lens the size of a forearm, Josh and Tabbi divided our group into pairs. My partner, Ted, had a searching look, a dreamlike quality to his voice, and a jet-black helmet he carefully buckled around his chin. He was in his fifties. That was promising. Even more promising, he was one of the guys who'd recently recovered from heart surgery.

"I'm hoping this week will get me ready to surf more with my brother-in-law," I told him. "The last time we paddled out together, it was almost head-high."

My comment was meant to intimidate, but Ted simply gazed at me, the way a person who has eaten a pot gummy might regard a caterpillar on a leaf.

"That's very cool. My goal is first, to feel the karma with everyone. And second, to work on my cutbacks."

Uh-oh, I thought. A "cutback" refers to pivoting your board nearly 180 degrees, so that instead of going down the line you're moving in the opposite direction, toward the "pocket," the breaking part of the wave. I'd never learned the mechanics behind this maneuver, let alone pulled one off. Already losing ground to my human yardstick, I borrowed a page from Matt's book and launched into calisthenics.

"Nice water," I remarked between jumping jacks. "Back in New Jersey, it's forty degrees right now."

"Oh, I'm from Oregon," Ted replied. "It's that cold all year round."

~~~~~~~~

A freckled British instructor named Naomi led me and Ted toward
the sea. She was a calm and forceful presence, an aquatic Mary Pop-
pins, and I felt confident we were in good hands.

But the paddle-out was brutal. It was at least four times longer
than Deal's, and to reach the main break we had to pass through a
series of smaller ones. It was impossible to traverse the whole distance in a single go. I'd wait for a lull, cross one impact zone, and get
walloped in the next. Once, in desperation, I forgot to check behind
me before ditching my board, and it missed Ted by inches.

"*No bueno*, man!" he yelled. Thanks to my longer board and unsur-
gerized heart, I made it out the back first, but the moment he caught
up, he swept his eyes across the mile-long beach, said, "Amazing!" and
paddled his blue 7′6″ onto a powerful right.

I, meanwhile, floundered. The peaks were West Coasters—gentle
and slow to break—and I had no problem committing. But it didn't
matter. I splashed desperately, shoulders aching, lungs bursting, only
for waves to billow beneath me like trains leaving the station. After
a half hour of watching me struggle, Naomi paddled over with prim,
authoritative strokes.

"Not to be presumptuous," she said, "but what if we went in a bit
and I gave you a little push?"

I hadn't been pushed on a surfboard since my second lesson with
Katie. Now, even with a boost from my surf governess, I rode only
three tiny waves in the ninety-minute session. Every so often I looked
back outside to see Ted cruising down a face, his helmet shining like

a marble in the tropical sun. I was collecting my sandals on the beach when he rejoined me.

"Isn't this awesome?" he asked, in the grateful manner of one whose karma is through the roof.

"Yeah," I lied. "Really great."

But flailing on a longboard while being pitied by an English-woman was sheer delight compared to what came next: video analysis. After breakfast, Tabbi and Josh pulled out iPads and we sat by the pool to watch the morning's session in slow motion.

I hadn't expected to wow anybody with my wave-riding footage. I had, however, hoped to view it without cringing so intensely that my gums hurt. Every clip was mortifying, the surf equivalent of a loud, public fart. The worst part was my pop-up. I'd practiced it thousands of times—in the water, in my office, on hotel-room floors. I thought I had it. But here I was, landing with both feet so close together they were practically touching. Where surfers like Matt crouched low to gain speed, letting the wave's energy flow through them, I stood as stiffly as a plastic army man. With my weight on the tail of my board, the nose spiked upward in a wheelie.

"That's how you lost your speed, by stalling out," Josh explained. I stared at the floor.

"Hey," he offered encouragingly, "at least you got some good wipeouts in."

"Yeah, thanks."

"I mean it. You need one really good wipeout a session. That's how you know you've been surfing."

Or maybe, I thought grumpily, *the way to know you've been surfing is to have successfully surfed.*

~~~~~~~~~~~

At Barefoot Surf, theory, coaching, and video analysis came in the morning. The middle of the day was too hot to do anything but rest. That left late afternoons and early evenings for "free sessions"—unguided surfing time where we could practice what we'd learned.

The main thing I learned the first evening in Costa Rica was that it wasn't just Ted who outsurfed me. Nearly everyone did. Ellie linked sullen turns on her swallowtail. The good-looking guy who had been late to class glided self-confidently into waves. Earlier that day, Dennis had mentioned that after putting martial arts behind him, he'd bought an at-home paddle training device. Now he zipped through the water like a fiend.

Cheater, I thought.

The hills of water turned rose-colored in the setting sun, and pelicans swooped to ride the air currents between them. The peaks were slightly smaller than they'd been that morning. It should have been lovely. But the packed lineup made catching waves impossible. In theory, surf etiquette rewards fitness and skill. If you can position yourself closest to the breaking peak, you get first dibs on the ride. As is often the case, however, what is described by those on top as a meritocracy feels to those on the bottom like a caste system. Every time I thought about paddling for a wave, some happy fit person had already taken it. I was beginning to think about giving up when a gentle, chest-high roller sailed my way.

This time, I didn't stall out. As I rose to my feet, I could see the open face before me. *I'm doing it!* I thought to myself. *I'm heading down the line. Amazing!*

Then I saw something that snapped me back to myself. A small, chiseled man with a thin mustache, a shaved head, and a look of angry determination was paddling straight toward me.

By Luis's definition of success—knowing why something is happening—I succeeded mightily over the next half second. I knew the guy with the mustache was trying to get out the back. I knew he hoped to thread the needle between my board and the breaking peak. I knew I technically had the right of way, and that such technicalities aren't always respected. Finally, I knew what I should do with all this knowledge: turn up the face to make room for him.

But this was one of those times when knowing how matters more—much more—than knowing why. We locked eyes. His expression said, *Get the hell out of my way.* Mine said, *If I could, believe me, I would.* A white line appeared between the horizon and the face; the lip, which had started off behind me, had surged ahead. *This wave's about to break*, I thought, just after it broke. I gave the guy charging toward me a final, helpless look before windmilling backward. Right before my feet lost contact with my board, I felt an ominous clunk. I swirled underwater, then surfaced and gasped for air. A shaved head with a thin mustache floated a few feet away.

"*Puta!*" he shouted, slapping the water with a flattened palm. He repeated the Spanish insult, then switched seamlessly to English. "Look where you're fucking going!"

In the way our puppy, Emily, could already tell the difference between a play-growl and a real one, I knew this was nothing like being called a kook at the dog beach. I wasn't sure this guy would hit me. But I was absolutely certain he was considering it.

"You shouldn't fucking be out here!" he said.

"I tried to give you some space," I said meekly, but this only enraged him further and he leaned in to my face.

An older surfer with a Santa Claus beard paddled over. "It's not this guy's fault, dude," he said in a mellow tone. "He had the right of way. You—"

"What the fuck are you doing, man?! This doesn't concern you." The bald guy's face was somehow packed with muscle, and every one of his facial muscles pulsed with rage. Shaking his head in preemptive memoriam, my would-be guardian slunk away. Only a handful of other surfers remained in the water—and they, too, were making themselves scarce. My odds of getting back to the beach in one piece were dropping.

"You know what?" I announced, as if I'd left something on the stove, "I really ought to go."

I leapt onto my board, paddling harder toward the beach than I'd ever paddled before. My sudden move surprised him, the way a seemingly dead possum springing to life might surprise a bobcat. Halfway to the shore I thought I'd made my escape. Then, in the way you can feel someone reading your book over your shoulder on a subway car, I sensed I was being followed. I looked back.

Face Muscles was chasing me down.

I had a head start and longer board, but his back and shoulders made even The Predator seem scrawny by comparison and he gained on me with every second. I got to the beach just moments ahead of him. As I struggled to lift nine feet of foam and fiberglass, he scooped up his shortboard and stalked toward me. I braced myself.

"Hey man," he said, "I'm sorry I got mad at you back there. I was just, like, really upset." I couldn't believe it. He sounded almost as chill as Ted. "It's just, my board got damaged. So, what are we going to do about that?"

Now I could believe it. He raised his board to display a small dent on its underside. But dings happen all the time—plenty of boards are pockmarked with them—and I was pretty sure I'd hit his rail, nowhere near the area he was pointing to. I looked around. Unlike the ocean, the beach was full of witnesses.

"I think," I said carefully, "we should just keep surfing."

The laid-back attitude vanished as quickly as it had appeared. "Twenty bucks," he demanded.

I thought about paying him to leave me alone. Then I remembered I had no cash on me. And I wasn't about to leave a crowded beach so the two of us could trek alone through a jungle to an ATM. I shook my head.

"Are you kidding?" he yelled. "You threw your board at me!"

"It was an accident."

"So, you admit you made a mistake."

"I fell. People fall."

"Yeah, but if you fall asleep while driving and kill someone, you could go to jail."

"I'll tell you what," I said. "If I fall asleep while driving and kill someone, I'll let you prosecute me."

It was the word *prosecute* dropped into a sentence that turned the tables. Surf World is not a casually trisyllabic realm. We'd crossed back into the real world, and we both knew it. "It's only twenty bucks," he whined. But I shook my head again, more firmly this time.

"You know what you are?" Face Muscles said. "You break other people's things, and you don't take care of it. *That's* how you were raised."

He stalked away, and I thought that was the end of it, that I had won. But just before disappearing down the beach, he turned and stared, committing my face to memory for later. Then, with a *this-isn't-over* glare, he headed toward the jungle trail.

~~~~~~~

"Excuse me," I asked from the front row of class the next morning. "Is the peak of the wave intrinsically steeper than the shoulder, or is its steepness a function of its height?"

Josh looked at me as though I'd given myself a wedgie.

"This is the shoulder," he said, extending a thick forearm almost parallel to the floor. Then he tilted his arm so it was vertical. "And that's the peak."

"Ah," I said. "So it's intrinsic."

He didn't reply.

In the surf session that followed, I hoped to work on my pop-ups. But I was too busy worrying I would bump into Face Muscles and that he would punch me. I'd even come up with a plan to avoid being punched. Years earlier, when I dated a girl from Mississippi, I learned to do a passable impression of her accent. If Face Muscles spotted me, I would slip into a southern drawl and insist he had the wrong guy.

"Ah sway-uh," I'd practiced in the mirror, "Ah've nevah seen you bee-faw in mah lahf."

It wasn't a bad plan, really. But practicing a Deep South drawl while keeping an eye out for assailants isn't helpful for one's surfing, and I again struggled to catch waves. On the handful of occasions when I popped up, my butt extended over my heelside rail, and my hands over the toeside one.

"Not to be rude," Josh said during video analysis, "but you're kind of surfing monkey-style."

That evening, I didn't run into Face Muscles. I even managed to catch a few unremarkable waves. But I'd never surfed back-to-back sessions on back-to-back days, and by the time I returned to my hotel room, I could feel my body falling apart. The tendons in my shoulders felt like pieces of plastic wrap stretched across a bowl. My hands and feet were covered in tiny cuts of indeterminate origin. I was so desperate for electrolytes that I bought a jar of pickles from the local general store just so I could take swigs of the juice. Worst of all was the board rash. While I relished not needing a wetsuit, my stomach rubbed against the beaded wax on the deck like a block of Parmesan against a grater.

Before bed, I FaceTimed Jacqui and found her sitting in a makeshift pen and crying, with Emily bouncing beside her. Our puppy had decided my wife was the most interesting thing in the universe and wanted to learn everything about her. This might have been cute, if Emily's learning process hadn't involved so many teeth.

"I'm wondering if this trip is even worth it," I sighed.

Jacqui, between sobs, looked directly at the camera for a very long time.

"Good to know," she deadpanned.

~~~~~~~~~

The following morning was sublime.

Maybe it was the practice pop-ups I performed on the beach. Maybe it was the fact that Ted finally started fading. Maybe it was the pickle juice. Whatever the cause, I caught thirteen waves in ninety minutes. When I popped up, I felt my back foot land before my front with the one-two rhythm of a snare drum. Instead of tilting backward in a wheelie, my rail gripped the wave in a handshake and took off down the face. On the final ride of the morning, I hot-dogged left and right as I headed into the beach.

"Doi-vid!" said Tabbi in her Tasmanian accent. "You were rip-peen' out there!"

"Well," I said humbly. Unable to think of anything else humble to say, I trailed off.

Seeing myself on camera brought me back to earth. My final ride to the beach was, in slow motion, a series of unglorified wiggles, less hotdog than Jell-O. Even so, it was unquestionably the best I'd ever surfed. The moment I got back to my room, I sent two carefully edited clips to Matt. Even if he had never seen the phenomenon in person, he now had video evidence that I could catch a wave.

"Nice!" he replied. "Finally going left!"

While the "finally" stung, even Matt agreed I was improving. I still didn't want to tell my brother-in-law I hoped to surf the North Shore with him in November. I worried he'd find it ridiculous. But his message had given me the confidence to do the next-best thing.

"Probably not Pipeline," Josh said, when I asked him whether my plan could work. "Pipeline would kill you. But you could think about Sunset Beach." He pulled out his phone and showed me a picture of a young, fit surfer dwarfed by a wave the size of a grain silo.

"That was me when Sunset was, like, five times overhead," he explained. "I don't think you'd like that. But overhead, a little more than overhead? If you work at it? I don't see why not."

Other than those who had vowed to be supportive when they married me, Josh was the first person I had told about my newfound ambition. I didn't totally trust him. He seemed like the type who enjoyed getting others into trouble. But he hadn't laughed at me. He hadn't told me to give up. There was reason to hope.

The fourth day was a rest day. On the fifth, my coach for video analysis was Chris, the quietest and most enigmatic of the camp's instructors. He peered at my slow-motion footage as if it were a magic eye.

"You outran that one," he said.

We were looking at my best wave of the session, and I remembered it perfectly: popping up confidently, heading down the line, gaining speed, flopping into the ocean only when the lip fizzled out. But seen from the outside, it was obvious my perspective had been faulty. Chris was right. I'd cruised past the shoulder, with its intrinsic lack of steepness, and traversed so far down the line that the pocket's churning power had wound up twenty feet to my left. I thought my wave was finished. In fact, all the good stuff had been happening behind me.

"So I have to go slower," I said.

"No," he replied. "You have to draw your line. You're only thinking about what *you* want to do. You need to do what the wave wants you to do. If it moves faster, you move faster. If you get out too far, you turn back toward the power source."

This idea—that surfing was not about imposing your will on nature, but combining nature's will with your own—struck me as fishy. It sounded dangerously like self-acceptance. Then, during that evening's free session, I spotted Josh catching waves and immediately understood what Chris meant. I knew instantly I was watching the best surfer I'd ever seen in person. Josh used his size to his advantage, throwing his bowling-ball stomach into turns, board whipping behind him like an afterthought. He was a sculptor, not a painter. He took chunks out of the wave. But what made Josh so beefily mesmerizing, so densely dazzling, was the connection between him and his raw material. In carving the face, he was creating something new while revealing something already there.

Feeling confident through osmosis, I tried a little artistry of my own. The next time my speed began to wane, I tried turning toward the pocket. It wasn't even close to a cutback. I slipped down the face, waited for the wave to catch up with me, then resumed traveling down the line. But while no one would call my ride a masterpiece, it was a brushstroke, a dance step, a first act of self-expression on a surfboard.

It definitely wasn't monkey-style.

~~~~~~~~~

Some people never leave a place like Playa Guiones. Near the spot where the jungle trail opened to the beach, I watched a young white couple with greasy hair attempt to clean a crying baby by dunking it into the sea. I could only assume they'd arrived for surf instruction and stayed. Frankly, it seemed tempting. Whenever Jacqui and I FaceTimed, I was brought back to the real world—the forces behind January 6th were mobilizing anew; an earthquake in Turkey had taken thousands of lives; Emily had escaped her pen and savaged our microgreens. But my flights were booked and my life was elsewhere, and the sixth day of surf camp was my last.

As I stepped onto the beach that morning, the waves boomed louder than ever. The vibrations in the sand went all the way up to my knees. A glum-looking surfer passed me in the opposite direction. Under each arm, he held a chunk of forest-green longboard that had been snapped in half.

"It doesn't look bigger than yesterday," Josh said from behind his camera, adding, "I reckon," in the British way that means, "I'm lying."

The salt water bathed the Rorschach test of raw skin on my stomach as I paddled out. My arms were numb from inflammation. It was obvious that everyone else was suffering, too. Yet we all made it. Twenty minutes into the session, we were hit with the week's biggest cleanup set and half a dozen boards were tossed like confetti toward shore. Even then, no one quit. Not even Prakash, the microchip designer in his fifties, who at one point rode a giant peak on his knees and facing backward. Fifteen minutes before our session ended, I turned to see Ken the jacked grandpa, his AARP biceps flexing as he assumed a warrior pose and roared on his foamboard down a six-foot face.

"Woo-hoo!" someone whooped.

It was me. By the standard I'd set—being the best surfer at camp—the week at Barefoot Surf had been a disappointment. By

Ted's standards, however, I was doing great. I was feeling the karma with everyone.

For the first few sets, I handled the size okay. Then I popped up and felt my lower back clamp tight. I'd surfed six tough days, and no amount of pickle juice could save me. Twice more that session I staggered to my feet, only to find myself as rigid as a mannequin. When I washed in an hour later, I walked so stiffly I might as well have been wearing a 5/4.

I was about to limp to breakfast when I spotted Ted gazing out at the water. I knew that look. It's the one every surfer gets when the waves are still good. It says, *Give me just one more chance, Lord, and I could totally shred.*

A voice surprised me. "You boys heading back out there?" I turned to see two front teeth overlapping in a grin.

"I think so," said Ted.

Josh looked at me. I nodded.

"Don't worry, I'll tell them to keep your food waiting," Josh said. Ted buckled his helmet and walked toward the water. I attached my leash and followed.

It took a quarter of an hour, but we punched through. A head-high peak flew toward Ted and he took off, racing left before effortlessly cutting back into the pocket.

Awesome! I thought.

I would have kept watching, but my reverie was interrupted by the coughing *chugaluga* of a motor. I looked over my shoulder to see a lifeguard on an ancient, mustard-yellow Jet Ski. I'd never seen him before. I didn't know Playa Guiones even employed a lifeguard.

"Okay?" he yelled above the crashing surf. I gave him a thumbs-up.

He didn't return the gesture. Instead, he raised his right index finger and slowly pointed toward the horizon.

I had just enough time to wonder what kind of wave a professional lifeguard would feel the need to identify. Then I looked back and found out. Trundling toward me was a monster among monsters, easily the largest wave I'd seen all day. I told myself not to go for it, but I was already paddling. I doubted I could make the take-off, but before I knew it I was on my feet.

It's easy to assume the reward for full commitment is unequivocal success. It's not. Sometimes you adopt a puppy and it upends your life. Sometimes you launch yourself over the ledge of the heaviest wave you've ever seen only to feel your shoulders, locked in place by your rebelling lower back, pitch at an alarming angle.

At the beginning of the week, I'd been wheelie-ing off the tail. This time I flew over the nose in a swan dive. For a bizarre instant, I was parallel to the face, at eye level with the ocean. Then my jaw smacked the water and I skipped like a stone until I was buried by the crumbling lip. I resurfaced with my head ringing as though I'd been punched in the face. Ted was still out there, shredding on his blue 7′6″, but I was done.

Which was okay. It was better than okay, actually. I'd gotten my really good wipeout in.

The next morning, before heading to the airport, when I walked into a coffee shop and saw Face Muscles waiting in line, I didn't approach him. But I didn't shy away, either. Instead I waited calmly, hoping he wouldn't notice me but knowing he might, and knowing, too, that if the worst happened, I'd forget about adopting an accent and face the danger as myself.

CHAPTER EIGHT

I Just Don't Want to Be the Guy Who Dies of Hypothermia in His Parking Space

"MY BIGGEST PROBLEM," Matt said matter-of-factly, "is that I have too much muscle."

I stared at my brother-in-law, then out the window of his truck into the predawn darkness, and wondered how this had become my life.

The literal answer was Surfline. Founded in 1985, the world's first private swell forecaster started off as an answering machine. For a fee, you could dial a number and hear a message describing conditions at any of twenty-two California spots. Compared to the previous state-of-the-art forecasting system—going to the beach and looking around—this was a revolution. The company thrived. By the time I took an interest in swell directions and wind speeds, Surfline was the global behemoth of wave prediction, with thousands of forecasts updated in real time on its app and more than five hundred cameras livestreaming around the world.

My brother-in-law and I felt differently about Surfline. I loved it. Deciding when and where to surf was prone to human error, particularly when I was the human, and I was happy to outsource my judgment to an algorithm. Matt, who didn't trust big pharma, big government, big business, big tech, or big labor, didn't trust big wave prediction, either. He sometimes called the app "Surf-lyin'," in a tone that implied the existence of a meteorological cabal.

So when, on the second Friday morning in March, Surfline predicted "good" Sunday-morning conditions for Rockaway Beach, ninety minutes away and across the New York State line, and merely "fair-to-good" conditions in New Jersey, I sensed an opportunity. The idea of actually taking a day trip with my brother-in-law made my palms sweat. In all the time I'd known him, not once had we ridden in a car just the two of us. But I could bluff. If I suggested we make the drive, Matt, who almost never left New Jersey and was skeptical of forecasts anyway, would decline. I'd get tough-guy credit for being willing to travel long distances in search of slightly better waves, without ever finding out what would happen if the two of us were stuck in a car.

I put my plan into action. Matt immediately texted back.

"I've had my best session ever in Rockaway. It would be an awesome morning there."

Fuck, I thought.

"Gets crowded," he added. "Earlier the better."

Fuck again. A cold snap had sent the air temperature well below twenty degrees, and the water temperature, which on the East Coast typically reaches its annual low in early March, was just above freezing. The last time I'd paddled out had been in bathtub-warm Costa Rican seas. Returning to hooded wetsuits and ice cream headaches was disheartening enough without adding "before sunrise" to the mix.

"Want to pick me up at 7 a.m.?" I ventured, picking the latest possible time I thought he would not object to.

"How about 5:30?"

Fucking, fucking fuck.

On Saturday night, Jacqui and I rented *The Kennel Murder Case*, a black-and-white mystery from 1933. It was a macabre choice, since Emily was watching with us, but the movie had modern pacing and a dashing lead performance by William Powell, and paying attention should have been easy. Instead, every ten minutes I reached for my phone to research the spot Matt and I would be surfing the next day.

The first article I encountered was a 2018 *New York Times* piece about crowded Rockaways lineups. *That's not too bad*, I thought. *I don't mind crowds.* Then I got to the part where a local surf coach described the time the water was so densely packed that he ditched his board to avoid a collision and its fin ripped off one of his pupils' eyelids.

First, who admits that sort of thing to the country's most widely read newspaper? And second, *eyelids*?

Most distressing of all were what locals referred to as "death sticks." In the mid-twentieth century, city officials had sunk hundreds of wooden, telephone pole–sized pillars into the Rockaway Beach surf. Their purpose—preventing erosion—was eventually usurped by rock jetties. But the sticks remained, protruding from the seafloor like needles from an acupuncture patient. At high tide, many were submerged completely. This meant you didn't have to be foolish to collide with one, just unlucky, unless you considered surfing Rockaway Beach to be foolish in the first place, which I was rapidly beginning to.

If fortune smiles, a death stick will merely impale you. If it frowns, your leash will wrap around the barnacle-encrusted pole and trap you beneath the waves. That's what happened to twenty-eight-year-old Charles DeVoe in the winter of 2010. A crowd of fellow surfers and local firefighters rushed to his rescue, but by the time they could untangle him, it was too late.

In the years since, the city had removed most of the sticks. But not all. And even this rare bit of welcome news came with a disturbing coda. When the heavy machinery arrived to rid their beach of deadly hazards, many Rockaways locals went berserk. They were certain that getting rid of the death sticks would ruin the waves. This belief was, to use a euphemism common in an age of anti-vaxxers and election deniers, "without evidence." But that didn't stop plenty of surfers from believing it.

Others enjoyed the sticks for their own sake. "It sounds kind of ridiculous, but it's kind of a rite of passage to run into them when you're surfing here," a filmmaker named Thomas Brookins told the *Times*. With all due respect to Mr. Brookins, no, that doesn't sound ridiculous. It *is* ridiculous.

So what did that make me?

I have a wife, two cats, and a dog, I thought to myself that night. *And I'm about to wake up before dawn to get in a truck that may or may not be sporting a militia sticker in order to drive ninety minutes with a person I've never had a nine-minute conversation with so we can surf someplace where my chances of dying are significantly higher than they'd be if I stayed home. How can I possibly take that kind of risk?*

I fell asleep after midnight, wondering how people with children work up the courage to cross the street.

~~~~~~~~~~

I stumbled downstairs the next morning, and had just pulled a slice of last night's pizza from the fridge when our living room was flooded with a blast of light. I tottered to the door to find Matt's truck on our lawn. It seemed that, upon realizing the driveway was full and the nearby street parking occupied, he'd improvised and jumped the curb.

Shielding my eyes from his headlights with a raised arm, I stepped outside. The air was a special kind of nasty, suffused with the cruel Northeastern dampness that makes people consider doing anything, even moving to Florida, to escape it. I'd swaddled myself in two down jackets. Still, I groaned and shivered as I hauled my thick wetsuit and board across the grass. Matt, standing by the door of his pickup, was wearing jeans, along with a hoodie featuring a picture of Skeletor, the villain from the *He-Man* cartoons.

"Hey," he said. "Your board gonna fit?"

After Costa Rica, I was more sensitive than ever to questions of length. I'd picked a 7′4″, epoxy-clad mid-length that could tuck into the pockets of steep waves in a way my longer boards could not. But my board was still too big to fit beside Matt's, a 6′0″ model designed by Hawaii shaper Jon Pyzel and called "the Phantom." Pursing his lips slightly, Matt hopped up into the truck bed, wordlessly grabbed my mid-length, and cinched it to his equipment rack with a heavy-duty twist tie. As I watched him work, fingers flying, I once again noticed the skull-and-lightning decal and wished I hadn't. On the back of his Skeletor hoodie, in large block letters, were nine words of text:

I DON'T LIKE BEING GOOD. I LIKE BEING EVIL.

We climbed into the truck. Matt hit the ignition, turning on the speakers, and what filled the cab was less a wall of sound than a mudslide. If forced to describe the genre, I would call it "adult men full of teenaged angst." Clocking my reaction, Matt turned the volume down just enough so I could hear him.

"You don't listen to Primus?" he yelled.

"This may surprise you, but no!"

"They're really good!"

We drove toward the Garden State Parkway, bass rumbling through the soles of my shoes like vibrations from a giant wave. *Why is it*, I thought, *that every time he describes something as "good," I end up less happy?*

I reminded myself that he was being generous. While we weren't partners in the water, or anything like it, most hardcore surfers would rather have a tooth pulled than allow a beginner to accompany them when the waves were good. Not only that, but in bringing me along, he was vouching for me. I imagined he felt the way I did when I took Emily to puppy class. Any accidents of mine would reflect poorly on him.

"I think I got a lot better since Costa Rica," I said, hoping to reassure him. "And the other day I swam laps for thirty minutes."

"I've been training, too," Matt said. "I usually get up at four to lift weights. Then I swim sets of five underwater laps with ten seconds between each lap."

"In a full-size pool?"

"Yeah," he replied, as though it were impossible to imagine swimming five underwater laps with ten seconds between each lap in anything else.

It was this talk of swimming that led to Matt's complaint about too much muscle. Apparently, the short-twitch fibers ate up oxygen and limited the number of seconds he could hold his breath. I looked down at my own swaddled body. "I don't think anyone's ever accused me of having that problem," I said. Matt chuckled, a bit too quickly for my liking, and there was a moment of uncomfortable silence I feared would last for the remainder of the drive. But he jumped back in.

"In that video you sent, the waves in Costa Rica looked pretty good."

"Bigger than I'm used to, but slow and mushy."

"Not like here."

"Definitely not. I was surfing a single-fin with side bites."

"How was that?"

"Pretty good."

Had a stowaway been wedged among the industrial-sized toolboxes in Matt's back seat, he would not have found our discussion captivating. Most topics remained off-limits. When Matt brought up stand-up comedy, which was adjacent to Joe Rogan, which was adjacent to vaccines, I steered us back to surf chat in a conversational cutback. Still, the fact remained: by the time we crossed Jamaica Bay and began looking for a parking spot, we'd spoken more in the past ninety minutes than we had over the previous two years combined.

The Rockaway peninsula juts from the bottom of Queens like a bad underbite, with an east-west angle perfect for picking up northbound swells. It's narrow, though—just two blocks wide in some places—and that makes it a parking nightmare. While we'd hoped to surf at the 92nd Street beach, reputed to be the area's best, every space within a half-mile radius was taken. Matt maneuvered the truck past Stop & Shops and Dunkin's as street numbers ticked down. I was about to suggest parking at a Family Dollar and hoping they didn't tow us, when Matt pointed.

"Over there!"

Just a few yards from the boardwalk, on 60th Street, a spot big enough for the truck sat empty.

"I've gotta make a U-turn. You hold it," he said.

"Got it," I responded. Then I hopped out of the pickup and realized I wasn't quite sure what I was expected to do. Standing in the open spot was easy enough. But I found it difficult to believe that a hardcore surfer, upon finding me guarding the only available parking space for miles, wouldn't try to bully me away with his car. I found it equally hard to believe that in such a scenario, the bully wouldn't win. I stood uneasily, prepared to defend our territory for as long as no one wanted to take it. The skinny streets made it impossible for Matt to turn his truck around quickly, and the skull decal on the window grew tiny, then imperceptible, as he drove farther from the beach. After two blocks, he hit an intersection, turned left, and vanished.

As if on cue, a gray Honda Civic emerged onto the street.

The driver was close enough for me to make out his smartly parted hair and glasses through the windshield, his shortboard on the back seat. He clocked the parking spot. Then he saw me, shivering slightly, with my hands tucked into my armpits for warmth. For a second our eyes locked like we were gunslingers in a Western. Then, slowly but deliberately, he advanced. Ten yards away. Eight yards. I could hear the *thwup-thwup* of his engine, count the scratches on his bumper. Five yards. I couldn't hold out much longer.

Suddenly, his determined look vanished and he drove away. For a moment, less triumphant than confused, I watched him go. Then I realized what he'd seen bearing down in his rearview mirror: a pickup truck large enough to crush his Civic into tinfoil, being driven by a guy with a Rasputin beard and a picture of an evil skeleton emblazoned on his chest.

"Nicely done," Matt said, hopping out of the cab and jogging straight to the beach. When he returned a minute later, he had a familiar, demented gleam in his eye.

"It looks good!"

"Good," in this case, probably meant terrifyingly unrideable. But joining forces to save our parking space had left me strangely optimistic. For the first time ever, Matt and I had worked together to achieve a common goal. True, the goal in question was to vanquish a middle-aged man in a Honda, but every great partnership has to start somewhere. Maybe today we would finally become a team in the water, too.

I walked to the truck to retrieve my wetsuit. Although I'd brought a thick fleece poncho to protect me from the elements while I changed, wearing it while donning my suit of rubber armor proved impossible, and I was soon standing shirtless in the cold. Matt, who hadn't bothered with a poncho in the first place, was equally exposed.

"WHY AM I LIKE THIS?" he bellowed into the offshore wind.

A year earlier, I might have mistakenly interpreted his cry as a sign of existential crisis. Now I thought I understood. Matt's question wasn't rhetorical, because he didn't know the answer. But he also didn't care what the answer was. Though I doubt he would have phrased it this way, he was acknowledging the absurdity of his condition—being the kind of person who woke before dawn to drive seventy-five miles to change his clothes outdoors so he could submerge himself in water cold enough to keep cheese from spoiling—without being bothered by it.

I found that kind of impressive. It was a type of equanimity I did not possess.

"Forget riding waves." I shivered. "I just don't want to be the guy who dies of hypothermia in his parking space."

"Hey, that should be the title of your next book!" Matt said. "Or at least a chapter."

~~~~~~~~~~

I saw it the moment I reached the boardwalk. It felt so unfair. The city had reportedly removed nearly all of them. Now, in the middle of the only surf break where we could find parking, stood a single gnarled post, a monument to needless danger.

"Death stick," I said darkly.

"I wouldn't worry about it," Matt replied. Too excited to do more than a handful of jumping jacks, he charged into the surf.

I understood his eagerness. The waves were what surfers call "corduroy"—perfect, evenly spaced ripples stretching to the horizon—and I could see barrels forming as they broke. But instead of following directly behind him, I embraced our separate roles. I was the guy who stood patiently in the parking space; he was the guy who drove off intruders with the truck. He hopped in the sea without hesitation; I lingered on the beach, waiting to see how local experts approached the problem.

I didn't have to wait long. A pair of bushy-mustached Brooklyn surf hipsters carried mid-lengths down the beach. At the first lull between sets, they eased themselves into a rip current formed by the crashing swell. I waited for the next lull and followed. I could tell immediately that I was stronger than I'd been during my last paddle-out in winter surf. When a new set appeared, forcing a do-or-die sprint toward the open ocean, I punched through and was out the back on my first try.

"Nice!" Matt said. "You're paddling way better."

"Thanks!"

Before he could say anything else, his expression transformed.

This is going to be oddly specific, but bear with me. In the final episode of season five of *The Sopranos*, Tony Soprano is drinking coffee on the patio of a fellow mobster's mansion when he spots a phalanx of FBI agents swarming in. His jaw doesn't drop, exactly. Instead, his face goes slack. His eyes become dinner plates. Without explanation, he spins 180 degrees and runs. That's how Matt looked: like Tony Soprano spotting a dozen feds. Leaning back on his board, he pivoted, kicked furiously, and hauled himself toward the shoreline. The peak almost knocked me off balance as it surged past. When I looked back, all I could see was the crest of the wave detonating halfway to the beach.

Then, far down the line, like an action hero outrunning an explosion, my brother-in-law shot into view. He summited the lip, hovered briefly atop it, and shimmied back down the face out of sight. It was at least ninety seconds before I saw him again. He was paddling toward me, against the current. The death stick was directly behind him. He didn't seem worried about it.

"How was it?" I asked.

"Amazing," he said. "Got barreled." A few months earlier, his flat tone would have confused me. Now, I got it. I'd never taken off on anything even close to that heavy, but I knew how it felt to have one's brain bifurcated by a wave, half your mind reliving what just happened, the other half imagining what might happen again. A new set rolled toward us. I raced toward a peak, hoping for a mind-splitting ride of my own.

I popped up and thought I had it. Then I watched as the lip grabbed my board and dragged it shoreward on a conveyor belt of doom. For a split second, I caught sight of my board's nose. "If you're looking down at your board," I remembered Josh saying in Costa Rica, "you're about to fall." Then I fell.

Over the previous eight months, I'd become a taxonomist of wipeouts, and I knew I was about to encounter a particularly nasty species. When you get stuck to the lip, the fall starts off oddly peaceful. Then the ocean swallows you and a switch is flipped to violence. Surrounded by the sea on all sides, you're shaken like a cocktail for as long as nature pleases. Perhaps if you wake up at 4 a.m. to swim underwater laps each day, it's easy to wait out this kind of holddown. If you're the rest of us, the only thing less pleasant than being thrashed while being suffocated is being thrashed while being suffocated while being frozen while being dragged toward an underwater death stick.

I clambered back onto my board frustrated and rattled. To my surprise, though, when I paddled back to Matt he was beaming. "I thought you had it!" he said. I'd gone for a legit wave, a wave even he would have been happy to ride, and leapt without looking. He'd noticed.

"You need to move closer to the peak," he continued. "There's a hook you can get into right by the jetty that sets you up for the barrel. It's really good!"

I understood enough to translate. He'd found a small, steep section, a kind of appetizer peak, that could slingshot a surfboard into the main peak with enough speed to shoot under the lip. For the first time, he was inviting me to join him, with his people, on his waves. I wanted badly to accept.

When I looked toward the jetty, however, I gulped. The hook broke straight onto the rocks. Anyone who wiped out there would be pulverized. This was not hypothetical: in 2009, a surfer was flung into a Rockaway Beach jetty and drowned. And that was an experienced wave rider, not someone who, less than a year ago, thought the Beach Boys lyric "Inside, outside, USA" was comparing domestic and foreign locales.

Then there were my fellow surfers. In Costa Rica, I'd learned that reading people is as much a part of surfing as reading the ocean, especially on crowded days. Who fights to get over the ledge? Who runs out of steam? Who indulges in performative lunging and then gives up? If the rider who has priority is likely to miss the wave, it's worth paddling anyway, so you can poach it when they fail. For this reason, even the most gracious surfer's inner monologue tends to be unsavory. *Weak. Fat old guy. Not a threat.*

Unfortunately, I was the morning's unthreatening fat old guy. There were about two dozen people in the water. All of them appeared to be in their twenties or early thirties and were, with the possible exception of those who had too much muscle, in perfect shape. They plunged into barreling waves as though it were no more difficult than cannonballing into a pool.

I turned back to Matt. He gave me a questioning look. *You coming?*

"Don't wait for me," I said. "I'll work my way toward you."

~~~~~~~~

At first I thought I might keep my promise. But the moment Matt disappeared into the two dozen wetsuits crowding the hook, doubt arrived. While these waves weren't the biggest I'd ever seen, they were unquestionably the steepest, with lips so heavy they made a sound like falling timber as they cracked. If I went over there and my pop-up was a millisecond late, a death stick would be the least of my worries.

The expert surfers gathered in an ever-tighter pack, leaving only one other person with me on the outskirts. He looked to be in his early forties, tall but not lean, with stubble instead of the caveman beard popular among winter surfers. His board, a single fin with side bites, was about the same length as mine, with a red decal that reminded me of a rooster's comb. Like me, he seemed suspicious of anyone who looked good in a wetsuit. After one particularly frightening set, I looked toward him and our eyes met. The connection was instant yet undeniable. We were in this together.

My new teammate and I didn't speak a word to each other. We

didn't have to. Over the next forty-five minutes, on the rare occasion when a shortboarder hadn't already claimed an approaching wave, he would offer it to me with an encouraging nod, or I would offer it to him. When I attempted a takeoff and inevitably fell, he'd be ready with a sympathetic glance. *You've got this. Next time.*

Matt, too, seemed to have found his crew. Every so often, I'd watch him being spat out of a tube before sprinting back to his hard-charging gang. He seemed, I thought, unburdened without me. I didn't mind. How could I? I'd discovered a kindred spirit of my own.

I bet the guy on the rooster board shops at farmers' markets, I thought. *I bet he knows the lyrics to* Sweeney Todd.

The sun rose, throwing a glare across the glassy surface. As though summoned by some cosmic bell, the best surfers paddled in. Clearly, they were attuned to the ocean in a way I wasn't, because within minutes the waves had dropped from head-high to chest-high and no longer barreled. My new friend flashed a determined smile. *This is our moment!* I paddled for a peak, and while my exhausted limbs failed me and I collapsed into the whitewash, I knew an encouraging nod of recognition awaited me on my return.

I was so happy to have found someone who understood what I was going through that for a long time I didn't wonder where Matt had gone. When I finally looked for him, he was standing on the beach. He'd already changed back into his Skeletor sweatshirt.

"Do you wanna stay out?" he asked, after a wipeout brought me close to shore. "I can film."

He was shivering, but his offer seemed genuine and I was having a good time. I paddled back out. As I floated alongside my kindred spirit, I could see Matt gripping his phone in gloved hands. I tried taking off on a few peaks, but the waves broke inside and I missed them. Finally, I popped up, only to be thrown shoreward by the lip.

It wasn't a bad wipeout. One second I was underwater, the next I was reeling my board back in. I hopped on and began paddling out, just like I'd done all morning. A large wave built on the horizon, and I hustled to get over it.

Two things happened during the next three seconds. First, I realized I would not, in fact, get over it. Second, my teammate decided to paddle for the wave. His technique, reminiscent of my own, left much to be desired. Arms jerking like Jackson Pollock splattering paint on a canvas, feet pedaling uselessly through the air, he wriggled toward the peak. Technically, he was moving in my direction. But I wasn't worried. There was no way he'd make it.

He made it.

For a moment, my kindred spirit and I locked eyes. He looked, I recall, as if he'd been unexpectedly shot out of a cannon. Then I braced for impact.

A few minutes later, back on the beach, I stood next to Matt. The rooster board had escaped the collision undamaged. Its owner was similarly unscathed, as was I. But my 7′4″ hadn't been so lucky. The rail had fractured at the point of impact, epoxy pieces smushed into the foam like the cracked shell of a hard-boiled egg.

"Can I see the tape?" I asked. Wordlessly, Matt handed me the phone.

I scrolled through the first clips, then reached the last one. In it, I crawled, clearly exhausted, toward the oncoming wave. The guy on the rooster board maneuvered into a takeoff spot. He paddled. His board planed. He rose to his feet. It was clear, watching the video, that I had plenty of time to dodge in either direction. Instead, I froze. The collision was imminent. I winced.

Then, abruptly, the camera swung downward and zoomed in, as though the person behind it had taken a sudden interest in sand. I looked up at Matt. He shrugged.

"I just figured . . . you probably wouldn't want that on video."

I'd never pictured my brother-in-law as the guy thinking about liability, or me as the one hoping my behavior wasn't caught on film. I cocked my head to one side, then nodded.

"Thanks."

He didn't reply, but his look said, *Don't mention it.* We walked back to the pickup. Matt jumped into the bed and took my board. My fleece changing poncho was in the cab, and I was about to retrieve it when I stopped, stood for a second, and leaned back in his direction.

"Matt," I said, as casually as possible. "What's that sticker for?"

He looked at the skull and lightning, then at me. I swallowed nervously.

"That? It's for a store called Born Scum. They do hardcore clothing, motorcycle gear, that sort of thing. You've never heard of them?"

"No," I replied. "I have never heard of Born Scum."

"You should check them out. Their stuff is really good."

"I bet it is," I said.

I was, of course, lying. But as my brother-in-law headed for the driver's seat, I realized that I'd never been happier to hear him call something "good" in my life.

CHAPTER NINE

Water Wizards

ON FEBRUARY 19, 2023, the most dangerous place in surfing was not the shallow reef at Tahiti's Teahupo'o or the mutant double lip of Tasmania's Shipstern Bluff, but a shopping mall in East Rutherford, New Jersey. There, at a three-million-square-foot complex called American Dream, a life-sized decorative helicopter piloted by a penguin from the *Madagascar* franchise snapped from cables suspending it above a DreamWorks-themed water park and plummeted into the giant wave pool below. Four people were injured. It's a miracle no one was killed.

The victims were technically swimmers; the pool was open for surfing only in the early mornings and late evenings, when the rest of the park was closed. Even so, I added "crushed by novelty cartoon aircraft" to my growing list of ways to die while on a surfboard.

I took a special interest in wave pools that spring, because not long after our morning at Rockaway Beach, Matt and I made plans to visit one. The pool we chose—an artificial outdoor reef in Waco, Texas—is America's second-largest, and the water would be a balmy seventy degrees. The real reason we decided on Waco, though, was that it didn't require either of us to invite the other on a surf trip. One of Jacqui's cousins was getting married in New Braunfels, a small city outside San Antonio, in mid-April. In mid-March, Matt's original travel plan—towing his Harley south and tooling around the Hill Country—fell through when his RV needed repairs. We'd already be less than three hours south of Waco; he'd already taken several vacation days. This made spending time at the wave pool an easy choice, no awkward conversations or vulnerability necessary.

"Do you think my brother-in-law and I need one room or two?" I asked the woman who answered the phone at Waco Surf.

"Oh, you'll have plenty of space," she said. "One should be fine."

She was confident and rooms were expensive, so I followed her advice. Only later, after I'd told Matt about the plan and it would have been awkward to change it, did I think about what I'd done. We'd left the mumble-and-nod frostiness of peak pandemic behind us. But going straight from a car ride to roommates was one of those ideas that made less sense the more I considered it.

While no evidence supported my belief, I was confident that the better I surfed, the better Matt and I would get along when not surfing. For this reason, improving took on even greater urgency as the wedding neared. On days when the ocean was flat in New Jersey, which was most of them that spring, I woke up early and drove the hour north to the American Dream mall, where I kept a wary eye on the giant inflatable Shrek hanging from the ceiling.

I could tell at once that there were many differences between waves in the ocean and waves in a pool. The former offer variety;

the latter consistency. Natural waves build slowly in the distance; machine-made waves are belched forth at the last second. Saltwater waves smell like whatever the land smells like near the water; pool waves, no matter what else they smell like, smell like the absence of salt. The biggest difference, though—and the reason some people think pools are the future of surfing—is that machine-made waves can be commodified in a way natural waves cannot. The one time I calculated how much each minute at the American Dream cost me, the number was large enough that I expunged it from memory and vowed never to calculate again. Yet I couldn't stay away. The promise of improvement, of opportunity, was too great. I attempted nearly as many pop-ups in each two-hour pool session as I had all week in Costa Rica.

Back in Washington, DC, I found a different—and far more affordable—way to keep working on my surfing. The William H. Rumsey Aquatic Center was around the corner from our house on Capitol Hill, and when Jacqui's job kept us there, I walked over carrying a small, finless foamie. Surfboards weren't technically permitted in the pool. But I hadn't spent my twenties as a precocious kiddo in our nation's capital for nothing. Voice dripping with deferential sweetness, I batted my eyes at the middle-aged attendant sitting behind bulletproof glass.

"It's just a kickboard, and the sign says kickboards are allowed. I promise I won't get in anybody's way." Once inside, I paddled back and forth in the lap lane, beneath a banner proclaiming HOME OF THE WATER WIZARDS, D.C.'S SENIOR SWIM TEAM.

The paddle-out at the dog beach was about fifty yards long. At the aquatic center, I started off paddling a thousand yards a day. It was brutal. Along with the expected muscle soreness came challenges I'd never imagined confronting on a surfboard. No one in *Blue Crush* or *Point Break* has to dodge teenagers taking running leaps into the deep end after school. On another occasion, I entered the locker room just in time to see a skinny older man slip a bathing suit over his Depends. He spent the next hour, all but inevitably, in my lap lane.

But I was soon putting in mile-long sessions, alternating between sprints and endurance work, and I could see the results. One afternoon, a Water Wizard, returning to the locker room after a training swim, caught me looking over my shoulder into the mirror and staring, in a manner frankly bordering on lascivious, at my new back muscles. He cut a wide path around me on his way to the showers, shaking his head, I imagine, at the kind of characters one encounters at a public pool.

～～～～～～

As helpful as indoor training was, I knew the real test of my improvement—the opportunity to measure my current self against my past one—had to come in the ocean. A few days before we left for Texas, I got my chance.

Matt was working that morning, and Jacqui had taken the car to DC, so I walked the mile to the dog beach alone. Sealed into my wetsuit, board balanced atop my head, I was huffing and caked in sweat by the time I reached the boardwalk. Even so, when I saw the waves my eyes lit up. Conditions were just as good as Surfline had predicted. The peaks, propped up by a gentle offshore breeze, marched toward shore in well-organized rows. Pockets zippered down the line, begging someone to fit a surfboard between lip and face.

I reached a hand across my body and gave my slightly more muscly shoulder an encouraging squeeze.

Even more than my paddling speed, I noticed the authority with which my outstretched hand caught the water, the arch in my back as I held my chest above my board. The sea remained a wintry gray, but the sun was shining, and each wave's trajectory was easy to track. I waited for a good one—stomach-high, smooth and glossy as lacquered wood—and paddled confidently to meet the breaking lip.

The pop-up was easy, the takeoff fluid. I didn't make the wave—overeager, I dug my rail and pitched forward—but just before I fell, I saw the lip unfurling before me. I'd been inches from the ride of my life. Instead of focusing on waiting out the hold-down, my mind jumped ahead to the next takeoff. *This is gonna be amazing.* I hurried to the surface, thinking only about the waves yet to arrive.

Which is why, by the time I noticed a floating white object skimming rapidly toward my face, it was too late.

In much the way knights errant once doted on their trusty steeds, surfers feel personal connections to their boards. Far more than mere conveyance, a surfboard is guardian angel, boon companion, and trusty sidekick rolled into one. So my shocked expression registered not just alarm but an acute sense of betrayal.

What the . . . ? How could . . . ?

The rail smacked me on the bridge of my nose. For all its graceful buoyancy, my board was as solid as a lead pipe, and the pain radiated from the impact and lodged itself between my eyes. I swallowed hard, expecting salt water. Instead, I tasted something warm, rusty, and sweet.

Hmmm, I thought. *This seems bad.*

It turns out the only thing more terrifying than frantically looking up one's symptoms on the internet is not being able to. As I pulled myself onto my board, making *hurgch* and *urgch* noises each time my mouth filled with blood, I tried to recall everything I knew about broken noses. First, as a preteen in summer camp, I'd been told your nose bone can shoot into your brain and kill you. Second . . . Actually, no, that was it.

I wiggled my nose. As far as I could tell, my brain had no bones in it. That was a relief. Still, the extent of my injury was far from clear. All I knew for certain was that when I pressed the mitten of my 5/4 suit against my face, dark-red droplets drizzled into the sea.

A minute later, I emerged from the ocean, startling a gray-haired man in a sweater vest playing fetch with his poodle mix.

"Excuse me," I said to him. "I know this is a strange question. But how much am I bleeding?"

It took the man a few seconds to adjust to his altered circumstances. He stared at my face. "Oh, not too much," he ventured. Then, with the stricken look of someone who realizes he has just dispensed medical advice, he asked if I was okay.

"Definitely," I said, not knowing if this was true. "I'm just trying to decide if I can paddle back out."

As the poodle mix sniffed my booties, its owner puffed out

his chest. We were no longer fretting about injury. This was man talk.

"Yeah, I'd go back out," he declared.

"Sweet," I replied. "Guess I'll do that." Giving him my best John Wayne look, I ambled back into the surf.

My pulse beat across the open wound as I paddled, each *lub* and *dub* landing a punch of pain between my eyes. I didn't catch many waves. The longer I stayed out, however, the more pleased with myself I became. Arriving at the beach, I'd hoped to practice takeoffs. Now all I wanted was to get a really good picture of my head wound and send it to Matt.

An hour later, back home and still dripping blood, I posed for selfies. I was deciding which looked most gruesome when I began to wonder if I'd suffered a concussion. It was the kind of question that seemed easier to answer after a nap, so I took one. When I awoke, the bleeding hadn't stopped. That's when I called an Uber to take me to urgent care. Thirty minutes later, I was sitting in a doctor's office being examined by a physician's assistant with a name tag that read CAMERON M.

"So, tell me what happened," he said.

Cameron M. was in his mid-twenties, dressed in athleisure and fashion sneakers, with a casual air that straddled the line between confident and aloof. But the minute I told him I'd been injured while surfing, he, like the dog parent of the poodle mix before him, switched into a low, guys-talking-guy-stuff tone.

"First time back in the water?"

"Nah, I surf pretty regularly," I said.

"Even when it's cold out? I would have been crying just being out there."

I decided I liked Cameron M.

"Hang tight, and the doctor will see you," he said.

Dr. Burman wasn't interested in guy talk. Instead, after learning I'd hurt myself surfing, he decided I must be a menace to society. This made me feel manlier than ever.

"You have to start being more careful," he scolded. "And you have to promise to stay out of the water for two weeks."

"Sure," I scoffed, in a way I hoped made clear what rebels like me thought of stuffed shirts like him. He sighed, went over the signs of a concussion, and gave me a butterfly bandage, which stopped the bleeding and made me resemble a boxer after a fight. In the Uber home, I finally sent Matt a picture of my swollen nose, thin lines of red still oozing from the narrow wound.

"Nice!" he replied.

It wasn't until the day before Jacqui and I left for Texas that Matt texted again. "I guess facial injuries are in this season," his message read. "A wrench slipped and got me pretty good." In the picture that followed, blood spurted from a dime-sized puncture in his forehead, forming a ruby river that gushed down his face toward his beard. His expression was stoic, as though posing for a mug shot.

"Did you need stitches?" I asked.

"Yeah, probably. But I just pulled a flap of skin over it and went back to work."

I flipped through my photos, taking a look at what, until thirty seconds ago, I had thought of as my red badge of courage. For a moment—just a moment, but still—I found myself wishing someone would drop a wrench on me.

~~~~~~~~~~

Upon arriving in historic downtown New Braunfels, Jacqui and I checked into the Faust, a charming, featured-on-the-wedding-website hotel that boasted Spanish Renaissance Revival detailing and a friendly resident ghost. Matt stayed across the street from a Home Depot. According to Jacqui's parents, his motel, part of a nationwide chain called AmericInn, was partially under construction, so he'd gotten a good deal. Also, his room had a kitchenette, which meant he could heat frozen pizzas instead of going out. He was reportedly very pleased.

Matt was a groomsman, so when I saw him the next morning, in a tiny Catholic church in the nearby town of Seguin, he was walking down the aisle. I almost didn't recognize him. He'd shaved his winter surfing beard down to the stubble. He took prudent, measured steps, as though the bridesmaid on his arm were made of glass. He played his part dutifully, processing toward the altar before taking his place among the groom's friends. But I could tell that my brother-in-law, who could dance along waves in head-to-toe neoprene, was suffocating in his suit and tie. He squirmed awkwardly, the way a penguin might if you dressed it in an actual tuxedo.

The bride reached the altar and the priest cleared his throat. He was an older man with thinning hair, kindly eyes, a thick Polish accent, and a belly he used as a shelf for interlaced fingers. He began his sermon by praising the happy couple for being young and good-looking. Then he paused meaningfully and gestured to us, their assembled guests.

"You think, over there, they are your friends?" he asked. "You cannot trust your friends. Trust Jesus."

He repeated this message in various iterations, swaying back and forth for emphasis as he detailed the ways Satan would attempt to drive a wedge between the bride and groom. As the sermon crept from ten minutes toward fifteen, I kept my eyes on Matt. As far as I knew, this was the longest he'd ever stood still.

I caught up with him at the reception, which was held in a barn-turned-event-space. The puncture on his forehead, I noted enviously, had healed into a ragged semicircle.

"You sure you shouldn't have gotten stitches?" I asked.

"I dunno," he replied. "By the time I had a doctor look at it, it was too late." Then he added, "I did need stitches over here with my eye, though. That was from getting in a fight in high school."

Matt didn't usually talk about his rebellious teen years. I perked up, eager for some grisly details.

"Wow. What happened to the other guy?"

"Oh, the other guy was fine. He was huge."

Matt must have enjoyed the party, because he left two hours early instead of his usual three. The next morning I joined him, Jacqui, and a few of their cousins on an outing to a swimming hole near Austin. The water was freezing—somewhere between 3/2 and 4/3 temperature—and I stood by the steps in my board shorts, dangling and withdrawing toes. Matt dove straight in and began swimming laps.

As I watched him slice through the surface, I thought back to what the priest had said. Was Matt my friend now? Perhaps not in the traditional sense. But we'd become, somewhat to my surprise, two guys who hung out regularly and pursued the same activity. Where did the Catholic Church rank that on the spectrum between friends and Jesus? Could surf buddies be trusted?

The priest hadn't made this clear.

CHAPTER TEN

Shrimply Irresistible

THE WEEK BEFORE MATT and I arrived in Waco, Donald Trump did. He didn't surf, obviously. Instead, he stood on the tarmac of the local airport before a crowd of thousands and made a solemn pledge.

"*I* am your retribution."

Trump's rally coincided, in a way that seemed less than coincidental, with the thirtieth anniversary of the Waco massacre, an FBI siege of a compound belonging to a cult known as the Branch Davidians. When they weren't arranging marriages between their group's leader and its young women, the heavily armed Davidians preached an anti-government gospel, and after the siege ended in a botched raid and dozens of deaths, Waco became a fixation of the Far Right. The most famous Waco obsessive was a Gulf War veteran and amateur computer programmer named Timothy McVeigh. On April 19, 1995, the raid's second anniversary, McVeigh and an accomplice blew up an Oklahoma City government building, killing 168 people, including nineteen children in a daycare on the second floor. It was the deadliest terror attack in American history and would remain so until 9/11.

Was Trump, in promising his followers a "final battle" against government persecution, presenting himself as the man who could finish what McVeigh started? Or was he merely looking for a rally site convenient to Texas's major metro areas? His campaign hinted at the latter motivation while clearly relishing the former.

One reason I'd avoided talking politics with Matt for the better part of a decade was that I found this sort of rhetoric terrifying, and I worried he found it fun. My brother-in-law wasn't a Trump supporter. But he also wasn't not. Years earlier, as the 2016 primary was in full swing, I'd asked him if he planned on registering to vote.

"Neh."

"Well, if you *did* register, who would you vote for?"

"Probably Trump or Bernie Sanders."

"Okay . . . um, why?"

"Because they're the most entertaining."

At the time I didn't think much about it. Sure, people like Matt existed—but how many of them could there be? Now, seven years later, Trump was a former president launching his third campaign for the White House, and his brand of political arson had spread across the country. Everything I thought I knew had been wrong.

We'd rented separate cars, and while Matt zoomed from Austin to Waco at Harley-on-the-Parkway speeds, I moseyed behind to stop at roadside attractions. By the time I pulled off the highway it was nearly dark. I'd imagined Waco Surf would be surrounded by cozy shops and locally owned barbecue restaurants, but in fact it had been built where land was cheapest, and I was soon lost in a morass of spotty cell service and barbed-wire fences with signs that said KEEP ON DRIVING. The landscape—farms and ranches stretching into the sunset—was gorgeous. Pastoral. All-American.

Still, any movie filmed there would have been about murder rather than baseball.

The history of Waco Surf, it must be said, is not entirely unmurdery itself. The property began as the BSR Ski Ranch, and its main attraction was a giant manmade lake with a cable tow for wakeboarders. (The fact that a wakeboarding resort was known as a "ski ranch" should have been a warning about the owners' attention to detail.) Over the years, the resort added a lazy river and an eighty-foot slide that launched riders through the air into a lagoon. But the real breakthrough came in 2018, when the Ski Ranch became the Surf Ranch and a two-acre wave pool opened to the public.

It was in September of that year that a young man named Fabrizio Stabile traveled—from New Jersey, as it happened—to shred the artificial surf. By all accounts he had a great time. Less than two weeks later he was dead, his brain eaten by *Naegleria fowleri*, an amoeba that thrives in poorly filtered water. The pool—which under Texas law had been classified as a lake—had no filtration system, and Stabile's parents were certain the Surf Ranch's negligence had killed their son. But they couldn't prove it. According to one former BSR employee, the day before the Centers for Disease Control arrived to test the water for amoebas, the Ranch's owners shocked it with a half ton of chlorine.

In the wake of the resulting scandal, ownership had changed hands, and the new management installed a purification system they promised was state of the art. Even so, as I wheeled my suitcase across the wooden bridge spanning the lazy river, I added "brain-eating amoeba" to my list of ways a surfer could die.

Apart from a lifeguard tower and a snack bar, the only building on the surf pool grounds was a two-story wooden ranch house about the length of a football field and the width of a basketball court. Its first floor was home to a combination surf shop, hotel check-in, and customer service desk. Most of the rooms, including ours, were on the second floor, where a long shared balcony faced the pool. I found Matt standing with his arms crossed on the railing, a rapturous look in his eyes.

"Whoa," he said, barely registering my presence.

"Whoa," I agreed.

Before us was the kind of sight that can almost make a person forget the possibility that an amoeba might soon eat their brain. A giant half-moon of water, a full city block in diameter, shimmered in the sunset. In its center waited three tiny, floating figures, their boards flush against a concrete wall. A high-pitched whine built, became a rumble, then a roar. Three punches of swell burst forth. One by one, the surfers took off, reached the bottom of the wave, and raced up the face, hitting the lip again and again. At the dog beach it was rare to see someone turn more than twice before the peak collapsed. These rides, on the other hand, lasted for what seemed like hours.

That night, we drove to Walmart to pick up groceries, passing one billboard for a Lone Star steakhouse and another for a seafood restaurant called Shrimply Irresistible.

"Who were those guys in the pool?" I asked Matt.

"I dunno," he said, with undisguised awe.

As it turned out, they were staying just two rooms down from ours. When we returned with our shopping bags the three of them were sitting on the balcony, Coronas in hand.

"I'm Johnny," said the one who had the most tattoos and was clearly the leader. He pointed to a tall guy with a walrus mustache—"This is Dougie"—then a shorter one with black, shoulder-length hair—"and that's Kenzo."

There's something about men with laid-back attitudes and diminutive names, the Donnies and Benjies and Tommies and Scotties encountered often in Surf World, that I find intimidating. Still, I figured if Matt could make it through a wedding reception, the least I could do was hang out with some surf bros.

"That wave looks pretty sweet," I said, launching into my best confident-dude impression and immediately wishing I hadn't.

"Yeah," said Johnny, as if concerned he might catch cooties. "It was . . . sick."

From a few feet away, I heard a chuckle. Matt and the other two bros were deep in conversation.

"Nah, dude. San Clemente is *Southern* California," Dougie said. "You gotta come surf it sometime."

He's already getting invitations? I thought. I recalled the way Matt had looked standing in his suit at the wedding. This was the opposite of that.

"You guys ever been to Jersey?" he said.

"Nah, bro. Good waves?"

"Yeah, 'specially in winter. You get a good south swell, south-southeast . . ."

At fancy parties in DC, it's not uncommon to realize the person you're talking to is scanning the room for someone more important. That's the realization I was struck with now.

"So," Matt asked, "you guys like living in California?"

"It's pretty sweet," said Kenzo. Johnny, seizing his chance to ditch me, jumped in. "Yeah, California's sweet, but it's run by idiots," he snorted.

"Matt," I said, "shouldn't we get the groceries into the fridge?" He reluctantly agreed.

Not everything is bigger in Texas. Our hotel room, for instance. Despite the assurances of the woman on the phone, the lion's share of floor space was taken up by a single queen-sized mattress; the second bed was a loft above the bathroom, which Matt had claimed before I arrived. For a few minutes we put away turkey, sliced cheddar, and Coke Zeros, trying not to bump into each other. Then Matt said, "I think I'm gonna go back out on the porch with the SoCal bros."

He grabbed a Corona and was out the door. A few minutes later, when I worked up the courage to rejoin them, Kenzo was telling Matt about his clothing-slash-lifestyle brand and Matt was discussing the fine points of East Coast barrels. I stood for a minute, self-consciously shifting my weight from side to side. Then I slunk back indoors.

That night, as Matt slumbered above me, I stared at the ceiling of a room not big enough for the two of us, as awkward and uncomfortable as a fancy-pants penguin without his tuxedo.

~~~~~~~~~

What Matt and I had witnessed upon arrival was called a "private session." The three SoCal bros, apparently flush with clothing-slash-lifestyle cash, had rented the entire pool for an obscene sum.

I'd signed us up for the more common public sessions, which were pricey but less outrageously so. Our first wasn't until 3 p.m. the day after we arrived.

"I'm gonna head into town," I told Matt that morning. "Wanna come?"

"Nah, I'll stay here and watch the waves."

I wasn't surprised Matt would rather spend the morning hanging with fellow hardcore surfers than watching me write about climate change in a coffee shop. What worried me was how unbothered I was by his choice. We'd been roommates for all of twelve hours. Already, we needed space.

I didn't return until just before our scheduled session. The water was about the temperature of the dog beach in early June, so Matt put on a neoprene top while I donned a full 3/2 wetsuit. We headed downstairs to rent boards—Matt chose a shortboard with a swallow-tail, I was goaded into a 6´6˝—before doing our jumping jacks on the artificial beach. Then we joined ten strangers in the shallow end.

A defining moment of ocean surfing comes when chaos snaps into order. One instant, the sea is churning and the peaks are unreadable and a young, fit local is about to steal your wave; the next, you're cruising effortlessly down the line. Pool surfing isn't like that. It's organized from the get-go. Robbie, a sinewy Waco Surf employee, split us into four groups of three and sent the first group to the center of the pool. As I watched from the shallows, surf etiquette was replaced by surf economics. Instead of jockeying for waves, three riders lined up, waited for the machine to pump out an artificial set, and took turns collecting their purchases. They could have been picking up pizzas.

I thought I'd enjoy the structured environment, but as I left the on-deck area and my spot against the concrete wall, I found the lack of chaos working against me. There were no sharks, no death sticks, no missing leashes, no angry dudes with quivering face muscles. Thanks to the new filtration system, there weren't even any amoebas. Resetting the wave machine took about sixty seconds, and with no fatal hazards to fill me with abject terror, I was free to dedicate that time to anxiety.

Will I wipe out? Will I miss the wave? If I'm the only one who misses a wave, what kind of look should I give the people watching from the shallows to show them I'm self-aware enough to feel embarrassed?

"Angle your board toward the beach cabana," said Robbie, sensing I was in trouble. "More. More. Now paddle!"

Distracted and still pointing in the wrong direction, I felt the wave flip my board before landing directly on me. The peak crumbled rather than crashed, so the hold-down was mild compared to a big wave in Jersey, but that did little to soothe my embarrassment. After failing to pop up for the first thirty minutes, I traded my board for a giant foamie.

Matt, meanwhile, got barreled on his second wave and immediately became our session's mayor. Ordinarily I liked watching people give my brother-in-law an extra half foot of room in the lineup, or pause their paddle-outs in admiration as he took off. I felt the way New Jerseyans feel when someone mentions Springsteen. *That's our guy!* But when the session wrapped up and we headed for the lukewarm hot tub, I found myself sulking as he held court.

"The thing about surfing is that once you start doing it, you just become happier," he expounded. Heads—many of them atop bodies covered in tribal tattoos—nodded appreciatively.

"It's a religious experience," agreed the broad-shouldered Texan with a chipped front tooth who had crossed himself before the session.

"That's true," concurred a real estate agent from San Francisco. "You have to manage the addiction, though. I have kids, but I ditch them to go surfing."

I looked around, hoping to spot a horrified expression. But my people—people who believed abandoning your children for a surfboard was irresponsible and examined the historical context behind Donald Trump's latest far-right tirade and could appreciate the ironic, self-aware perfection of "Shrimply Irresistible"—were nowhere to be found. This was an asylum for surf lunatics. Matt was part of the ruling class, and I was the one feeling embarrassed and resentful on the outskirts.

When I returned from breakfast at the snack bar the next morning, I found Matt sitting on my bed, eating a tortilla with peanut butter. To my surprise, he was watching the news. It was a typical broadcast—war, crime, disaster—and it made me feel awful. *The world is falling apart, and I'm here surfing.* But if Matt had similar thoughts he never expressed them. The stream of calamity seemed to surge past him, the same way waves surged past me on my too-short board. The closest Matt ever got to acknowledging the brokenness of the world came when, during our first session of the day, the lifeguard played Blink-182 over the poolside speakers.

"They should play more heavy metal," he said.

And later that morning, they did.

~~~~~~~~~

Shortly before leaving New Jersey, I'd asked a progressive student group at Baylor, a large Christian university in Waco, if they'd be interested in having me speak on campus while I was in town. I figured left-leaning young people in a red state would find it encouraging to hear from a former Obama speechwriter. Also, part of me must have known that after a few days surrounded by shredders, I'd be looking for a confidence boost.

The proposed campus visit got kiboshed by the school's administrators, who apparently saw me as an outside agitator. But the student group's president happened to be an amateur videographer, so I hired her to come to the pool and film. Halfway through our second full day, just after the session that featured plenty of heavy metal, Matt and I sat at a picnic table and watched the footage.

It was worse than I'd feared. On the advice of the guy behind the rental desk, a wrinkled baby boomer from Hawaii named Lenny, I'd switched to a longer board, a 7′0″ model called a Pickup Stick. It helped. But I still missed half of my waves, and though I technically caught the remaining six, it would be a stretch to say I rode them. Where Matt swooped up and down the face, I slid into the flats and watched the breaking lip race on without me. I glanced toward him, just to see his reaction, but he averted his eyes. It seemed my surfing was too painful for him to bear.

That night, we returned to Walmart to restock the mini-fridge. Matt moved swiftly and purposefully through the aisles. Turkey. Popcorn-based potato chip alternatives. A zero-sugar energy drink called Celsius, which came in a variety of flavors, each the color of poison. I'd never shopped with anyone so immune to impulse purchasing. I, on the other hand, had not become a Category Four to life insurers with discipline and self-restraint. Each time we passed Cheez-Its or chocolate bars, I reflexively reached out a hand, only to withdraw it under my brother-in-law's gaze. The best I could do was sneak a small bag of low-carb, low-calorie gummy candies, which I opened the moment we left the store. They were squishy and apple-flavored. In the parking lot I offered one to Matt, who tried it and nodded, impressed. Then, catching himself, he scanned the ingredient list.

"I'm trying not to eat soy," he explained. "I hear it lowers testosterone."

I raised my eyebrows. For the first time since we arrived in Waco, we were back on my turf. "Actually, I don't think that's true," I said. "I heard that about soy and testosterone, but I looked up a few studies, and they all said it doesn't make a difference."

"Well, you can find studies that say both things. It's like anything."

Maybe it was being excluded by the SoCal bros. Maybe it was the suggestion that testosterone was not my area of expertise. Maybe it was the way my brother-in-law was echoing the kind of post-truth, non-logic logic that, when employed by people like Joe Rogan or Donald Trump, put our public health and our democracy at risk. Whatever the reason, my mind began building toward a snap.

No, you cannot find studies that say both things about anything. That's the whole point of studies—to find out the truth. And just because someone claims to have done a study that proves the earth is flat or climate change isn't real or a vaccine isn't safe doesn't mean every study is equally valid. Some people are worth listening to, and some are not. End of story.

I knew saying any of this out loud would torch our entire Waco trip. Even so, it took all my self-control to stay quiet. "Maybe so," I muttered, trying to pack a manifesto of frustration into just three syllables.

Matt didn't reply. But he must have noticed something was off. We loaded the car in a state of all-consuming discomfort and drove for several minutes, neither of us saying a word. Just when the silence had become suffocating, Matt spotted something out the window.

"Shrimply Irresistible," he chuckled to himself. "That's pretty good."

~~~~~~~~~~

The first session of the following day was nearly identical to those that preceded it. Matt tried a new board, one several inches shorter than his go-to Pyzel, and proclaimed he'd never surfed so well in his life. I stayed on my Pickup Stick and failed to improve. Afterward, we got turkey and bread from the mini-fridge and sat at a picnic table by the snack bar, watching the video of the session.

Matt was right about his surfing. His turns, which threw buckets of spray onto anyone foolish enough to stray too close, were sharper than ever. I, meanwhile, kept sliding down the face two seconds into what should have been a twelve-second ride.

Matt was almost done with his sandwich when he swallowed thoughtfully. Then he paused in the way one does when they would rather not say something.

"You gotta square your shoulders," he blurted out.

In all the years I'd known him, I couldn't remember him offering me advice about anything. Over the previous ten months—during which I'd thought about surfing nearly every day, taken a half dozen lessons, traveled internationally for a surf camp, followed at least twenty Instagram surf influencers, and subscribed to four instruction-based channels on YouTube—it had never occurred to me to ask him for help. He was a natural athlete, in outstanding shape, who was also, when it came to risk, a crazy person. I assumed any suggestions he might share would be impossible, life-threatening, or most likely both.

"Aren't I already looking down the line?" I asked skeptically.

"Your head's pointed that way. But your torso's facing toward the bottom of the wave, so that's where you end up going. If you angle your shoulders the way you want to go, you'll stop slipping."

"Maybe," I said. None of the would-be gurus who'd watched me surf had mentioned squaring my shoulders. But nothing else was working. On the second wave of our first afternoon session, I felt the board plane beneath me. As I rose to my feet, I twisted my shoulders ninety degrees, as if I were sprinting down the line rather than sidling along it.

Suddenly, effortlessly, the face opened up. What shocked me most was the sensation not just of speed, but power. I'd resigned myself to watching from the flats as the juiciest part of the wave passed me by. Now, with my tail lodged firmly in the pocket, it was like attaching an afterburner to my board. When the power source began to outrun me, I found myself roaring forward on instinct to catch it.

Twelve to fifteen seconds later, I toppled of my own volition into the shallow end of the pool.

"Hey, look at you!" Matt said. His tone was more pleased than impressed—he spoke the way you might address a child who's learned to operate an E-Z Bake oven—but I didn't mind one bit.

In lieu of an on-campus event, Baylor's progressive students had invited me to a pizza place that evening. I enjoyed the conversation at dinner. There's a special kind of optimism you find only in people under twenty-five, a belief, as yet unrefuted by reality, that they might be the secret ingredient. Even so, I found myself itching to get back to the surf asylum. I had another day of waves to look forward to.

The next morning, as I returned to the balcony with my breakfast burrito, I ran into Johnny. He was surrounded by suitcases and busy stuffing a shortboard into a bag.

"You guys headed back?"

"Yup."

"Nice."

He knelt down, carefully zipping the bag. Then he looked up.

"I saw you out there," he said.

I waited, hoping for a conjunction. *And, you were totally shredding. So, I have more respect for your skills. Yet, I could hardly believe it was you.* But as he turned back to his luggage, it became clear his sentence was complete, less "you belong" than "you exist." I headed for our room.

Then I turned around. *You can do this*, I thought.

"Hey, man," I said. "Have a good one." I extended a fist.

There was no danger Johnny would become my friend, or even my buddy. But I held his gaze, and he offered a fist of his own. We pounded and parted ways.

~~~~~~~~~~

For our last full day in Waco, I signed up for three sessions, thirty-six waves, an embarrassment of riches. With so much abundance, there was no need to worry about failure. If I missed a takeoff, I'd get a second chance, and another after that.

For the first time since I'd started surfing, I remembered the rides more clearly than the wipeouts: the wave opening up along-side me as I squared my shoulders; the sensation of reverse gravity as, in a topsy-turvy Humpty Dumpty, I flew up the wall; the union of board and water as I pushed off the face to turn. Halfway through our second session, Matt caught the third wave in the set and I the fourth. We paddled back together to the lineup, and the words tumbled out of me.

"I feel like I don't deserve this!"

He chuckled. *Is he telling me he knows exactly what I'm feeling? Or that he can't imagine how I feel?* I wondered. I might have asked him, but just then a rider wiped out after missing a cutback and Matt launched himself onto the newly empty wave. That evening, I signed us up for a fourth session. Other than dinner, which I ate at a nearby taco truck because our mini-fridge was nearly empty, I didn't leave the pool and its grounds all day.

The next morning, our last in Waco, Matt and I headed down to the rental rack and Lenny pulled out my user-friendly board. "You know, you're the best on the Pickup Stick I've ever seen here," he said. "A lot of people who take those can't even surf."

"Oh," I said, brain short-circuiting with pride. I took a step toward the doors.

Then I stopped short. For a long time now, I'd been wanting to share something with Matt. I just hadn't known how to do it. Now, an opportunity had opened up.

"I talked about this with a coach in Costa Rica," I said to Lenny, making sure Matt was in earshot. "But he was a crazy British guy, and you grew up in Hawaii and seem like an adult. So, if I keep at it, do you think I could surf the North Shore by the end of this year?"

Lenny crossed his arms—despite his age, his biceps were the size of soup cans—and furrowed his gray eyebrows.

"Early season," he muttered. "Big, but not too big. Sunset Beach, maybe." He bobbed his head from side to side, then looked at me.

"Yeah," he said, loudly enough for Matt to hear. "I think it's possible."

~~~~~~~~~~

For his grand finale the next morning, Matt joined a "pro session," which, while not private, was longer than the standard ones and packed with specialty waves. For ninety minutes he launched airs and crouched low into barrels while I filmed from my phone. Then the regular session began and I suited up.

"I've gotta pack real quick," he said. "Then I'll take the suitcases down and come watch."

As I jogged into the shallows, I could feel a familiar whir as my brain made room for anxiety. What if I forgot everything I'd learned? What if I didn't make a single one of my final twelve waves? What if I had to return home less confident than ever in my progress? But to my surprise, instead of continuing downward, the spiral got stuck. Even stranger, the feeling that came over me was not one of confidence but acceptance. *Maybe I'll suck today. Maybe I won't. I can't control it. Might as well do my best.*

The first six waves were rights. I caught about half of them, and after each successful ride I scanned the edge of the pool. Matt was nowhere to be found. *Don't be silly*, I thought, pushing aside disappointment. *He's packing.*

I was about to paddle for my second left, the turbine going from whine to roar, when I looked up and saw him. He was sitting on the concrete retaining wall in a brand-new Surf Ranch hoodie, one blue-jeaned leg dangling over the edge. *Here we go*, I thought. But my arms were numb from exertion and I missed the wave. The next one wasn't much better. I struggled to lift my chest off the board and was pitched over the falls. Another two wipeouts followed. Before I knew it, the hour had flown by and I had just one wave left.

This is it, dude, dig deep, said my inner surf bro.

Where did you come from? I thought. Then the machine began to bellow, and I paddled more fiercely than I had all trip, and I caught the wave.

From the pocket, wiggling up the face, I could see Matt watching. I crouched low, sliding toward the flats before angling up again.

The top of a wave, closest to the lip, is where the water moves fastest and surfers generate the most speed. For a tenth of a second I stood there, a conquering hero surveying his concrete domain.

Dude, do a cutback! said the surf bro.

I appreciate your enthusiasm, but I don't yet know how to do a cutback, I replied.

I went for it anyway, which is how I confirmed that my inner bro's confidence was misplaced. Throwing both forearms above my head and balling myself like a turtle in its shell, I nose-dived, then bounced along the concrete bottom until the wave passed by and the water went still. As soon as I got my head above water, even before gasping for breath, I looked for Matt. He was nodding in approval.

Thirty minutes later, we stood in the parking lot by our separate cars. "This was fun," I said. Just as I had with Johnny the day before, I held out my fist for a pound. Matt tapped it with a fist of his own. Still, I could tell his gesture was cautious. I wasn't sure what, but something about the moment had left him ill at ease.

"Nah," he finally said. "I'm giving you a hug."

~~~~~~~~~~~~~~~

CHAPTER ELEVEN

Beanbag

ON THE FLIGHT BACK TO DC, I watched a clip from the pool, paying particular attention to an impish wiggle at the end. I had turned a surfboard! It was a tiny turn, a mini-turn, a soupçon of a turn, but a turn nonetheless. The passenger beside me shifted. I angled my screen, hoping he'd glance over.

"That's not you, is it?" he would ask.

"Well, actually . . ."

"That's incredible!"

"Oh, it's not hard. You just have to square your shoulders."

My neighbor pulled out a book, so I never got to wow him with my humility. But that didn't stop me from replaying the clip, sliding my finger left to right across the screen like one of those rats they teach to push buttons for cocaine. Thirty thousand feet in the air, I remained a full-time resident of Surf World.

Then the wheels hit the tarmac and the real world returned. "Call me please," read the text from Jacqui. I assumed Emily had done something destructive; her most gremlinesque chewing episodes always seemed to occur when I was surfing. But the moment

Jacqui answered, I knew this was more serious than a half-eaten running shoe. I'd never heard her sound so terrified.

As with most things involving conspiracy theories, the short version of what happened is pretty long. But here goes.

Shortly after taking over Twitter, Elon Musk announced he'd discovered something shocking: the company's anti-misinformation team was working with the deep state to censor conservatives. To prove his claim, Musk leaked a carefully selected batch of internal Twitter emails to writers of his favorite online newsletters. These newsletter writers then turned around and released a fraction of the batch to the public.

Even without context, the "Twitter Files" showed mostly what you'd expect: people making judgment calls, sometimes successfully and other times not. But that reflected a quaint understanding of scandal. Musk and his allies started by reaching a verdict—Twitter's ex-employees were out to get them—and only then began searching for evidence. It was an investigative method that left no room for reason or doubt. Any new piece of information was either proof of a conspiracy, proof of a cover-up, or discarded as irrelevant.

On its own, the story would have fizzled. So politicians kept it in the news. In March 2022, Jim Jordan, the Republican in charge of the House Judiciary Committee, held a hearing so some of the Musk-friendly writers could air their claims in an official setting. In April, one of those writers admitted that many things he said under oath were not exactly true. The committee's Democrats, in a ham-fisted but typical bit of bluster, sent a letter reminding the writer in question that lying to Congress is a crime.

To Musk and company, this letter was further proof of their

claims, another example of the regime persecuting a man for bravely telling the not-quite-truth. One member of the growing anti-anti-misinformation movement looked into the process by which the letter had been conceived, scrubbed metadata from the Word document, and reported the name of the letter's author: congressional aide Jacqui Kappler.

This happened to be inaccurate. While Jacqui had created the original document on her computer, like most things on Capitol Hill it had been revised by a small army of staff and approved by a lawmaker. Whether one thought the line about lying to Congress deserved blame or credit, someone else had penned it. But the outrage machine doesn't worry about accuracy. What matters is that it's fed. Now, my wife was on the menu.

Politics, as the saying goes, ain't beanbag. But when did it become Russian roulette? Ten years ago, while members of Congress were frequently targeted by name, their staffers almost never were. And they're not the only ones suddenly in the crosshairs. There was the TV weatherman in Iowa bullied into early retirement because he talked about climate change; the Stanford disinformation researcher forced to move her family into hiding; the law enforcement personnel in a Cincinnati FBI field office shot at after Trump was indicted; the nurses at a Boston hospital sent into lockdown by a bomb threat because their workplace treated transgender youth.

"Don't worry," I reassured Jacqui on the phone. "There are, like, twenty of these stories a week. Nineteen of them don't lead to anything."

"What if we're the twentieth?"

"Then we'll get a ton of death threats and probably have to move."

"Oh good," she said.

As soon as I got home, I hurried inside and locked the door. Then we sat down and checked the internet to see whether our lives would be ruined. Some guy left nasty comments on one of my Instagram puppy pictures. Another, realizing I was Jewish and assuming Jacqui was as well, started an anti-Semitic smear campaign against her. But he got only four likes, the online equivalent of pulling the trigger and hearing the *click* of an empty chamber, and the outrage machine lumbered on. As night fell, we sat on the couch, pets in close proximity, and gradually untensed.

"Hey," I said.

"Hey," Jacqui said.

I exhaled deeply, thinking about everything we'd gone through, and looked into her eyes.

"Did you see the way I turned on that wave?"

~~~~~~~~~

Having informed Matt, in my roundabout way, that I hoped to tackle the North Shore in November, it was time to test my skills in more consequential surf. The best place to do that in Central Jersey was the Manasquan Inlet.

Like Frank's Deli, or Southside Johnny and the Asbury Jukes, the wave at Manasquan is regionally rather than internationally famous. But when waves approach from the perfect angle, bouncing off the unusually long jetty, they compound themselves into supersized rights that peel for hundreds of yards. On good days, surfers from across the mid-Atlantic swarm the inlet in search of a challenge. At the beginning of May, when Surfline called for head-high waves and good conditions, I finally felt ready to join them.

"Want to meet at sunrise?" I asked Matt.

"It's gonna be really crowded," he replied. "How about first light?"

I had not known such a time existed. Even so, I gamely approved.

"And I'm gonna bring my friend Vito," Matt added. "Is that cool?"

I gamely approved again, but this time I didn't really mean it. While I wasn't against my brother-in-law having friends, after our Waco trip I'd begun to think of us as a pair of adventurers, like Frodo Baggins and Samwise Gamgee, or Butch Cassidy and the Sundance Kid. The idea that some interloper might turn us into a trio—or even worse, that Matt might not consider us a duo in the first place—sent an annoyed *pfft* of air through my teeth.

"There's a reason it's 'Lewis and Clark,' and not 'Lewis and Clark and Clark's friend Vito,'" I groused to Jacqui.

"What about Sacagawea?"

Seeing she would be no help, I huffed into the yard to put new fins in my board.

The only Vito with whom I was familiar was a character in *The Sopranos*, so I pictured Matt's friend as a plus-sized middle-aged guy in a tracksuit. Instead, a half hour before sunrise the next morning, I pulled into a parking space to find Matt standing beside someone I sincerely thought was a teenager. Then I remembered that people in their mid-twenties now look like teenagers to me.

"Young Vito, meet David. David, meet Young Vito. Vito's an apprentice electrician. We're working together on a job in Rumson."

Vito's brown hair, unmarred by graying or male-pattern baldness, was arranged in a ponytail. His lean torso and wiry limbs left little doubt that life insurers would smile on his application. His eyes, free of wrinkles, eagerly gazed at my brother-in-law the way our puppy gazed at my wife. I opened the trunk to retrieve my changing poncho, my lips pressed in consternation.

"At least 5/4 season's finally over," I said to Matt, running a leg through my 4/3 wetsuit.

"Yeah," agreed Vito. "It's about time."

"So, *Matt*," I said pointedly, "Jacqui told me your dad wasn't feeling well. How's he doing?"

"He's doing okay," Matt replied. "They took him to urgent care, though, just to test him for flu."

"Has he taken a Covid test?"

"Yeah. It's not Covid."

"That's good," I said.

"Didn't have 'The Vid,' as much they want him to?"

This last remark came from Vito, and my head snapped in his direction. What really got to me was not the suggestion that shadowy forces would turn their awesome might toward ensuring a seventy-year-old suburban lawn care enthusiast came down with coronavirus instead of a cold. It was the snicker that followed. The implication was obvious: anyone who found his theory implausible was a mindless sheep. I wondered, sometimes, if Matt felt that way about me.

Perhaps if the prospect of surfing Manasquan hadn't shaken my own confidence, Vito's self-assurance wouldn't have bugged me. By the same token, if my wife hadn't so recently become a target of the casually conspiracy-minded, I might not have cared about "The Vid." Even now, I couldn't hold Vito responsible for the state of our national discourse. I could, however, dislike him. And that's what I decided to do.

"Ready?" Matt asked the moment my gloves were on. Before I could answer, he began trotting down the road that ran along the inlet to the beach. Vito jogged next to him, practically panting with enthusiasm, his shortboard nearly identical in length to Matt's Pyzel. I sulked behind.

For once, I hadn't asked the internet whether anyone had died at the spot Matt and I would be surfing. As I reached the shoreline, though, it became obvious how someone could. Where most New Jersey jetties prevent beach erosion, the one at Manasquan protects a channel deep enough for a commercial fishing fleet. This makes it a different beast. Cutting between river and sea, as long as the Empire State Building is tall, the inlet jetty is a solid mass with ends Tetrised from T-shaped, concrete chunks. These "jacks"—so called because they resemble the classic toy—spike into the air and water at random, in a way suggesting the engineer was hired due to connections rather than merit. A powerful rip current had built alongside the wall, and Matt used it as a conveyor belt to get out the back. Vito followed him.

I did not. Big waves usually don't break directly onto rips, because the water flowing out neutralizes the water flowing in. But there are exceptions to the rule, and if I mistimed my paddle-out, one of those exceptions could launch me into the concrete. I scooted a dozen yards to my left before entering. That way, if I was flung backward, I'd be well clear of the jetty.

The downside of forgoing the rip current was that it forced me to battle the sets head on. I was about two-thirds of the way out the back, and beginning to seriously worry about exhaustion, when the sun crept over the horizon and the ocean's surface became a sequined dress of light. I kept paddling, half-blinded, gasping for air.

Suddenly, as though a curtain had been raised, a wave reared up and blocked the sun. On its face was Matt, knees bent, left hand grabbing the rail of his board, right hand almost touching the water. I could feel my own arms moving, yet he seemed entirely still. Then he came unstuck in my mind and hurtled forward, inches ahead of the thunderous, crashing lip.

For a moment, transfixed, I forgot to paddle, and a wall of white-water swept me backward. By the time the next lull arrived and I finally made it out, Matt was on his fourth wave of the day. He was catching them hungrily, surfing them in a hurry, as though making up for valuable seconds lost to parking lot chitchat.

"It's walling up!" he yelled, passing me as he paddled back to his takeoff point.

I had no idea what that meant. Then the first wave came toward me and I understood. While all East Coast peaks are steep, these grew vertically, like tombstones being pushed upward through cemetery grass, before collapsing all at once. The waves were as close to unrideable as it's possible to come without being unrideable. Each takeoff required the surfer to perform a feat of perfect timing, like snatching a quarter from a crocodile's jaws. Even after getting out the back, I remained concerned a cleanup set would hurl me into the concrete. Each time a wall emerged I defensively paddled outside, sprinting over it to safety.

It was after one of these sprints that I looked behind me and caught sight of Vito's head bobbing in the carnage, his ponytail swirling like a leaf in a storm drain. I watched the waves work him over, holding him down for several seconds at a time. I knew what he was going through: the cold water bursting through gaps in his wetsuit, his brain pleading for air. I checked quickly to make sure Matt couldn't see my face. Then I broke into a satisfied smirk.

It took a while, but Vito finally retrieved his board. I was surprised to see him paddling toward me with his legs splayed wide, struggling to balance. *He's just as hopeless as I am!* I thought. Even more so, in a way. Where I had the good manners to be ashamed and terrified, he thrashed the water with a giant grin on his face.

"You get any good ones?" he asked when he reached me.

"No," I said coldly, adding, "it's walling up."

"All right!"

Not even pausing to catch his breath, he swung around and launched off a head-high lip. It ended disastrously—the wave crashed, and moments later his surfboard flew, riderless, straight into the air. But when I looked right, I saw that Matt was impressed. For Vito, commitment came naturally.

Over the next thirty minutes my brother-in-law drifted toward the center of the break, where the waves were even steeper and bigger than those nearer the seawall. Vito followed, apparently oblivious to fear. His wipeouts were frequent and spectacular—he called to mind a slender bar-goer being thrown from a mechanical bull—but he never strayed far from Matt. While the two of them were vastly different in skill level, anyone watching from the beach could tell they were a pair.

Not that they cared, but I was surfing pretty well myself. No one would mistake me for an adrenaline junkie. I let plenty of opportunities pass rather than risk a wall collapsing on top of me. But for the first time surfing with Matt in New Jersey, I wasn't a tourist. When I finally paddled into waves, I did so aggressively, without regard for the consequences. Each takeoff attempt hurt in a new way: bruised triceps; leash tangled around knee and cinched tight during a fall; leg colliding with fin in a manner that, had I not been wearing a wetsuit, would have sliced me like a pot roast. But I didn't let the pain stop me. Brushing off each near-injury, I charged back to the lineup with forceful strokes, determined to catch the next one.

I was finally surfing Central Jersey's most formidable break. And I belonged out there. And Matt didn't notice.

~~~~~~~~~~

I didn't have my smartwatch, so I marked time by how chilly I became. I was losing feeling in my fingers when Matt rode a wave in all the way to shore. I wasn't sure if he'd gotten cold, or grown fed up with the ballooning crowd, or simply caught his fill. From my position outside the breaking waves, I saw him carry his board back to the parking lot. A few minutes later he returned in his Skeletor hoodie and watched me and Vito from the beach.

At a different time in my life, in a very different setting, I'd been the young hotshot, the energetic up-and-comer. The usurper. Now, the roles were reversed. For months, I'd surfed where Matt wanted, when he wanted. I'd paddled out in hurricane swells and below-freezing temperatures. We'd even shared a hotel room. And apparently none of it mattered. This upstart had put our duo at risk.

A peak emerged. The line running along the lip was nearly horizontal, and the rising sun shone directly in my eyes, so it was hard to know where it would break. Even worse, it was the very beginning of a set. Wiping out on the first wave after a lull is like tumbling out the back door of the first truck in a convoy. You'll be walloped, and walloped, and walloped again. Ordinarily, there was no way I'd take that risk.

But these were extraordinary circumstances. I'd worked too hard to let some ponytailed puppy with thoughts about the deep state take my place.

The wave walled up. For a moment, my board swiveled down the line and I thought I might make it. Then the ocean's power welled beneath my feet and I thought I might go over the falls. Neither of those things happened. Instead I felt, I can only imagine, like an ant who has the misfortune to be standing atop a Jenga tower when someone loses a game. There was a rumble below me, followed by a sheer drop, the shock of cold water, and the thud of fiberglass against ribs as my board knocked the wind out of me. Then the wave shoved me under and the hold-down began.

I surfaced struggling to breathe, my head about to implode and explode simultaneously, a palm-sized ache where my wetsuit pressed against bruised ribs. Already, the next wave was crashing in front of me. I dove. Not deep enough. Another long hold-down began, this one accompanied by the knowledge that it wouldn't be the last.

It was after the third wave of the set, or maybe the fourth, that I realized I wasn't alone. Vito must have gone on one of the set waves, too. He was sputtering and gasping for breath, and for the first time looked decidedly unhappy with his circumstances. In a rare moment between pummelings, he noticed me as well. His eyes went wide—*Can you believe this is happening?*—before the next wave smacked him.

I'd been telling myself the same story about Vito all morning: *I am not like you. I believe in science and know the danger posed by misinformation and would never consider riding a shortboard before I'm ready.* Now, as the last wave of the set finally came through and our joint suffering ended, I began to wonder, *Have I misjudged him?*

I decided the answer was no. I'd assessed him correctly. What I'd failed to do, however, was assess him completely. My newest thought didn't replace the ones I'd been thinking all morning. Instead, it layered over the others, the way a filter changes an image through a lens.

I am not like you. And also, we are just two schmucks in an ocean.

When the set finally ended, Vito and I paddled into shore, stumbled onto the sand, and uncuffed our leashes a safe distance from the breaking waves. After taking a quick breather to confirm we were still alive, we joined Matt and began the trek back to our cars.

When we arrived in the parking lot, Matt was quiet. I knew him well enough to know that part of him was still on those faces, in the middle of those rides, unwilling to break the spell by talking to mortals who would never truly understand. Vito and I, meanwhile, jabbered incessantly, aimlessly, reliving the injuries we'd suffered and the takeoffs we'd almost made.

After a round robin of fist bumps, we changed into civilian clothes. Matt and Vito drove off to their job site. I lingered for a moment, enjoying the sun that had finally risen, a kind of second light.

~~~~~~~~~~~~~~

There is something strange, something Rip Van Winkle-y, about returning to a person you share a bed with when you've been through something dramatic while they remained asleep. I lay awake, eyes open, every thought mirrored by its opposite. I'd survived a consequential wave yet hadn't caught one. I'd proved myself to Matt yet he didn't seem to care. I'd been certain Young Vito was my enemy yet felt we were on the same side.

Ordinarily, such unresolved uncertainty would have tortured me. But this time—perhaps from exhaustion, perhaps from growth— I found myself smiling. I looked down at Jacqui's head resting on my shoulder.

You have no idea how much has changed, I thought. And then I fell asleep.

CHAPTER TWELVE

The Honda Odyssey

STEVE BANNON, IN AN EARLY anti-globalist rant, once claimed people in New York have more in common with people in London than with those in Kansas City. This isn't true.

What is true, and what Steve Bannon should have said, is that regardless of where they live, people with status on their preferred airline have more in common with each other than they do with people who show up two hours early for a flight. One sunny June morning a few weeks after paddling out at the inlet, I arrived at Newark's Terminal C fifty minutes before departure. After checking my bag at the premier desk, confirming that my suitcase had been tagged with a bright orange PRIORITY label, and breezing through TSA pre-check, I walked briskly to my gate, reaching the line right as Group Two was boarding. Matt had been waiting there for ninety minutes.

"I thought you wouldn't make it," he said.

"Nah, I had plenty of time."

He checked his ticket and frowned. "I don't think I'm in Group Two."

"You're with me. It'll be fine."

Matt looked worried his fellow Group Fives might grab pitchforks, but my plan worked. We boarded the flight together, and after taking my seat across the aisle from him, I unwound with a *New York Times* article about the growing popularity of outdoor bathtubs. I was reading about Tina, a Tampa Bay autopsy technician who found that long soaks in a clawfoot oasis helped her live in the moment, when I heard a chuckle. I glanced over to see Matt holding a copy of the morning's *New York Post*.

"I love their writing," he told me, laughing again. "Hilarious. Straight to the point."

Leaning closer, I saw that the story he was reading involved a homeless man and a former felon beating each other up on Eighth Avenue. I was struggling to phrase my next question so it didn't sound like "What the fuck?" when we were interrupted by a salvo of wet, percussive coughs. The jowly man in the row ahead wasn't covering his mouth, not even as a gesture. And these were not mild allergic reactions, but deep, virusy bellows. I reached into my backpack and pulled out a KN95.

The moment the mask was across my face, I was transported back in time by the sour stench of breath, the official smell of peak pandemic. A feeling came rushing back, too, the sense that I was making a political stand whether or not I wanted to. This was bad enough in 2020, when I wanted to. Now, three years later, my goal had nothing to do with public health. I just wanted to lower my own odds of getting sick. Yet surrounded by my maskless fellow passengers it was impossible not to feel foolish, a mewling nanny-stater begging for a national dress code.

I stole a glance at Matt. He was avoiding eye contact. He was also, of course, unmasked. *I wonder*, I thought, in the clinical manner of a prisoner who's already been sentenced, *if a trip to California was such a good idea.*

~~~~~~~~~~

Perhaps if I'd taken Matt's approach to surf training—hurl yourself off waves until you're either dead or competent—I might have been comfortable going straight from Waco to the North Shore. What I had proposed instead was a phased approach. We'd go to the West Coast in mid-June, spend the summer and fall in New Jersey, take one more tune-up trip in early October, and then, finally, be ready for the main event. Such gradualism was not in Matt's nature, but Waco had piqued his interest in surf travel. He agreed to the plan.

For our first phase, a week in Santa Cruz, California, had seemed ideal. Compared to four days in Texas, the trip would be a chorus line of baby steps: slightly further from New Jersey; slightly bigger waves; slightly higher chance of shark attack; slightly more time in close proximity.

What I'd failed to appreciate is how quickly increments of change add up. By the time we landed in San Francisco, every decision felt like a wedge issue. At the car rental I received a free upgrade, and was examining Audis and BMWs when a voice echoed across the concrete distance of the garage.

"Let's go with this one," said Matt, standing beside a white Honda Odyssey.

For those unfamiliar, the Odyssey is a minivan designed to serve as a rolling storage unit for suburban families. I walked over and peered into the cavernous interior. You could easily fit a brood of children in there, along with a few of their friends, assorted pets, beach chairs, skis, bikes, tennis rackets, golf clubs, a cooler full of snacks, and a smaller car you might actually want to drive. I took a longing, backward look toward a BMW. Matt gave me what I'd come to think of as his salt-of-the-earth expression: arms crossed, faint smile, slow nod.

"Yeah," he said. "This one's gonna be way more practical."

I thought about putting my foot down and demanding the car of my choice. Ninety minutes later, I swung the Odyssey into a tiny parking space not far from Santa Cruz. After donning our 4/3 wetsuits, we headed across the parking lot to investigate a local break known as the Hook.

One reason I had suggested we visit this part of California was its friendliness toward surf craft of all sizes. Several of the best breaks in the area, the Hook included, are known as "longboard waves," with slow, easy takeoffs and gentle faces for languid gliding. Matt could bring his Pyzel from Jersey, while I could rent a board like the one I'd ridden in Costa Rica without feeling ashamed of its length.

What I hadn't considered was that to catch a wave, even a longboard wave, you must first reach the ocean. In New Jersey this was easy: I pointed myself toward water and walked. But the Hook was at the bottom of a sandstone cliff towering forty feet above the sea. I crossed the street, joined Matt by a flimsy wooden fence, and peered skeptically downward, my nine-footer balanced precariously atop my head.

"Nice," Matt said, looking at the surfers catching waves.

"Mrmm," I said, looking at those same waves smashing against the rocks.

At the bottom of the path was a weathered platform from which surfers could launch themselves into the sea. It was unwise to idle there—the whitewater would drill you into the cliff—so Matt waited a few yards above. For a moment I thought we might paddle out together, and by doing so strike an unspoken truce: between luxury SUV and practical minivan, mask and no mask, *Times* and *Post*. The moment I drew near him, though, he hopped in the water and headed for the break.

The ocean was greener than in Jersey, the air perfumed with the sweet, briny bouquet that hits you right before you slurp an oyster. While it was a long distance to the takeoff point, the waves were spaced far apart, which made the paddle-out easy. I was grateful for this, as it allowed me to focus on being concerned. Only a few hours into our trip, our cultural cold war had erupted, with skirmishes across the front. What would the situation be a week from now?

Then I reached the break and a peak came and I caught it.

If the waves in Manasquan had been like tombstones rising from a cemetery, the waves at the Hook were as soft and round as pillows beneath a duvet. The swell cupped my board, carrying me gently shoreward. I stood and sailed down the line, as blissful as a Tampa Bay autopsy technician soaking in an outdoor tub. I paddled back to the lineup and took off again and again. I never grew anxious I might miss the wave. I never needed to. For the first time in my life, I surfed as though surfing was just something I did.

What on earth were you so worried about? I wondered.

~~~~~~~~~~

That evening, in our two-bedroom rental condo decorated in the style known as "It's an Airbnb, what do you expect?" I came downstairs to find *SpongeBob SquarePants* on the TV. Matt wasn't in the living room, so I assumed he'd been flipping channels and had forgotten to turn the television off. Then he appeared from the kitchen, plopped down on a chair, and turned up the volume. He watched until the episode was over. Then he started watching the next one.

"Groceries?" I interjected.

One thing about my brother-in-law, I thought as we drove to Safeway, *is that he acts as though all his preferences make the same amount of sense.* The minivan had actually been a good call. We could throw my longboard in the trunk instead of strapping it to the roof. On the other hand, there was *SpongeBob* and not wearing masks around sick people and the tattoo I'd somehow never noticed before, on his leg, of a 1940s-style pinup girl with accompanying text that read, inexplicably, "HA!" Even on our brief shopping trip, it was difficult to make sense of his notions. For example, why did he forgo coffee for Celsius energy drinks, which were more expensive than coffee, and then decline to split a twelve-pack of Coke Zeros on economic grounds?

"My plan is to save up enough to make my house payments for a year," he informed me. "That way when I break my body riding my bike or surfing, I'm covered."

"Wouldn't it be better to not break your body?"

"Meh," he shrugged. "It's gonna happen sooner or later."

This was a level of stoicism, or madness, or both, that I just couldn't fathom.

"Well," I said, still bitter about the Coke Zeros. "As long as you have a plan." We headed back to the condo, and the groceries hadn't even been unloaded before the TV was on and playing *SpongeBob* yet again.

Matt awoke the next morning with a cough, and I felt sorry for him. Just not immediately. First, I thought, *See! Masks work!* Then I thought, *It'll be nice to have something to slow him down.* Then I felt bad about the first two thoughts. Then I made a mental list of all the ways I'm a good person so I didn't have to feel bad. Then I felt sorry for him.

I'd hired a local guide, a tan guy in his early twenties named Nate, to show us around. We started at Pleasure Point, a famous spot—and a famously crowded one—a half mile west of the Hook. Standing on the cliff, Nate pointed seaward.

"Over there is where the wave breaks first. We call that First Peak." He angled his hand a few degrees to the left. "Over there is where the wave breaks second. It's called Second Peak." Finally, he pointed to the right, where a lone shortboarder was being demolished by a steep, violent-looking wave about a hundred yards from shore. "That's where the sewer pipe used to be."

"Let me guess," I said. "Third Peak?"

"No," he said. "It's called Sewers. Everything's gonna be solid today, so where do you want to start?"

"Sewers!" said Matt.

Nate eyed my longboard. "You sure?"

I gave him a look that said, *The unspoken social contract between my brother-in-law and me dictates that he decides where we surf, and in exchange if I start drowning he might try to save me.* Nate got the gist of this, if not the details, and we descended the rocky steps. Halfway down the cliff the trail forked. I regretted my decision, but it was too late. I took one last, wistful glance at the longboarders gliding along Second Peak, then veered right toward Sewers.

Nate was from the Dylan school of surf instruction. "Missed it!" "You fell off!" "You made it!" But after Waco, I knew where to go for guidance. Matt connected instantly with the wave, turning as though a preexisting groove had been worn into the face. As he paddled back, I flagged him down.

"Any thoughts for me?" I asked.

"You're angling your takeoff away from the peak," he said, out of breath from his thirty-second ride. "Angle toward it instead."

This seemed like bad advice. Where Jersey breaks distributed their power evenly, Sewers broke over a small, concentrated section of rocky reef in a way that reminded me of the car going over the cliff at the end of *Thelma and Louise*. Matt was telling me to jump in the back seat.

And then I tried it, and it worked. Instead of nudging my board down the line as I paddled, I headed straight for the foaming lip. Connecting with the pocket was like opening a waist-high lock with a nine-foot, fiberglass-clad key. A few seconds into the ride, the seafloor must have changed, because the face lengthened. I turned right, gliding for another ten seconds before finding myself in a deep, flat channel. This was another benefit of reef breaks—paddling back out to the lineup was easy—and I beamed in triumph as I passed Nate.

"You made it!" he said.

That afternoon I walked downstairs to find Matt watching *Dr. Phil*. The guest was an influencer from Florida. During the pandemic

she'd lost advertisers after spreading misinformation about vaccines, and now she'd been invited on live television to talk about
how no one paid attention to her anymore. Matt seemed not to
notice this irony.

Keep your mouth shut, I admonished myself. *You just had another
perfect surf session. Why risk it?* But the words left my mouth before
my thoughts could restrain them.

"It's weird that people are still talking about vaccine stuff," I
blurted out. While my language was neutral, my tone was unmis-
takably not.

Matt didn't take his eyes off the television. "Yeah, well, they're
talking about other stuff, too," he said, in a tone that wasn't exactly
neutral, either. Several more minutes passed, with neither of us saying anything. Then the show ended and we went to lunch.

Capitola's main street was criminally tacky—half the stores sold
cheap souvenirs, and half of the remaining half sold dreamcatchers—
but like so much of California it was redeemed by weather. It was one
of those sunny, coastal afternoons, just warm enough for a T-shirt,
when the fog has lifted and you can't help but feel that the ocean
breeze is rooting for you.

"I might have to move here," Matt said.

"Good idea," I replied. "You get good surf all year round."

At last, I thought. *A conversation in which we're not on opposing
sides.*

"Although," Matt added, "I do like to do things other people aren't
doing. So if I moved here, I probably wouldn't even surf."

I was simultaneously impressed and befuddled. My brother-
in-law had found a way to take the opposite position from mine,

even when, only seconds earlier, he'd taken that exact same position himself. We reached our destination, a Tex-Mex restaurant. Matt ordered a chicken burrito, and I a shrimp one.

"This is pretty gross," I remarked once our food arrived, looking down at my plastic tray.

"Yeah, mine too," he said. "Do you think Trump will go to prison?"

The question wasn't entirely out of nowhere. A few days earlier, the former president had been indicted in federal court for hoarding top-secret documents at his private club. Still, this was new territory. Even during the years I worked in the White House, Matt had never expressed an interest in my opinion on current events. I phrased my answer carefully.

"Based on what I've seen," I said, "I think he *should* go to prison. But I don't know if a Florida jury will convict him." When Matt said nothing, I grew bolder, analyzing the case from all angles—politics, personalities, legal questions. He sat there, listening, until he was finished eating and we stood to leave.

Okay, I thought, as we stepped into the California sunshine, *this has to count*. We'd been able to discuss something other than surfing without descending into petty disagreement. Not only that, but we'd talked about one of the most controversial subjects in the news. It felt like a major milestone.

Only that evening, as I lay in bed and he watched more *Sponge-Bob* in the living room, did I realize. I'd never asked him what he thought.

By the middle of the next day, I'd begun to feel the way a mermaid might. So long as Matt and I remained in the water, everything was idyllic. Life on land was constant struggle.

"Want to grab a couple of beers to go with dinner?" I asked hopefully that afternoon, as we passed a brewery near the Airbnb.

"I'm trying not to drink alcohol after exercise," Matt said. "It reverses all the gains you made." I bought a bottle of beer anyway, but by the time we got back to the condo I knew I wouldn't enjoy it. It sat in the fridge unopened, a tiny idol of shame.

That night, sick of Capitola, I suggested going to downtown Santa Cruz for dinner, and Matt countered that he'd rather get pizza nearby. *How does pizza fit into maximizing gains from exercise?* I wondered. But I held my tongue and we picked up a Hawaiian pie not far from where we'd gotten our burritos the day before. It was awful, like eating ciabatta dipped in fruit juice, and I made passive-aggressive faces as I chewed.

"This reminds me of that death-metal song 'Pineapple on Pizza,'" Matt said, taking a second slice. "Have you heard it?"

"I have not."

"I'll play it!" Our condo was soon filled with the sound of a hundred thousand droning bees, and the track lasted, if I remember correctly, millennia. Later that night, Matt watched *SpongeBob* again, coughing fitfully throughout the episode.

I awoke at first light with a runny nose, a low fever, and sinuses that felt like they were encased in five millimeters of neoprene. When I came downstairs, Matt was watching an MTV talk show in which a young woman with a laugh borrowed from a psychotic dolphin reacts to viral videos.

"I checked the forecast this morning," I told him. "Maybe we try Second Peak."

He waited for the *eh-eh-eh-eh-eh* of laughter to subside. "Probably gonna be a ton of people there," he said warily.

"Yes, well, if there are a ton of people there, it's probably for a reason."

"But maybe not."

"But probably."

Another Gatling-gun peal echoed from the television.

"But maybe not."

We ended up heading for a different break twenty-five minutes north. The moment we got into the car, Matt turned on his death metal playlist. As our Odyssey lumbered down the highway, I massaged my congested sinuses and tried to confine our conversation to a safe space.

"Yesterday I wiped out so hard my bootie came off," I said.

"Hey, at least it floated. That's the good thing about neoprene. If you get knocked out by your board, you'll float to the top where someone might find you. In board shorts you just sink to the bottom."

"Glad we're wearing wetsuits," I said.

"Yeah, well, with a wetsuit, you look like a seal, so the sharks will get you." Then he added, "You should listen to the Joe Rogan episode with Kelly Slater. He gets into this stuff."

Matt knew, even if we'd never exactly discussed it, what I thought of his favorite podcast host. Was he needling me? Or did he genuinely think I'd enjoy the interview? I wasn't sure. But I was in an ungenerous mood. Days into the trip, hours into the illness I'd picked up from him, everything he did annoyed me. Even the fact that Matt called the break we were driving to "Steamer's Lane" rather than "Steamer Lane" was aggravating. *How can he get the name of the area's most famous surf break wrong?*

Steamer Lane—so called because it was once full of steamships and not, as certain people would have you believe, because it is owned by a steamship—is flanked by a cliff long enough to form a small peninsula. This natural viewing platform is where, in 1885, a crowd gathered to watch three Hawaiian princes surf below. It was California's introduction to what would become its official state sport.

Today, Steamer Lane is famous not just for its history but for offering variety despite containing just four peaks. The first wave breaks only during massive swells. Because it indicates that big-wave surfing is on tap, it's called Indicators. On the far right, another breaks just a few feet from the cliff face, forcing hotshots to take off through a narrow slot. It's called The Slot. Nearby, a third peak breaks near the tip of Lighthouse Point and is called The Point. The fourth peak is more longboard-friendly, especially on smaller days. It sits about halfway between Indicators and Lighthouse Point and is known, because of course it is, as Middle Peak.

On the morning we arrived, Indicators and The Point weren't breaking, and The Slot appeared suicidal, but inviting pillows beckoned from Middle Peak. Eager to get back in the water, I popped the trunk to grab my board. Matt, meanwhile, began his calisthenics routine. This was his typical pre-surf ritual, one I'd seen him perform countless times, but today I found it irritating, like watching a theater kid do vocal warm-ups.

"I'm gonna get a head start down the steps," I muttered, and without waiting for his reply headed for the cliff.

It was the first time I'd ever gotten out the back before him, and I assumed he'd try a few waves with me at Middle Peak before heading to The Slot. But when he finally got in the water he zoomed right past me. I took this as a personal slight, and then a three-foot wave headed toward me and nothing felt personal anymore.

Here's what it's like to ride along the open face of a world-class wave on a nine-foot board when the surf is up but gentle: Imagine sitting on the grass for a picnic. Not just any picnic. A picnic on a day in early summer when the sun is shining and a slight breeze blows puffy clouds with interesting shapes across the horizon and you're wearing a shirt that is comfortable and seasonally appropriate and (you know this without even having to confirm it) makes you look great without looking like you're trying and also, on top of everything, you just took your first bite of a really good sandwich. Now imagine all that but you're flying.

As I paddled back to the lineup, an otter popped above the water to regard me, so close I could make out each dripping whisker. It lay on its back, happily ripping the legs off a wriggling orange crab. Using its webbed hind feet, it had pinned a second crab to its belly in a macabre on-deck circle. The otter and I each took a moment to appreciate the ocean's bounty. He tossed his appetizer's shell into the water and snatched his helpless second course. I caught another wave and flew.

I was having so much fun that at first I didn't even wonder where Matt had gone. Then I pretended not to wonder. Then I wondered.

I found him by The Slot. It was easy, really. I looked for the scariest takeoff point, one no person who understood the relationship between actions and consequences would seek out, and there he was. Matt wasn't the best surfer in the ocean that morning. Santa Cruz is packed with blond teenagers, Aidans and Coopers and Tylers who have been surfing nearly every day for a decade by the time they're old enough to drive. But my brother-in-law inched deeper—closer to the cliff, further inside, at greater risk of being caught in the impact zone—until he reached a spot even the teens wouldn't dare approach.

When the set came, he paddled furiously. For a second, extending from the water's surface, he looked like he was heading straight for the cliff. But a tiny slice of the face surged past the rock, and he skirted onto it. Then the wave opened and he claimed his prize, roaring past the humbled Aidans and Tylers, spray billowing off his rails with each turn.

After a surf session this good, there's no way things won't get better for us, I thought, and for a few hours we resembled two friends having fun together. We took a pleasant drive to the Santa Cruz boardwalk before returning to our condo. Later, when I came downstairs after a nap, *Seinfeld* was on. But our era of good feeling didn't last. By evening, my sniffles had returned with a vengeance, and when I suggested we go out to eat, Matt insisted on defrosting chicken tenders instead.

"Since we did Steamer Lane today, maybe we should go back to Pleasure Point tomorrow?" I ventured, changing the subject back to surfing.

"I dunno. Steamer's Lane was pretty good. Gonna be a ton of people at Pleasure Point."

"Well, if there's a ton of people there, it's probably for a reason."

"But maybe not."

"But probably."

"But maybe not."

I got in our family-friendly minivan and drove a long way to eat bad Chinese food on my own.

~~~~~~~~~~

By our final night in the Airbnb, Matt was over his cold and practically bouncing with pent-up energy. I, meanwhile, had developed achy joints to go with the sneezing and congestion. My body, which had crossed the line past sore a long time ago, felt like a phone on low-power mode.

"For tomorrow, I'm thinking Waddell's is the move," Matt declared.

He was referring to Waddell Creek Beach, a break several surf-shop employees had told us about. They described the spot in a way that was odd for humans and typical for surfers: while they sounded highly enthusiastic, not a single element of their descriptions was enticing. The beach was an hour's drive north, usually choked by fog, colder than spots closer to town, unsuitable for longboards, unremarkable for shortboards, pockmarked with submerged boulders, and home to a seal population large enough to attract great whites. Thanks to low tide, the highlight of the area—a big, left-breaking reef—would be unsurfable in the early morning. By mid-morning the winds would kick up and ruin the waves. I couldn't think of a reason anyone would travel from Santa Cruz to surf there. Which is exactly why Matt wanted to.

The Honda Odyssey

"I bet it'll be less crowded," he said.

For a reason, I thought. But I no longer had the energy to argue.

The next morning, I awoke before dawn to the sound of dolphin-like laughter ricocheting from the television again. For several minutes, I lay in bed and wallowed. *If he wasn't here, there's no way I'd surf today*, I thought. Then I limped downstairs. Matt nested contentedly on the couch, finishing his eggs. The only light in the room came from the TV.

Ignoring my brother-in-law ignoring me, I staggered to the kitchen and ate like a wounded animal. A half-empty jar of peanut butter sat on the counter. A handful of tortillas sat in the fridge. I smeared the former on the latter and gobbled. Then I took a long, hard look at a slender white can I'd purchased mostly as a joke. There was a still a cup of cold brew left in a bottle. But I was feeling desperate. I leaned into the living room, cracked open the Celsius, and smiled wanly.

"Fuji apple pear," I announced. Popping three Advil into my mouth, I washed them down with a giant swig.

On the drive to Waddell Creek, I learned the difference between Celsius and coffee. When you drink coffee, you become caffeinated. When you drink Celsius, the world around you becomes caffeinated. By the time we stood on a high cliff above the beach, the ocean and sky were jittering.

"Let's follow that guy!" I insisted.

"Which guy?"

"The guy with the longboard," I said, hopping out of the car and heading along a dirt path. "He looks like a local. He'll know where to go."

191

By the time I realized there was no guy with a longboard, and I had in fact been in the grip of an energy-drink-and-fever-induced hallucination, we were already halfway down the cliff. Matt was silent as we trudged back uphill, red-brown soil filling our sandals and staining our legs. He turned toward me. I figured another passive-aggressive duel was about to begin.

"Look!" he said. He pointed toward a barely submerged fringe of rock a hundred yards below. A gray figure cruised along the reef's edge, staying just outside the impact zone. It was huge, far too chunky to be a shark. Yet it sliced through the water with extraordinary grace.

"A bull elephant seal!" I whispered to Matt. We stood in silence, just able to make out the thick, watermelon-shaped head that sat atop an even thicker body. There were no surfers in the nearby water. There was no one else on land. Just us.

A set rolled in. The seal turned toward shore and lunged forward. Then it caught the wave, stopped swimming, and surfed all the way to shore.

"Whoa," Matt said softly.

"Yeah," I said.

If he wasn't here, I thought, *there's no way I would have seen this.*

We headed a half mile up the coast, to a long beach with sand made dense and cement-like by fog. From the moment I paddled out there, it was obvious Waddell Creek was not for me. I got thrown off the first wave I went for, and when I came up, a shortboarder with close-cropped hair was in my face.

"Dude! You gotta look out," he snarled. After a week of catching waves with fluent ease, I felt like a tourist again, watching Matt snag rides and knowing I didn't really belong. After an hour, he had caught his fill and headed back toward the parking lot. I followed a few minutes later, discouraged.

"You didn't need to come in," he said, when I reached the minivan.

"You sure?" I asked.

"Yeah," he said. "I'll stay in the car and turn the heat up."

Determined to redeem myself, I paddled back out and did even worse than before. For thirty minutes I bobbed on the surface, too tired and nervous to go. Then, finally, I took off on a small inside peak, the kind of wave I'd made plenty of times in Jersey, and got pounded into the sand. As I dragged myself and my board back toward the Odyssey, I felt more defeated than I had in months.

"How'd it go?" he asked. I slid my longboard into the trunk.

"Terribly." I slumped out of my wetsuit, then tramped toward the open window to see if Matt wanted me to drive.

Before I could reach him, though, a new song came blasting over the car radio, a wall of sound that stopped me in my tracks.

"Taylor Swift!" Matt said. "I love her!"

"Yeah?" I said, shocked. "Me too."

For the first time in the eleven years I'd known him, Matt turned up the volume on music I didn't consider deeply unfortunate. It was a classic, not pop Taylor but country Taylor, and he cranked it loud enough to drown out every doubt and embarrassment in my head. The chorus kicked in. Unable to help himself, he grabbed an invisible guitar and started jamming.

Later that day, we'd go looking for great white sharks from a distance and fail to spot them. We'd hunt for souvenirs for Jacqui and for Samantha, Matt's girlfriend. We'd wind our minivan through the

Santa Cruz mountains to a charmless airport hotel, hanging foul-smelling booties to dry in our separate rooms.

But as far as I'm concerned, that parking lot by Waddell Creek was where our surf trip ended. With Matt, on air guitar, serenading me to "Love Story," as I gazed at yet another view I would have missed without him, counting waves I might one day catch.

CHAPTER THIRTEEN

Try That in a Small Town

FOR REASONS I'VE NEVER UNDERSTOOD, when my wife means to say "minor miracle," she says "mild miracle" instead. I kind of love it.

Mild miracles were everywhere that June. There was the Trump indictment in Florida. There was the week the Wagner Group, Vladimir Putin's army of mercenary thugs, turned against him in a short-lived but satisfying revolt. Most mildly miraculous of all, when I returned from California to New Jersey, it was 3/2 season again. I held up the beast I'd battled in the parking lot before my first surf lesson, the shame-garment that had tried to kill me. Then I slipped it on so effortlessly it might as well have been a pair of silk pajamas.

"Matt and I are headed to Deal," I said to Jacqui, traipsing through the living room in skintight neoprene without a trace of self-consciousness. She was on the couch, drafting a memo on her laptop, but took a moment to look up as I passed.

"So, are you and my brother . . . friends now?" she asked, not so much against the idea as flabbergasted by it.

"Well," I replied carefully. "We're not *not*."

I found talking about friendship with another man embarrass-ing, like admitting a crush in eighth grade. Yet the change Jacqui noticed was undeniable: while Matt and I had never formally agreed to spend more time together, it was as though we'd signed a treaty in Santa Cruz. The waves were sometimes flat—it was summer, after all—but if he was free, and I was free, and conditions were halfway decent, we'd surf together. Small talk in the parking lot; surf session; fist bump; drive home. The most remarkable thing about it was how unremarkable it was.

At the end of June, two tropical storms, Bret and Cindy, began tracking north toward Jersey. Early one evening, Matt called me after work.

"Could be decent. Let's try Spring Lake."

For the first time I could remember, I arrived at the boardwalk minutes ahead of him, so before throwing on my wetsuit I checked the waves. They were pretty big. They weren't good. Bret and Cindy were still hundreds of miles to the south, and the ocean frothed in anticipation of their arrival. Water sloshed in strange directions. Chest-high peaks were difficult to tell apart.

"I might check Belmar and see if it's better," I said to Matt on the phone. "What do you think?"

"Sure. Give it a shot."

Curious, I noted, a field researcher of myself. *You feel the need to ask for his permission before scouting somewhere else.* I hadn't doubted my assessment of the conditions. I'd been surfing for a year; I knew garbage waves when I saw them. But while Matt and I had never discussed the details of our tacit agreement—that's what made it tacit—his having final say over surf spots seemed like a key provision. For all the progress I'd made, the ocean, and New Jersey's ocean in particular, remained his turf.

Matt arrived across the street from Crazy Michael's surf shop an hour before sunset. He jumped down from his truck and we ambled together to the boardwalk. While conditions in Belmar weren't perfect—a current pulled north, and peaks burst from the seafloor like geysers—I was confident it was a big improvement from Spring Lake.

"Looks . . . interesting," I said, not wanting to state a strong opinion until I knew his.

"Looks good," he said, and went to get his wetsuit.

Although summer season at the Jersey Shore technically goes from Memorial Day to Labor Day, the big crowds don't really descend until July 4th, and weekdays in late June are often empty. We paddled out alone. A year earlier, that would have freaked me out. *What about Freya? What about Barry? Shouldn't we spread the risk around?* Now, though, calculating the odds of a shark attack seemed silly. Why worry about something that would probably never happen?

A right came out of nowhere, and Matt leapt to his feet. For a few seconds I couldn't see him, and when I finally did, he was far down the beach. He paddled back in what seemed like seconds and was soon on a screaming left. Then, as though attached to a giant windshield wiper, he did the whole thing again in reverse. I didn't do so badly myself. Pulling against the current, aiming for the breaking pocket the way Matt had taught me to in Santa Cruz, I caught several shifty peaks.

It was one of the longest days of the year, and I had just started to think about how much I was looking forward to dinner when the first raindrop rippled against the ocean. I was facing seaward, toward a cloudless horizon, but the moment I looked back at land my breath caught in my chest. The sky over Spring Lake had gone dark. A single, massive cloud, as water-dense and rageful as the Atlantic on which I floated, rolled toward us. A flash split the air. As I'd learned to do at summer camp, I began counting Mississippis. At six Mississippi, the thunder bellowed.

How many Mississippis are there to a mile? One? Three? Five? It was one of those facts I would have sworn I knew until the moment it became relevant.

I looked frantically for Matt. It was unlikely he hadn't seen the lightning. It was impossible he hadn't heard the thunder. But when I spotted him twenty yards away, he was paddling through the impact zone, his expression completely unconcerned. He hopped on one pitchy wave, then another. When a third wave sent him flying in my direction, I tracked him down.

"Hey! Don't you think we should go in?" I had to yell to be heard above the driving rain.

"Nah," he yelled back. "I don't think it'll hit us." He offered no evidence to support his opinion, and he didn't wait to hear mine. As a second bolt arced through the sky, he zipped outside and caught a lurching right.

I was suddenly angrier at my brother-in-law than I'd been in a very long time. I didn't expect to be treated as an equal. I could put up with him deciding where we surfed, or when we surfed, or how long we stayed out. But we were clearly in danger. While he might not mind being one of the two tallest objects in a lightning storm, I did. Surely, in a friendship, that ought to count for something.

That's it, I thought. *He doesn't care what you think, so you don't need to care what he thinks. It's time to go in.*

I repeated this argument several times, and each time I found myself quite convincing. But my body refused to agree with my brain. The thunder was only three Mississippis away now, yet I floated in place. I didn't want to be struck by lightning. I didn't want Matt to think I was a wuss. *Curious*, I noted. *Judging by your actions, you consider the second prospect more frightening than the first.*

Matt, meanwhile, was charged by the storm. He snatched rides more quickly than ever, racing back through the impact zone after each one. Ten minutes passed. Fifteen. The whole time, he acted like I wasn't there.

It was only once the sun sank below the horizon that he caught a final wave. I paddled in behind him as fast as I could, scrambling to the sand in near darkness. My mouth was dry as we walked back to the parking lot, and I struggled to peel off my wetsuit with trembling fingers.

"That was pretty good," Matt announced, somehow already behind the wheel of his truck. "See you next time."

I'd long ago realized that regardless of the arena—politics, culture, or anything else—outsiders study insiders with anthropological intensity, then are surprised to discover that the insiders don't think about them at all. Maybe that's what had just happened. Or maybe Matt had been sending a message: *This is what you get for having the audacity to suggest we paddle in early. This is how much fun I'd have if you weren't here.*

I wasn't sure. And I would sooner have paddled out naked than asked him about his feelings, or told him about mine. Instead, as

I peeled off the neoprene and pulled on my clothes, I was left to wonder.

What, exactly, does surfing "together" entail?

~~~~~~

The following Saturday was a rarity. While the waves were big enough that Matt would have eagerly surfed them, he was too busy with work. After our lightning-storm session, I was frankly relieved he couldn't make it. Instead of driving to Deal at first light, which Matt would have made me do if we were paddling out together, I slept in and arrived at the dog beach at nine.

It was the first weekend in July, and the weather was perfect, with brilliant sun and seventy-degree water. The stomach-high waves were as clean as I'd ever seen them, each as distinct and regular as a heartbeat, as gently rounded as a smile, with a glossy, porcelain sheen. There were lots of foamies in the water. I could hear Matt's voice in my head, insisting we traverse New Jersey's coastline searching for someplace empty.

No thank you, I thought. *This place is crowded for a reason.*

The feeling of warm sand against the soles of my feet brought me back to one year earlier. The summertime dog beach held a special place in my heart, and not entirely in a good way. This was the site of my earliest embarrassments on a surfboard, my kookiest moments, my most glaring ineptitudes. It was like middle school. The birthplace of humiliation.

Now I had returned. And I was ready to triumph.

As if on cue, my thoughts were interrupted by a banana-yellow foamboard and a familiar voice. His hair was longer, and the snug fit of his wetsuit suggested he hadn't done much winter surfing. But there was no mistaking my fellow VAL from the summer before.

"See that guy?" Troy said breathlessly, pointing to a round-faced shortboarder. "He's a YouTuber!"

"Wow," I replied politely. But I'd already drawn a line between Troy and me. He remained an audience member. I was a player now. I wanted waves.

I knew how to get them, too. Most people in the water hadn't paddled out since the previous fall, and they took up familiar positions near the jetties. What they didn't know—and what I did, thanks to a long 5/4 season—was that winter storms had shifted the sandbars beneath us. New waves were breaking. I spotted my reference point, a pair of trash cans on the beach about halfway between the jetties, and drew an imaginary line running perpendicular to the shore. Then I paddled until I had become a point on the line and waited.

A year earlier, when I sensed the flower of fear opening, I would turn and paddle blindly toward the beach. It was like shutting my eyes right before a baseball hit my glove. This time I paddled steadily, deliberately, checking over my shoulder to see what the breaking wave would do. I rose to my feet, flew into the flats, angled up to the lip, then dove back into the pocket before hopping into the surf.

As I paddled back out for a repeat performance, Troy watching in amazement, I could feel, just for an instant, a familiar instinct kick in. *Don't get too full of yourself. There's a big difference between a chest-high wave at the dog beach and an overhead one at North Shore.* But my doubts were aristocrats from before the revolution. They still existed; their authority did not.

I totally fucking deserve this, I thought.

For the next twenty minutes, surrounded by strangers, I surfed my own private peak. I decided that, as the discoverer of my wave, I'd earned the right to name it. I could have called it anything. Stepping Stone. Sign of Progress. Neptune's Bounty.

I named it Trash Cans. I was a surfer now.

No secret spot stays secret for long. Troy inched toward me, and a few other VALs followed. I didn't mind. Their bulky boards were always out of position, their legs splayed for balance, their hips too far back. If I wanted to be generous, I let them flounder for the wave. If I didn't, I snatched it for myself.

It was amazing how confident I felt with Matt not around. When I surfed with him, I was the outsider who couldn't help but notice my own shortcomings. Now, as the insider, I could spend my time noticing others' shortcomings instead. When a flabby guy about my age warned me he'd spotted a fin, I rolled my eyes. *Some people see fins everywhere.* When a pitchy East Coast peak plunged the nose of Troy's board into the water, turning it into the fulcrum of a yellow foam trebuchet, I did not think, *There, but for the grace of God, go I.*

I thought, *Fucking kook.*

About an hour into the session, I was paddling back to the take-off point when I looked toward the popular kids' jetty and was met by a piercing blue stare. The Predator! He sat on his familiar turquoise longboard in his usual spot, far outside, waiting to poach the choicest peaks.

When he finally took off, though, I was stunned. The Predator was human. Where Josh's board had snapped off the lip and Matt's danced along the face, The Predator's glued itself to the pocket and churned monotonously forward. Even worse, when he wasn't riding, he stayed fixed in one spot and hoped waves would come to him. I could still only dream of surfing as well as he did. His athleticism and stylish crouch put him in an entirely separate league from people like me. Still, he was a gatherer, not a hunter. I could see that now.

As my idol worship faded, I began to pay more attention to others in the water, surfers I recognized but had never particularly admired. Tilda Swinton, for instance. She scanned the horizon as though peering into a crystal ball, putting herself in the path of incoming sets minutes before they arrived. Ditto a big bald guy on a yellow swallowtail. He crisscrossed the beach, yet always seemed to be in the exact spot where the best wave was breaking. These were my new heroes—not necessarily the youngest or strongest, but the ones who never stopped moving.

I surfed until noon, and while my arms grew sore, I never flagged. When I finally caught a ride to the beach, I found myself trembling not from exhaustion, but from a sense of possibility.

"How was it?" Matt texted that afternoon.

Why, I wondered, not for the first time, *are his simplest questions the most difficult to answer?* The morning had been transcendent, glorious, affirming, and not just because it was the best surfing day of my life. Twelve months earlier, I'd surfed to forget I was depressed. This was different. Snagging waves at will, gliding down shoulders and soaring up faces, made the whole concept of depression seem ridiculous. I couldn't believe I had once stood on train tracks and seen the appeal of not living. I knew it without having to think about it: I wasn't that person anymore.

Matt was part of that. If it hadn't been for him, I never would have come this far. Yet it didn't escape my notice that when I finally reached a moment I'd once thought of as unreachable—when I finally felt like a Jersey surfer, when I finally felt reborn—it was without him.

~~~~~~~~~

Jacqui tended her garden that summer the way I tended my levator scapulae. When she took the car to the plant store, Matt would pick me up in his truck and we would drive together, usually to Deal.

"Did you always like being an electrician?" I asked him one afternoon in the middle of July.

"At first I hated it," he said. "I got this apprenticeship while I was trying to figure out how to do something with guitar. But the music thing didn't happen, and after a few years I learned to love what I was doing."

"That sounds frighteningly grown up," I said. He chuckled.

Just then, a Range Rover with New York plates swung right onto Ocean Avenue, cutting us off. The driver was being more rude than dangerous, but even so, Matt honked his horn and scowled.

"Try that in a small town!" he grumbled.

"Uh . . . what?" I asked.

"'Try that in a small town.' It's an expression. You say it if someone's a jerk to you."

"And, you're a fan of the song it comes from?"

"I haven't listened to it."

"Do you know the story behind it, though?" When he didn't

say anything, I continued. "It's a country song. All the verses are about mob justice, and the music video was shot outside a courthouse in Tennessee where there had been a lynching, so lots of people were offended, and then the guy who sings it said he was being canceled and the song went to the top of the charts. It was a whole thing."

"Hmm," Matt said, in a way I took to mean he would stop using the expression when I was around, but would continue using it in general.

If this had been an isolated incident, I wouldn't have given it much thought. The more time we spent together, though, the more I noticed his willingness to entertain ideas I found slightly unhinged. The views he expressed—about living off the land; or whether taxation is theft; or the logic of vigilantism; or the wisdom of traveling to Peru to rejuvenate one's organs via stem cell therapies illegal in the United States—couldn't really be described as conspiracy theories. Nor, despite the prevalence of the word, were they the products of misinformation. It was more that kernels of truth had become cobs of confident opinion. *Where is he getting this from?* I often wondered.

The short answer was usually Joe Rogan's podcast. The long answer was more complex. While Matt would never have described himself as libertarian—he wasn't one to join movements, even those dedicated to standoffishness—he seemed receptive to any argument that involved taking matters into his own hands. Pandemics could be defeated with exercise and clean living. Financial security could be achieved by trading crypto. Looming societal breakdown could be rendered irrelevant by a gun.

Matt didn't act on most of these opinions. He didn't own fire-arms, for instance, although that was probably because he lived in New Jersey rather than Texas or South Dakota. For the most part, I treated his views on current events the way he treated mine about swell direction and fin placement—by saying, "Hmm, maybe," and changing the subject. What worried me as the summer drew to a close was what his worldview meant for us as surfers. I'd assumed that while our skill levels were different, we wanted the same things out of the hobby we shared. Now I realized that wasn't true. For Matt, surfing was a temple to rugged individualism. Paddling out alone wasn't just about catching more waves or braving the ocean's fury. The solitude, and the self-reliance that came with it, were in and of themselves the point.

I took the opposite view. At Loch Arbour, one break north of the dog beach, sand had piled against the long jetty all winter and created what was, by Jersey standards, an unusually gentle wave. A spot that had gone unloved the previous year—Katie paddled there to escape the crowds—was now the region's unofficial longboarding capital. It became my go-to when Matt was busy.

I liked Loch Arbour's waves. I liked its spirit of shared enter-prise even more. The core group of regulars—a half dozen women not much younger than me—traded waves happily, taking turns and cheering whenever VALs struggled to their feet. Their de facto leader, an athletic blonde named Steph, was easily among the region's best surfers. By the sport's law of the jungle, she had the right to belittle the incompetent and steal rides from the weak. But she didn't. Her in-it-together spirit—practically socialist by surfing standards—set the tone for the entire break.

Occasionally, I tried to get Matt to surf Loch Arbour with me, but it never worked. Where I saw community, he saw a crowd.

We never stopped surfing together. I still couldn't imagine paddling out at the North Shore without him; I doubted that Matt, who almost never left New Jersey, could imagine getting to the North Shore in the first place without me. But while I didn't tear up our tacit agreement, I began grumbling more frequently about its contents.

"Want to try Darlington?" he asked one morning at the end of August. "I've heard it's pretty empty, even on good days."

"Okay," I said. But I made sure to sound grouchy. I'd never even heard of Darlington, and I stewed the whole way there.

As it turned out, the spot wasn't far—just a few beaches north of Hathaway—and was indeed uncrowded, with only three other people out. But I knew immediately there was no risk I might have fun. The wave broke far outside, past a jetty fringed in wooden pylons reminiscent of the Rockaways' death sticks, and the lip pitched almost perpendicular to the face. The pocket zipped right so quickly it might as well have been emailed. I groaned inwardly and paddled out.

Some surf breaks turn out to be better than they appear from the beach. Darlington was much worse. The waves slamming against the pylons, theoretically rideable, offered no margin for error. The waves everywhere else, theoretically safe, were unrideable. Even Matt spent a great deal of time bobbing fruitlessly, paddling south before the current pulled him north again. *He should feel bad about his decision to drag us here*, I thought. But I'd surfed with him long enough to know he didn't. Thousands of riders had descended on the Shore; almost none of them were nearby. That, for Matt, was its own reward.

I was staring at him, willing him to let us paddle in and try somewhere else, when I heard a voice behind me.

"Hey!" I turned around to see a scrawny guy on a shortboard. He looked even younger than Young Vito, with a patchy brown neckbeard, a haircut he appeared to have given himself, and the hollow, aggressive eyes found almost exclusively in men who resent their fathers.

"Hey," he repeated. "Is this your first time surfing?"

For a moment I thought he was sincerely asking. Then I realized he had just thrashed me with what was, for a hardcore surfer, the world's most devastating insult.

He started up again before I could respond. "You're too close. Don't paddle near me."

"Okay," I said, rattled. "That's fine."

A minute later I joined Matt. When I told him what had happened, he shook his head and said, "Ridiculous."

In the try-that-in-a-small-town world of surf spots, where one's worth is determined by skill on a board, it's rare that a very good surfer takes the side of a very mediocre one. I was grateful to Matt for sticking by me. Still, back in the parking lot an hour later, I couldn't shake an uncomfortable thought. *Does the neckbeard guy have more in common with Matt than Matt has with me?* There were differences, obviously. That dude was an asshole; Matt was not. But weren't their philosophies disturbingly similar? The iconoclastic urge to paddle out at a break most people found unpleasant. The wariness of an interloper overstepping his bounds. The desire to go it alone.

Maybe it's time for acceptance, I thought. *Matt is who he is. You are who you are. Nothing is going to change that.*

I told Matt I was done for the day. I was lying. Instead of going home, I went straight to Loch Arbour, threw my wetsuit back on, and had a wonderful time.

CHAPTER FOURTEEN

Sparring with Hurricanes

I NEVER MEANT TO BUY a board made by a company with the same name as my therapist. It was pure coincidence. Then again, if that was true, why was I so careful not to mention surfboard Stewart to human Stewart on our Zooms?

To my conscious mind, what mattered was not my new board's name but its dimensions. It was seven feet—the shortest I'd ever ridden—with thinner rails built to knife into the wave face and a narrow, upturned beak for surviving sudden drops. Designed for full commitment, the outline was equal parts aspirational and reflective. My board was a self-portrait of a person I had not quite yet become.

Less symbolically speaking, surfboard Stewart was built for hurricanes. A year earlier, when I watched The Predator wade waist-deep into the water and splash, I thought he was kind of crazy. I still thought that. But now I was kind of crazy, too.

Imagine being a werewolf, only you don't know when the full moon will arrive or how long it will last. That's the inner life of a New Jersey surfer as summer turns to fall. While meteorologists will tell you the Atlantic hurricane season runs from June through November, surfers know the truth: it runs from whenever the first big storm arrives until the last one clears. In between these unpredictable bookends, the East Coast is (if you ignore the constant threat of devastation) a paradise of consistent swell, clean waves, and comfortable water temperatures. Hurricanes are to Jersey surfers what the midnight-sun summer is to Icelanders, a period of unmatched abundance combined with the ever-present knowledge of future scarcity. People go nuts.

I had an additional reason to take this particular hurricane season seriously. In every important respect—fitness, skill, courage, ability to say "gnarly" without feeling foolish—I felt almost ready for overhead Sunset. But on the North Shore, almost ready can quickly become almost alive. Although autumn waves in Jersey would have nowhere near the power of a big Hawaiian swell, they could at least serve as an approximation. I thought of them the way a boxer thinks of sparring partners before a fight.

～～～～～～～

The season began with a climate change miracle. After tearing through the Dominican Republic in late August, Franklin limped from the Caribbean to the Atlantic as a mere "minimal tropical storm." But gobbling moisture from the unseasonably warm ocean like Popeye chugging spinach from a can, it rebuilt into a hurricane. Within three hours, it had leapt from Category One to Category Four. By the first Wednesday in September, Franklin was parked outside New Jersey and sending waves our way.

I would have been much happier taking on the Franklin swell alone than going with Matt to Deal. I suspected he felt the same. I wanted to surf Loch Arbour; he didn't want to babysit. For a long time, I thought about the best way for us to clear the air, have an honest conversation, and suggest that the two of us take a much-needed break from each other. Then we went to Deal.

It was ninety minutes before sunset when we parked near Hathaway Avenue, and Matt waxed his board with typical impatience. As we scurried down the bluff to the beach, though, I could tell something was off. He wasn't trotting ahead of me. That was unlike him when the waves were big. Each time his foot touched the ground, he winced.

"You okay?" I asked.

"My back," Matt said. "I pulled it pretty bad yesterday."

He stretched for longer than usual. As he struggled to touch his ankles, I noticed the beginning of a widow's peak in his hairline. His beard had a dab of gray, too, like a spot of mold on an otherwise fresh block of cheese. I was just a few weeks from my thirty-seventh birthday. But it had never really occurred to me: Matt was getting older, too.

A teenager on a potato-chip shortboard raced into the surf, took a flying leap, and ducked under an approaching wave. Matt took halting steps toward the water, lowering himself onto his Pyzel without his usual sprightliness before paddling outside.

I remained onshore, scanning the water and choosing between the lesser of three evils. To my left was a sideways current more powerful than any I'd previously encountered. Water rushed through the rocks of the north jetty like paper through a shredder. In the center, the evil was a rip, which turned the surrounding water into a gauntlet of collapsing, lopsided peaks.

The evil to my right was the wave itself. It arrived on its own private schedule, just once every fifteen minutes, and seemed designed in a lab to imperil surfers. While its size was terrifying—easily eight feet, maybe ten—what really scared me was how it broke. First, the lip shot out a fist of foam just powerful enough to knock a rider off balance. A moment later, this initial jab was followed by a powerful hook that sent an avalanche of whitewater, along with anyone caught up in it, surging into the boulders of the south jetty. No one was even trying to ride that wave—it was clearly unrideable—so I would have to choose between remaining in the center or heading north. Although neither option seemed promising, the rip was empty, while a pack of a dozen surfers battled the north-jetty current. Trusting the wisdom of crowds, I paddled in their direction.

The surf was even gnarlier than I'd expected. I could dive my Stewart's beak beneath the pummeling fists of the impact zone, but once I got out the back, maintaining my position became a full-time job. It took me ten minutes to feel confident I wouldn't be swept into the jetty, ten minutes to start hunting for waves, and another ten to decide that these two objectives were mutually exclusive and it was best to focus on the first. Only as the sun was setting did I finally start looking for Matt.

I had a good idea of where I'd find him. He wouldn't chase the giant peak by the south jetty—even he would know that was suicide. Like me, he'd be forced to choose between a crowd to the left and chaos in the center. I knew which one he'd pick. I spotted him halfway between the jetties, searching for a decent wave inside the rip.

It wasn't going well. Everything was against him. He had to paddle nonstop just to avoid being caught in the current, and the peaks he hunted appeared with little warning. Then there was his form. A surfer's gait—the tempo at which their arms wheel through the water, the angle of their hands, the acceleration between the beginning and end of their stroke—is as identifying as a fingerprint. I knew what Matt looked like in the water. Today, he didn't look like himself. He slogged through the ocean with less power than usual, each movement restricted in concession to his sore back.

For forty-five minutes, I watched him struggle in vain. Finally, he gave up and headed toward me. *It's really happening*, I thought as he paddled closer. *He's about to join the rest of us.* He drew twenty yards away, then ten. I could see the defeat in his eyes. Then, suddenly, he wheeled on his Pyzel Phantom and paddled in the direction from which he'd come.

I wasn't sure what he was doing. Then he crossed the invisible line running through the beach's center, and I knew. He had his eyes on the south jetty, with its unrideable wave. He was going to try to ride it.

Because his paddle strokes were labored and the current strong, he approached his target in slow motion. That gave everyone around me time to realize what was taking place. One by one, a dozen of my fellow surfers looked up from their private struggles, transfixed.

For someone who loathed crowds, Matt had a showman's timing. Right as he set himself up outside the rocks—a place where, if he fell, there would be no escaping disaster—the far-off peak began gathering strength. On my side of the break, twenty-four eyes widened. The wave roared toward him, building in height and vehemence, enraged by the presence of a challenger. Spray feathered off the crest like sparks from a knife being sharpened. I'd seen Matt take off hundreds of times, yet even I wondered, *Is he really going to go?*

He went, and I could tell at once that his position was off. Right before he could leap to his feet, the lip punched his board, knocking him flat. I knew what it felt like to lose one's agency to the ocean, to have free will ripped away by a breaking wave. But I'd never seen it happen to Matt. Now it was happening at the worst possible time. Transformed into a helpless object, a piece of detritus, he clung to his board as the lip hurled him toward the rocks.

He was halfway over the falls when something seemed to bolt upright inside him. Chest springing off the deck, head snapping toward the bottom of the face, he paddled more ferociously than I'd ever seen him paddle, clawing at the water like a man buried alive. He caught up with the breaking lip, which should have been impossible. Then he passed it. Grabbing his outside edge, he sprang into a crouch. For a moment, his board left the water's surface. He hovered in midair. Then he jammed his inside rail into the face and took off, roaring clear from the detonating peak. With the jetty safely behind him, he leaned into the wall of water, shot skyward to the lip, cut back, raced into the pocket to regain speed, and shot skyward again.

His ride took him all the way across the beach, and as he rocketed past, a dozen heads turned as though leashed to his tail. I stopped watching Matt surf, and started watching the surfers watching him. One let out a low whistle. Another's jaw literally dropped.

Matt hopped off his board by the north jetty. Ignoring the current and his injured back, he turned around and paddled as though nothing had happened. Anyone seeing him for the first time would think he didn't care about having a witness, let alone an audience. For a moment I thought so, too. Then I saw him subtly angle his board in my direction.

"Nice!" I said, as he drew within earshot.

"Yeah, that was pretty sweet." He paddled off in search of more waves.

This time, though, only eleven heads turned to follow him. The man whose jaw dropped had shifted his gaze to me. He didn't say anything. He didn't have to. His look said it all.

You know that guy?

Hurricane season was just a few hours old, and it was already getting the best of me. But as I paddled to stay in place, arms aching, back numb, with no waves to show for my effort, the corners of my mouth curled in satisfaction.

Yeah, I thought, surprised by just how proud I felt. *I know that guy.*

~~~~~~~~~~

Hurricane Franklin flipped a switch marked DIVINE WRATH. In July, Matt and I had usually surfed together twice a week. By the first full week in September, we were often surfing together twice a day. Not every hurricane swell was the same. Some were heavier than others. Most were bracketed by forerunners and leftovers slightly smaller than the main event. But only slightly. The waves were always big, and always good, and always there.

It was this relentlessness, even more than the swells' size or power, that stood out. It reminded me of those high-intensity interval fitness classes in which bursts of all-out effort are punctuated by recovery periods that are almost but never quite long enough. And with no way of knowing how many stormy sparring partners the season would bring, I didn't dare take a day off.

If I wasn't surfing, I was eating. At the start of hurricane season, I'd made a promise to myself: to maximize performance, I would pay more attention than ever to nutrition. But my pledge arrived pre-broken—I'm fairly sure I was holding an ice cream cone as I made it—and anything with calories, from buffalo chicken pizza to shrimp quesadillas to Junior Mints, was quickly rebranded as "fuel."

One afternoon during Franklin's leftovers, I walked to El Sabor Oaxaqueño, a Mexican restaurant near our house. I ordered a plate of beef ribs smothered in salsa roja, and had just unrolled the foil sleeve protecting a stack of warm tortillas—my vegetable—when I reached for my phone and opened Spotify. I don't know what made me do it. Maybe it was seeing Matt claw himself onto so many perfect waves. Maybe my principles had been worn thin by exercise. Maybe I just needed something to pass the time while I worked through an enormous lunch. Whatever the case, I did a quick search, thought, *Am I really doing this?* and threw myself over the ledge.

"Okay, I admit it. He's a great interviewer," I told Matt two days later. We were at Deal again, bobbing in Hurricane Idalia's forerunners, and I wasn't lying. There was something about Joe Rogan's tone—a contradictory blend of childlike curiosity and don't-bullshit-a-bullshitter frankness—that made me want to keep listening. By the time the episode was over, I hadn't just learned more about his guest, surf legend Kelly Slater. I felt like I knew him.

"I'm glad you liked it," said Matt excitedly.

"I'm glad I gave it a shot," I conceded.

I was ready for a new topic, but he had other plans. "If you thought that one was good, there's lots of other episodes you should try," he said, a bit too evangelically for my liking. A bulging right appeared and I, happy for a break in the conversation, paddled after it.

I'd been struggling to figure out the waves all morning. They were steeper than anything I'd encountered, in or outside of New Jersey, and I kept rushing my takeoffs. This one was no exception. I popped up early, before I had enough momentum, and stuck to the lip. I remained calm enough during the hold-down to regard my own submerged form with disinterest. *Looks like you won't be doing any breathing for a while.* That was a form of progress. But I still returned to the lineup frustrated.

"I keep getting hung up," I complained to Matt.

"Yeah," he said. "Anyway, he just did this great episode about the Maui wildfires, and about how the government screwed up. I think you'd like it."

Change the subject! I thought. But he was excited, and I didn't want to hurt his feelings.

"Who was his guest?"

"He actually had two of them. B. J. Penn—he's an MMA fighter who ran for governor of Hawaii, he's been hit in the head a lot—and this woman who used to be in Congress named Tulsi Gabbard—"

"Oh, she's the worst!"

Even before the words tumbled out of my mouth, I regretted them. But the comment was too direct to take back, so I tried to do the next best thing and surround it in a pillow fort of verbiage.

"It's just, she ran for president as a Democrat, and then she lost the primary and became this right-winger, and now she's a huge conservative media personality, so it just feels like she'll say anything to get attention."

I waited nervously for Matt to reply, but he said nothing. Instead he looked miffed, like I'd insulted a friend of a friend, and paddled grumpily toward the north jetty. As soon as his back was turned, another giant right appeared. *Slow down*, I reminded myself as I paddled for it. The peak scooped me up, and instead of taking off immediately I looked down the line, sinking my inside rail before I stood. I didn't ride the wave perfectly. Unprepared for its steepness, I slipped down the face. But my Stewart made the drop. I stayed on my feet, zooming clear as the thundering lip exploded behind me.

I leapt off my board as I neared the beach, pumping my fists underwater. *Holy shit!* I'd never ridden a wave so violent, so powerful, so obviously born of a storm. I still wasn't ready for the North Shore. But I was slightly more almost ready, and that felt like a very big deal.

Then, like a sad trombone at the end of a flourish, a thought.

I wish he'd seen it, though.

~~~~~~~~

Hurricane Lee followed close behind Idalia, and Matt and I continued paddling out every day. Sometimes he invited Vito along and I pretended not to mind.

Matt's ponytailed protégé had improved a lot. Because he launched himself at everything, his ratio of rides to wipeouts remained low. But more than once I saw Young Vito reel in a fragment of hurricane stroke by stroke, yank himself over the ledge, and make it onto the face in a wild, improbable leap, like a man vaulting through the open window of a moving car.

I admired that. And as I started to pay Vito more attention, I realized his tenacity was not his only impressive trait. There's a surfing term for the quality he possessed, a rare metaphor in a lexicon not known for poetry. "Stoke." Synonyms get you almost all the way there—excitement, enthusiasm, passion for wave riding, zest for life—but not quite. Vito had an inner fire that roared on good days and bad. No bruising wipeout or fruitless session could extinguish it. His answer to the question *Is this worth it?* wasn't contingent on success.

On a few occasions, I tried paddling with Vito-like abandon, hoping that caring less about my results would improve them. It didn't really. I caught lots of good waves on my Stewart. I missed lots of good ones, too. But I found that caring less could be its own reward. One afternoon, walking from our house to the Oaxacan restaurant, a thought stopped me in my tracks.

When you do things joyfully, you enjoy them more!

Then I wondered, *Is this the most blindingly obvious epiphany in the history of epiphanies?*

It wasn't, though, at least not to me. And not, I expect, to plenty of others as well. At some point in my adult life, at least among many adults I spend time with, it became fashionable to obsess about how terrible everything is. The instinct behind this trend—to broaden one's circle of concern—was noble. As Martin Luther King famously put it, "We are caught in an inescapable network of mutuality, tied in a single garment of destiny." But when did our mutual garment become so funereal?

Obviously, the state of the world hadn't helped matters. On the rare occasions when I wasn't surfing or eating, I was still working on my climate change project, and the latest reports about our planet weren't just worrisome. They were mind-bogglingly terrifying, like watching a tractor-trailer begin to skid out of control. There were moments when surfing a hurricane swell felt like dancing to the fiddle as Rome burned.

I mentioned none of this to Vito. Just once, I brought it up with Matt. "The season's been awesome so far," I said. "But what if we start getting nonstop Category Fives slamming into the coast three months straight every year?"

He considered this for a moment.

"Let's hope that happens!"

I was never able to see it like that. I didn't really want to. But I did, in a strange way, embrace a new double life. The more fun I had surfing climate change–fueled waves, the more passionate I felt about protecting our planet. It made me appreciate how much is left to save. Not long ago, I'd often felt that the happy warriors I knew were in denial. How wrong I'd been. To love life in a world full of tragedy doesn't make you complicit. It makes you complete.

Once I allowed myself to admit they existed, I began to cherish the moments of unbridled perfection the ocean brought me, diamonds sparkling so brightly they changed the way I thought about the rough. One morning during the tail end of the Lee swell, Matt and I were out at Deal when I heard screaming.

"Whoa!"

"Did you see that?"

"Fuck!"

I turned to find a pod of bros gawking at a dolphin. It disappeared deep below the surface. Suspense mounted. Suddenly, it launched vertically from the water, high into the air. For a moment the dolphin hung there, ocean-slick and slate-gray. Then it flipped, dove headfirst, and leapt again. It was the kind of natural wonder I never imagined I'd see in person—and certainly not in New Jersey.

A few days later, Matt and I made plans to go to Deal, and he brought Vito along, and I didn't mind. The two of them searched for lefts near the north jetty, while I tried a spot not too far from the south one. I'd been floating for no more than a minute when I looked to my right and realized I was sitting three feet from The Predator.

I'd never seen him at Deal before. He wiggled his chin slightly in a nod of recognition. *He remembers me!* I thought. While I'd readjusted his place in my mental pecking order, he remained a lord of the dog beach, a celebrity of my surfing life. It felt gratifying to be considered a peer.

Several minutes ticked by. The swell was due east, and the waves were walling up, rendering most peaks unrideable. I started to get antsy. I could tell The Predator was antsy, too.

Then we both saw it. A chest-high right, steep but manageable, with the wall tapering off just to our left. We were both in the perfect spot to catch it, and the perfect spot to ride it if we did. I was slightly closer to the breaking section, which gave me priority, but just to be sure of my surroundings I glanced The Predator's way. He clocked the peak, then me. He could see I was going. He paddled anyway, cutting me off.

This, among surfers, is an act of blatant disrespect. It says, *I've seen you in the water. And I have so little regard for your skill, or for you generally, that I'm going on this wave whether or not you do. Because I am one hundred percent confident that if you try to catch it, you'll fail.*

A year ago, I would have shrugged. He was the king. Let him have what he desired. But times had changed. I pulled through the water as hard as I could.

I caught the wave. For a second, as The Predator was paddling and I was gliding forward, we looked directly at each other. My glare said, *Step off.* His said, *Make me.* At the last moment, he leaned back, stalling the tail of his board and letting me through. I popped up and put my weight over my front foot—it was like pressing the gas pedal—and my Stewart shot down the line.

I imagined, and hoped, that this would usher in a short period of friendly competition followed by lifelong mutual respect. But when I paddled back to the lineup and offered The Predator my own chin-nod of recognition, I got nothing in return. For the rest of the session, he dropped in without even pretending to care about priority, forcing me to bail on rides that should, under surf law, have been mine. I was annoyed. At the same time, when it came to human reference points, I could think of no clearer sign of improvement. The Predator—The Predator!—saw me as a threat.

An hour later, back on the beach, I told Matt and Vito what had happened.

"Who's The Predator?" Vito asked. I described him.

"Oh, that guy! It's ridiculous. He does that all the time."

"And he's not even that good a surfer," Matt added.

"Or, I'm a *great* surfer," I suggested.

Matt waited an appropriate amount of time before laughing. Vito and I joined in. We stood on the beach for a while, stoked to be there, a happy little crew.

~~~~~~~~~~

"You know," I admitted to Matt a few days later, "I wasn't sure what I thought about Vito at first."

"Yeah?"

"I don't know if you remember, but he said that thing about 'The Vid.' It wasn't a conspiracy theory, exactly, but—"

"He was kidding."

"Hang on, what?"

"Yeah, Vito got the Covid shot really early. He actually left his old company because they didn't take health stuff seriously enough. He just jokes around like that. To fit in."

"Oh," I said.

Matt watched as I exhaled slowly, a deflating balloon of self-righteousness.

~~~~~~~~~~

As the season reached the apex of its madness in mid-September, Matt and I paddled out together so often that I began to lose track of which hurricane we were surfing. My inner monologue resembled that of an adventurous bisexual who's bad at saving numbers in his phone. *Is this Margot or Nigel? Nigel or Ophelia? Ophelia or Phillipe?*

With so many hours spent floating in close proximity, it was impossible to limit our conversation topics to surfing. We still didn't talk about the Covid vaccine—that remained our third rail—but we covered just about everything else: which of his middle school teachers was his least favorite; whether he preferred working for himself or contracting with another company; whether his girlfriend's pressure campaign to get him to buy her a puppy for Christmas would succeed. Neither of us intended to "open up." Both of us would have shuddered at the phrase. But it was a natural consequence of being in the same space for so long.

"Other than you," I announced to Jacqui, "your brother is the person I've spent the most time with over the last twelve months. And it's not even close."

"Hmm," she said. "That's terrifying."

It was, a little bit. But it was also kind of nice. They say familiarity breeds contempt, and in some cases that might be so. For me and Matt, though, familiarity bred familiarity. One Saturday morning—I think it was as Nigel sent forerunners toward shore—I had a surprise for him.

"So," I announced, "I listened to that Joe Rogan episode you mentioned, the one about the Maui wildfires."

"Whoa! What did you think?"

A dozen sessions earlier, I would have answered Matt's question strategically, by changing the subject or mumbling something noncommittal. But I was confident we'd turned a corner. So long as I was careful to remain diplomatic, I could be honest with him.

"He's still a great interviewer," I said. "And I know you and I might feel differently about this . . ."

And then I heard myself say, ". . . but that was some of the dumbest shit I've heard in my entire life."

Okay, I thought, *that wasn't as diplomatic as I hoped*. But it was too late to stop now. "Like, at one point the MMA guy said everyone would be happier if Hawaii's Big Island was full of casinos and Formula One tracks, and the government knows this but won't let it happen because they want to keep the economy depressed so they get a better deal on renting Pearl Harbor. Not to be rude, but that's totally nuts."

For a moment, my brother-in-law said nothing. If there had been a set coming, of any size, I would have sprinted for it just to break the tension. As it was, all I could do was wait.

"I told you," he finally said, "that guy's been hit in the head a lot."

Matt's answer, I noticed, was a diplomatic one. And while he changed the subject after that, this time he didn't paddle away.

About a week later, there was, at long last, a brief lull between storms. Surfing anything under waist-high now felt like vacation, and I was grateful for the respite. Matt and I planned to take our final tune-up trip, our last big test before the North Shore, at the end of September. My back and shoulders needed the time off.

I thought the waves might be too puny for Matt to want to surf at all. But that evening, he texted me as soon as he got off work.

"Want to drive down my way, to Mantoloking?" he asked.

It was the first time Matt had asked me to join him at a break in his part of Jersey, and I could instantly see why he liked it. Tucked into a long, thin barrier island ninety minutes from both Manhattan and Philadelphia, Mantoloking is as close as the Garden State gets to isolation. Too small to be considered a town, the borough's population is, as of the last census, a mere 331. Surfing there was Matt's version of getting off the grid.

Unlike most other Jersey breaks, Mantoloking has no jetties, just miles of beige sand and green-brown waves. This particular evening, the swell was so insubstantial we could paddle out anywhere. Even Matt had brought a longboard, and the inconsistent sets left long chunks of time during which we had nothing to do but talk.

He was telling me about his cat, Coco, and her habit of hiding in the rafters for hours on end, when I heard a buzzing sound above us. I looked up to see a hovering quadcopter drone, its red camera light blinking.

"Now's your chance to do something cool!" I yelled.

And Matt, at the exact same time, yelled, "The government!"

I thought about that moment a lot afterward. He was kidding. But he was also expressing something about himself he took seriously. And he knew that I knew he was kidding. And he also knew that I knew he was expressing something about himself.

To put it much more simply: it was the kind of joke that only works when two people know each other.

For the rest of the evening, we caught puny peaks and meandered down the line. Once or twice, Matt yelled, "Party wave!" and hopped on alongside me. We surfed long after the sun went down, only riding in when it became difficult to see our own boards. Matt threw his longboard in the pickup. I stashed mine in my SUV. For a moment, we stood there, the only two in the middle of nowhere, surrounded by the dark.

"Hey," Matt said, "I'm glad you could make it out tonight."

It was, I realized, the first time he'd ever suggested he was happy to have surfed with me.

"I'm glad you invited me," I replied.

I felt more almost ready for the North Shore than ever.

CHAPTER FIFTEEN

Le Snake

I WAS IN THE BACKYARD scraping old wax off my board when I learned that our senior senator had been indicted. New Jersey is no stranger to corruption. Given the state's history, some might argue corruption has New Jersey's spare key. But these particular allegations—that Robert Menendez, chair of the Foreign Relations Committee, had met with foreign agents and taken gold bars as a bribe—were almost cartoonish, the kind of thing a crooked councilman in Gotham City would do.

"Holy crap," I mumbled.

"*Grrrrrrrf*," replied Emily, who had grabbed the still-damp cuff of my leash and begun a game of tug-of-war.

"Drop it," I admonished. Then I made a series of *tchk-tchk-tchk-tchk* noises, the way you do when you want to feel self-righteous about your dog ignoring you.

The day after the news broke, Congressman Andy Kim, a Democrat from a district bordering ours in Asbury Park, announced he would leave his seat and run against Menendez for the Senate. This was exciting for several reasons, not least of which was that Jacqui and I knew Andy. He was just a few years older than me. We'd worked together in the White House, and I'd campaigned for him when he flipped a seat from red to blue in 2018. We'd occasionally meet up in DC for dinner or drinks. I hoped he'd win.

Less exciting was a comparison that, in the wake of Andy's announcement, I couldn't help but consider. For the past fifteen months, I'd defined courage as a willingness to ride heavy waves. But running a long-shot campaign against a corrupt sitting senator, with a powerful party machine lined up against you? That was courage of a different category. Andy's bravery improved the lives of others in a way that mine, at the moment, did not.

I was struck, too, by a related thought: *There's an open congressional seat in a district just a few minutes' drive from our house.* Like many people who have worked in politics, I'd often wondered what running for office would be like. But it had always been hypothetical. No real opportunities had come up. Now, one had. A handful of people asked if I'd be interested in running, and one of those people was me.

I made some calls. To my surprise, while a few mentors and confidants implied I was being ridiculous, none said it outright. Several were downright encouraging. What most amazed me was the speed with which questions of why became questions of how. How many hours each day would be spent raising money? How many candidates would join the race? How quickly could we rent or buy a house on the other side of the district line? Winning wouldn't be easy. But as I thought through these small-picture questions, it was impossible not to notice how plausible contending would be.

"I'm eighty percent sure I'm going to want to do this," I told Jacqui after a long day of investigation.

"Okay," she said, in the tone that's her marital shorthand for *You're describing a decision in numerical terms because you haven't thought it through yet.*

"Maybe even ninety percent," I said.

First, though, Matt and I had a surf trip to take.

~~~~~~~~~

We had planned to go to Ireland. We'd arrive at the end of September, spend seven days battling brutally cold water crashing over shallow rock, then show up in Hawaii a month later, confident and battle-tested. But the forecast didn't cooperate. According to Surfline, every break on the Emerald Isle was destined for the same fate: unseasonable cold, punishing rain, and dangerously strong onshore gales.

It wasn't fair. For the first time, I was, without reservation, looking forward to a surf trip with my brother-in-law—and now we'd be spending most of it cooped up inside and unable to surf.

Two days before our flight to Dublin, I scrolled through Google Maps, hoping to change our itinerary and knowing Matt would object. If being in an actual lightning storm hadn't deterred him, there was no way he'd let Surfline boss him around. I composed a text, deleted it, recomposed it, deleted it again. Suddenly, a green bubble appeared.

"I'm looking at the forecast. Doesn't seem good."

I was delighted. I couldn't remember a time we'd ever so clearly thought alike. I was also impressed. Matt, handed a golden opportunity to do something dangerous and unpleasant for basically no reason, had chosen not to. I took this as a sign he was growing as a person, by which I meant he was becoming more like me.

Just a few months ago in Santa Cruz, even the most minor decisions had been headaches. It's hard to imagine a decision more major than "Where on the entire planet do we want to travel forty-eight hours from now?" This time, though, I was excited. I opened the Surfline app. The world was our oyster.

"What about Morocco?" Matt suggested.

"Flights don't work. Bali?"

"Too far. El Salvador?"

"Too hot this time of year. Iceland?"

"Iceland?"

Okay, maybe not *all* the world was our oyster. But even this, in its own way, was encouraging. When our surf-destination wish lists failed to overlap, it didn't feel like proof of a great divide. For once, our differences didn't mean anything. We simply worked things out.

We settled on Spain's north coast. Tacking a last-minute flight to Bilbao onto our existing Dublin itinerary was cheap. Even better, Jacqui and I had once planned a trip to the area. Although Matt and I wouldn't be dining in fancy restaurants or hiking through Basque Country hillsides, it was surprisingly easy to repurpose a romantic vacation with my wife into a surfing strike mission with her brother.

The closer our new-and-improved trip got, the more excited I became, and not just because Surfline said the waves would be solid. Matt had never been to Europe before. He'd never crossed an ocean of any kind. When it came to hurricane swells and Celsius energy drinks, he'd broadened my horizons. This was my chance to repay the favor.

I was so eager for our trip to begin that I agreed to ride with him to the airport, even though it meant getting there preposterously early. His father was behind the wheel, Matt was navigating, and his mother and I were in the back seat. For the first half of the drive, my three in-laws mostly talked among themselves.

Then, just as we exited the Parkway onto the Turnpike, Matt swiveled his head toward me and said, "I was just looking at the forecast for Ireland. It's not bad!"

I opened Surfline. The forecast was entirely unchanged.

"Guess it's too late to switch things up," I replied warily.

"We could rent 5/4 wetsuits and hoods. Maybe we'd find good surf."

I wasn't sure what had gotten into him, so I pretended the conversation had run its course even though it clearly hadn't. The tactic seemed to work—he didn't bring up cold-weather gear for the rest of the ride—and eight hours later, we arrived in Dublin for our connecting flight. As we left the plane and exited onto the tarmac, we were hit by a blast of freezing dampness. Through the windows of the shuttle bus to the terminal, we could see rain plinking gloomily in all directions.

"Looks like we made the right call," I said, eager for him to confirm we were back on the same page.

"I dunno. I would've just packed different."

That evening we landed in Spain, and it became impossible for anyone, even my brother-in-law, not to see how wisely we'd chosen. Driving east to the surf town of Zarautz, a setting sun presided over a cloudless sky. The air was a crisp and comfortable seventy-five degrees. To our left, the Bay of Biscay shimmered in the evening light. In all other directions, a tessellation of fields and forests unspooled for miles before merging with the towering yet elegant Pyrenees.

"So," I said, as proudly as if I'd designed the landscape myself, "what do you think?"

"Meh." He shrugged. "It's nice, I guess."

I had never before asked my brother-in-law what he was thinking, and I wasn't about to start. That didn't stop me from developing a theory, though. *I* was supposed to be the one who second-guessed big decisions, the one who rerouted itineraries based on things like weather and common sense. Matt was the one who sought out gnarly, empty breaks and surfed messy winter waves until his fingers went numb. These were not merely his preferences. They were his principles. And like most of us, he dealt with violating them by pretending he hadn't.

No minivans had been available at the rental desk, so we wound through the capillaries of Zarautz's historic district in a gray SUV and parked on a narrow street. I'd booked us a two-room condo in a nineteenth-century apartment building, and after unloading our luggage, I made a big show of heading out the door.

"I'm going to try to find pintxos," I declared. "Want to come?"

"What are you finding?" Matt asked. He was preparing for tomorrow morning's session, and the apartment echoed with the *thocka thocka* of wax scraping across his board.

"Pintxos. They're a local specialty. Little plates or snacks. Like, a piece of bread topped with ham or seafood."

The *thocka*s ceased. He opened his mouth a little, as though getting a head start on disgust.

"What kind of seafood?"

"Sardines. Anchovies. Sometimes smoked salmon."

His mouth opened further, then closed abruptly, as though he was worried a sardine might fly in.

"I saw a pizza place across the street. I think I'll stick with that."

Forty-five minutes later, I found myself sitting alone in a bar crowded with happy, chatting Europeans, contemplating a second glass of wine and staring at an empty plate. Today didn't count, I decided. After all, it had been spent entirely in transit. We still had time for a promising start.

~~~~~~~~~

The next morning, I found our SUV's side-view mirror dangling from the driver's-side door like an arm yanked out of its socket.

"Oh, shit!" Matt exclaimed. He had followed a few steps behind me.

"Someone must've clipped it overnight," I said.

He sucked in air through his teeth, then looked at the wires, thinking electrical thoughts.

"I should call my insurance company . . ." I continued.

"Have you thought about replacing it?"

". . . or the guy from the car rental. His business card's in the glove compartment."

"I'll see if they sell car mirrors on Amazon."

I fished the keys from my pocket and pressed the unlock button. Nothing happened. I circled the car, trying each handle. Still nothing.

"Crap," I said.

"What now?" Matt asked. He had his phone open and was scrolling Amazon for parts.

"I must have left the lights on last night. The battery died. It won't unlock."

"That's not good," he murmured. Then he added glumly, "I don't think we can get a replacement mirror in time."

With no better ideas, I walked laps around the car, pulled handles, and swore. A small crowd gathered at a nearby intersection, and though I flashed my most disarming smile, none of the onlookers smiled back. A few began speaking softly in Basque, a language that is full of *sh* and *th* sounds colliding with *k* sounds, and is particularly ominous when muttered. After pacing for a few more minutes, I turned back to Matt. I figured he'd be on his phone, perhaps searching for nearby mechanics. Instead, he'd shifted his attention to a point halfway down the block.

"Did we have a silver car or a gray one?" he asked quietly.

"Gray, I think. Why?"

He gestured with his head. Down the street was an SUV with a matte finish and twice as many side-view mirrors. Other than that, it was identical to the car whose handles I'd spent the last several minutes vigorously yanking. I pressed the unlock button again. Two orange lights flashed. I walked over to our rental. The driver's-side door popped open.

We drove slowly past the crowd of stone-faced locals, neither of us saying a word, and continued deeper into the historic center. I began to chuckle.

"Well, that was an adventure!"

Matt didn't reply. He looked angry and embarrassed. He remained silent for half a minute, then softly cleared his throat.

"I don't think," he said quietly, "that cars are allowed in this part of the city."

I took stock of my surroundings: a truck unloading a delivery of fresh vegetables; tourists enjoying breakfast along the medieval plaza; a pedestrian staircase where one might expect a street. Also, several signs with exclamation points and the Spanish words *Centro Histórico*.

"You know what?" I replied. "I believe you're right."

Ordinarily, Matt's mood improved as we neared the ocean. But when we finally walked into a surf shop so I could rent a board, he seemed twitchy. Less than ninety seconds after we arrived, he plopped down on a brown leather couch, then immediately sprang to his feet.

"I'm gonna check the waves," he announced, already halfway out the door. A few minutes later, I was about to take my rented mid-length and join him when the shop's owner stopped me.

"You shouldn't go out now," he said. "The tide is too low. Not surfable. I'd wait a few hours and try again."

Boardless, I crossed the street. Matt was standing on the mile-long stone esplanade that overlooked the beach. He was easy to spot, and not just because he was doing stretches in a crowd of strolling Europeans. To keep the sun out of his eyes, he'd recently purchased a floppy black baseball cap secured to his head by a chin-strap. While the hat apparently served its purpose, it also looked disconcertingly like a baby's bonnet.

"The surf-shop guy says to wait," I announced. We both looked out to sea. The low-tide waves pitched sharply against exposed sand, closing out instead of peeling down the line.

"No," Matt said, "I'm going out now." His voice held an edge I hadn't heard before. "Too many waves are going unridden."

"We're gonna do two sessions today either way," I ventured. "Why not wait?"

He sniffed. "Sounds like down-the-beach syndrome."

In a literal sense, the affliction to which he referred, common among surfers, describes those who never catch waves because they're always paddling to what they insist will be a better spot. More broadly, it's a mindset, a refusal to enjoy what you have in the perpetual search for something better.

Maybe he has stay-in-place syndrome, I thought. But the tips of Matt's fingers jittered in frustration as he stretched, and for the sake of peace I gave in. Hurrying back across the road to the shop, I grabbed my rental board, tucked it beneath my arm, and jogged back to the spot where Matt had been stretching. The whole thing took three minutes, round trip.

He was gone.

For a moment I stood, confused, and scouted. Maybe he'd run to the bathroom? Maybe I'd taken a wrong turn? I waited several minutes, but he didn't appear. I was about to work my way along the esplanade when I noticed Matt's drybag wedged against the concrete. Raising a hand to shield my eyes from the morning glare, I looked toward the ocean just in time to see a surfer taking off on a pitchy wave. He was wearing a baby-bonnet cap.

I couldn't believe it. Matt often paddled out ahead of me. But he never, ever ditched me. I stomped into the sea, trying not to notice the sense of betrayal and hurt beneath my anger. Paddling out wasn't easy—just as we'd been warned, the waves were punchy and steep—but after a few minutes, I reached him.

"Hey," I said, in an irritated tone. "I was looking for you."

"Oh. I went out."

His voice was nonchalant, as though I'd asked him which movie he'd watched on the plane. But I saw through him, and he knew it. Before I could say another word, he launched himself over the cracking lip of a chest-high left.

During hurricane season, I'd relished watching Matt ride waves, and not just because I got to live vicariously. I felt that by observing his experience, I was completing it. Chefs need diners; authors need readers; Matt needed me. Not this time, though. Almost vindictively, I turned away and took stock of my surroundings.

The view was stunning. Burnt-orange sand fringed cobalt-blue water. The beach, fronted by the seawall and the cheerful shops of the promenade, ran more than a mile with no jetties to mar it. To the east, mist-shrouded mountains formed the cupped palm of a bay. To the west, a stone barricade separated the ocean from a winding cliffside road on which you expected, at any moment, Audrey Hepburn to zip by in a convertible. Instead, I saw Matt paddling back with an I-told-you-so expression.

"The waves are great!" he announced.

"Meh," I replied. "The guy in the shop said it's better a few blocks north."

I paddled down the beach, toward the green hills in the distance. There was no doubt about it. Zarautz was the most beautiful place I had ever seen from the deck of a surfboard. And I had never, while lying on the deck of a surfboard, wanted so desperately to be anywhere else.

~~~~~~~~~~

Around two in the afternoon, right when the surf-shop owner said the waves would get good, an unexpectedly giant swell arrived, surging water into the break and turning the bay into a giant toilet bowl being overzealously flushed.

"This wasn't in the forecast," I said defensively.

"Surf-lyin'," Matt replied.

We sat on the seawall looking grim, surrounded by other equally grim-looking surfers. Far outside, obscured by the spray of giant, crashing waves, a solitary figure had somehow managed to punch through the impact zone. He wasn't getting long rides, or even good ones. But he had the ocean to himself.

"Let's try it," said Matt.

I was skeptical, but he had the final say in surf spots. For fifteen minutes I battled stampeding walls of whitewater, making no progress but refusing to admit defeat while Matt was still out there. Duck-diving, he got farther than I did. But the sets were punishing and there were no lulls between them. When he finally turned around and washed toward shore, I knew I could paddle in.

We returned to the seawall. The solitary surfer was still out there, catching giant, unruly waves. Matt watched him enviously.

"One day," he said.

"My goal for next year is to ride a shortboard," I said. And then, without meaning to, I added, "Either that or run for Congress."

I'd never intended to mention my newfound ambition to him. But there was no going back. As I explained the situation, his mouth opened slightly, as though I were again describing seafood. I finished, and he took it all in.

"That's so cool!" he said. "I'd register to vote just to vote for you."

"Thanks," I said, surprised. "Why?"

"Because you're, like, a regular guy. You walk the dog."

The relief that swept over me was personal rather than political. For a moment, the morning didn't matter. It felt like we were a team again. But the sense of camaraderie faded quickly, and when it came time for dinner and I suggested we go out together, he told me he'd already made plans. "I picked up a frozen pizza," he said, adding, in a Super Mario accent, "It's-a quattro formaggi."

"Sounds adventurous," I replied, more harshly than I meant to. I ate outdoors, alone, on the edge of the plaza I'd driven through illegally in the morning. By the time I got back to our apartment, Matt had long since gone to sleep.

~~~~~~~~

Lineups in northern Spain were composed primarily of two groups: Spaniards very good at surfing, and Germans so unbelievably stupid you had to wonder how their grandparents pulled it off. On the second day of our trip, Matt found himself among the former and I the latter.

For our morning session, we'd driven up the coast to the city of San Sebastián, where we parked near a beach called La Zurriola. Set in a small half-moon of water, flanked by a stone jetty on one side and a headland on the other, the break was like a double Manasquan Inlet. Swells gushed into the bay, then ricocheted off both sides. The result was a spot with multiple personalities. On the left, sheltered by a favorable angle, was a kiddie pool with waves so puny they were barely rideable. On the right, just a dozen yards away, overhead peaks steamed toward shore.

"Whoa, that looks good!" said Matt, his eyes on the big ones.

"I don't know if I can make it out over there," I said.

"You'll make it," he said, but his tone was more *stop whining* than *you've got this*. The moment our boards touched the water he took off without looking back. I scraped toward the horizon into a patchwork quilt of impact zones, where I was pummeled from all directions until I ran out of steam. I sat on the beach, recovered, and tried again with the same result.

Ten minutes later, I was in the kiddie pool surrounded by Germans. Wobbling on their foamies, they called to mind a herd of Teutonic piglets fumbling in a pen. One had donned what appeared to be an old-timey leather football helmet. Another, as he hugged his board for dear life, wore a full canvas rucksack. As a wave no more powerful than a cocker spaniel neared him and he began to capsize, he flashed me a look that said, *What do I do now?*

Mine said, *Where do I even start?*

That evening in the apartment, Matt showed me a video he'd taken on his GoPro. He'd caught a big right near the headland, giving him a perfect view of San Sebastián as he hurtled down the open face. I couldn't imagine what it was like to see that with your own eyes, to harness so much power, so effortlessly, for so long.

"Cool," I said flatly. I wondered if he'd ask me how my day had gone, and when he didn't, I added, "There's another restaurant I want to try tonight. It does baby squid. I assume you're not interested."

"No thanks. I already know I like frozen pizza. Why would I try anything else?"

"But you only know you like frozen pizza because you've tried it."

"Exactly." He paused for a moment, then raised an eyebrow. "Are you, like, angry that I'm eating pizza?"

"No," I replied. "Don't be silly."

An hour later, I took a forkful of squid and thought about how righteous my anger was. Matt was entitled to his choices. But my choices were objectively better. How could he not recognize that crossing the Atlantic to eat dinner from the frozen-food aisle means leaving part of life unlived? How could he not see that trying new things—precisely *because* you're unsure whether you'll like them—widens the angle of your inner lens?

Maybe I was just hungry or bitter about my failed paddle-out or on my second glass of wine, but the conflict between pintxos and pizza began to feel like part of a larger schism. It's often described as a clash between globalism and populism. But that, I decided, was not really correct. The true dividing line is between those who embrace the terrifying hugeness of the world and those who fight to shrink it.

Also, I thought, *and this is totally unrelated, but why does Matt never offer to split his quattro formaggi with me?*

I learned the next morning that my brother-in-law, in his own way, was also pondering questions of culture.

"I thought I'd like Spain," he said, "but I feel so weird here. I hate being a gringo."

"Good news!" I replied. "I'm pretty sure the word *gringo* is used in Central and South American Spanish, not Spanish Spanish. So you have nothing to worry about."

If Matt found this helpful, he didn't mention it. We decided to go to France.

The French border, just a half hour from Zarautz, was one of those European ones that you can cross without a passport or even noticing. Still, I hoped a new country might mean a new start. The early feedback was encouraging. Ten minutes after reaching Gallic asphalt, we stopped for gas at a Carrefour shopping plaza and Matt threw up his arms in delight.

"This is basically Wegmans!" he exclaimed, referring to his favorite supermarket back home. Not long after, he discovered a boulangerie whose grilled-chicken sandwich he liked almost as much as the ones he made himself. It was a bit strange—most people's favorite thing about France is not that it reminds them of New Jersey—but the fact remained. My brother-in-law was a Francophile.

After taking a look at French waves, so was I. We parked our car on a high stone bluff above a break called Lafitenia, grabbed our boards, and wound down a footpath to the rocky beach. The green hills formed a *V* framing an ocean with the grayish tinge of a blue jay's crest. What really made me swoon, though, was a flat deepwater channel extending from the beach. With no whitewash or current, paddling out was a breeze, and I reached the center of a small cove feeling positively springy. A wall of water approached in a spirit of bonhomie, as though it might kiss me on both cheeks. I pivoted my board and took off.

"Nice turn and burn!" Matt yelled as I paddled back. For some reason, the French riders only went right, so the two of us had the left to ourselves. For the first time all trip, we were happy simultaneously.

As the tide dropped, a different class of surfer joined the crowd. Bony, chiseled, with faces made for taking drags of unfiltered cigarettes and staring into the abyss, these newcomers fixated on a rocky headland far outside, where no peaks were crashing. Then, as though they'd heard a whistle audible only to grim-looking French people, they began paddling in that direction. Just as the first riders reached their destination, the tide whooshed out, revealing skewers of red-brown rock underneath. The water churned in a drumroll. Waves began breaking off the reef.

The new takeoff section was narrow. Wary of being shish-kebabbed on the rocks, I sat just to its right, and for a minute Matt joined me and observed. Then a set rolled through and he lunged like a dog flushing a pheasant. His ride took him all the way to the beach.

"Wow, I really liked that!" he said upon returning. It was the most enthusiastic he'd been all trip. "It doesn't seem like much, and the rocks are really shallow, but it shoots you forward fast."

He turned toward the peak, eager to catch another, but the crowd had grown and the takeoff point was mobbed.

"I think I have to go deeper," he announced.

By "going deeper," he meant getting closer to the peak, just as he had at The Slot in Santa Cruz. He maneuvered one yard to his left, then another. Before long, he'd drawn nearer to the porcupining rock than even the bravest French surfer dared go. I could see he was being unusually precise with his movements—paddling in spurts, pulling up at the last second, measuring distances and timings in his mind. Matt was so focused, in fact, that he failed to notice the shortboarder coming up behind him.

It was a carbon copy of the guy who had yelled at me in Darlington—same scrawny frame, same ragged brown hair, even the same neckbeard. He drew within a foot of Matt's board, then startled him by leaning into his face.

"Why are you going so deep?" His accent was almost cartoonishly French.

"I dunno," Matt replied, trying to keep things friendly. "I just thought it'd be a good spot."

"Are you . . . *le snake*? Do you feel at home here?"

The shortboarder added something I couldn't understand, but which included the word *maison*. Matt, realizing he was in trouble, raised his hands in a hold-no-weapon gesture.

"It's cool, man. Take any wave you want."

"Humph," snorted the Frenchman, glaring until Matt retreated from the lineup. I paddled over.

"Want to head back to the cove?" I asked.

"Nah, I think I'm done," Matt said. He went in quickly. I followed. We plodded up the footpath.

"What do you think his problem was?" he finally asked as we neared the parking lot.

"I think he was just mad you're a better surfer than he is," I said encouragingly.

"If we'd gotten in a fight, I would've won," Matt declared.

"Oh yeah," I agreed. "He didn't look like the fighting type."

By the time we were halfway to the Spanish border, I was trying to turn the incident into an inside joke. "What are you, *le snake*?" I asked, as Matt passed a Peugeot on the highway. He played along at first—"You feel at home here?"—and I was surprised to discover his French accent was much better than mine. But the bit quickly wore thin. He'd been rattled. The next day we went to a different spot on the French coast, and when a small pack of locals showed up, Matt was so careful to keep his distance I worried he might paddle back to Spain.

~~~~~~~~~~

That afternoon, I got a phone call I'd been waiting for. A political friend who knew a lot about New Jersey was on the line.

"It's great you're thinking about running," he said, before listing all the reasons I shouldn't. Vindictive local party bosses. Time away from home. Negative ads that make tens of thousands of strangers hate you. His final point was sadly inescapable in an era of broken campaign finance.

"What do you think the number would be?" I asked.

"For a primary in this district? Three million. Maybe four."

It was a lot. Still, as I paced the cobblestone streets, my steps grew steadily more determined. *I could do this.*

I smiled as I walked. And as I walked, I realized I was smiling not at the thing sparking my enthusiasm, but at the enthusiasm itself. Eighteen months earlier, I'd struggled to find the courage to get out of bed. I was convinced the best was over, that the world and I had peaked. Now, upon hearing of a potential new adventure, the first thoughts to pop into my head were full of evidence-free optimism. I could help. I could matter. I was ready to rejoin the world.

Then another, less familiar thought struck me: *Yes, you could do this. But should you?*

I stopped walking. Should we sell our cottage in Asbury Park, a town we loved, to move across district lines? Should Jacqui and I upend our lives together so I could hit the trail? Should I call everyone I'd ever met and ask them to donate money—in a year when democracy faced existential threats—so I could have a slightly larger chance of winning a primary campaign against people with whom I basically agreed?

I was excited to dream big again. But this specific ambition summoned a disturbing phrase to mind: *down-the-beach syndrome.*

By the time I returned to our apartment an hour later, I was ninety percent sure I didn't want to throw my hat in the ring. There was no way to know for certain if, by not running, I would be making the right choice. But I also knew that if I made the wrong choice, it would be okay. I was thirty-seven years old. There was plenty of time.

~~~~~~~~

All week, Surfline had called for a monster swell to arrive on the second-to-last day of our trip. Even I was skeptical. Outliers in the long-term forecast usually return to normalcy as lead time shrinks. But this one didn't change. The night before, the app predicted double-overhead waves at Zurriola. That was easily twice as high as anything I'd surfed before.

"Maybe we should head back to France," I said. "It's only supposed to be six feet there."

"Nah," said Matt. He was done crossing borders. "Zurriola's the move."

His tone made clear that it was useless to argue. Besides, a small part of me agreed. If I could tackle a double-overhead wave in Spain, an overhead one in Hawaii would be substantially less intimidating. I lay awake in terror most of the night, but when morning arrived, I downed a tortilla, chugged the Celsius I'd stowed in my checked luggage for exactly such a moment, and headed to the beach with Matt.

The rucksack-wearing German was nowhere in sight. Even some of the Spaniards had stayed home. I didn't blame them. The waves were so massive they were difficult to comprehend. It seemed more reasonable that the bay was full of tiny surfers riding waves of normal size. It was only once my feet touched the sand, and the vibrations from the crashing lips shot past my knees, that the enormity and violence became real to me.

Matt went straight for the biggest peaks. I knew I'd never be able to paddle out behind him, so this time I headed for what had until recently been the kiddie pool. Even there, the walls of water were now chest-high, and it took me several minutes to fight through. Then, careful to stay outside the breaking waves, I paddled in search of Matt.

I found him on the left side of the beach, near the headwall. He was paddling too hard to say much, but he nodded and waved when he saw me. I fought my way to him, always keeping one eye on the advancing swell, and finally reached him during a brief lull.

"Big," I panted.

"Yeah," he said.

The peaks, as tall as ranch houses, careened about the cove in strange directions. Some broke almost perpendicular to the beach. Matt seemed to have the angles figured out, and he caught a few large rights. But his balletic grace had been sacrificed for something more intense and practical. He surfed like a man defusing a bomb.

I had almost worked up the nerve to try a takeoff of my own when I saw something that stopped me. A Spanish surfer, lithe and athletic, charged for a set wave, clawing for the ledge and trying to get onto the face. He almost made it. But not quite. On a peak of that size, there is nothing as dangerous as almost but not quite making it. The lip snatched him at the highest possible point, then flung him at full speed toward shore. It was like watching someone get chucked out a second-story window. He flew off the wave and hung in midair for ages, limbs frozen and useless, wings without feathers. Then he slammed against the ocean and was swallowed by the foam.

If I rode a wave that size, it would make the whole trip worth it. But I'd only get one chance. If I fell and landed in the impact zone, there was no way I'd have the strength to paddle back out.

"They're good," Matt said, returning to the lineup.

"Yeah?" I said.

"You gonna go?"

"Maybe," I said.

I wanted to say more. To admit that the week meant to get us stoked for the North Shore had left me feeling the opposite. To apologize for my insistence that he share my definition of adventure. To wonder if we were asking too much from each other.

I doubt I would have said these things no matter how much time we had. But Matt's eyes went wide, and when I looked toward the horizon I knew we had no time. Coming toward us was the biggest peak we'd seen all day, at least two feet more giant than the giants around it. Wordlessly, we started sprinting. There was no question of riding this wave. It was going to break too far outside. The only question was whether we could get up and over it before it broke.

I'd paddled hard before, but this was a new level of wildness, a surge of adrenaline I didn't know my body could produce. My breath was ragged. I couldn't feel my arms. The wall rose before us, towered over us, blocked out the sun. I kept going. I was almost there.

I'm gonna make it, I thought.

"We're in trouble!" Matt yelled.

And that was the last thing I heard before the lip pitched me through the air.

CHAPTER SIXTEEN

Nothing's Worse Than Knowing Too Much

FOR A LONG TIME I WAS WEIGHTLESS. In free fall. Bracing myself to hit the water with a full-body slap. But the impact never came. The crashing lip, as powerful as a jackhammer, blasted through the surface, and I flew down the resulting sinkhole until my right hip bounced against the sand. Then the sea washed over me like a coffin lid and the hold-down buried me alive.

At first I held it together. *Don't worry. Wait it out.* But I'd developed a mental hourglass during hurricane wipeouts in New Jersey, and I could feel it running dry. I'd never been underwater this long before. I'd never pinwheeled so violently. I raised an arm, expecting to punch through the ocean's surface, but all I felt was more ocean. Water streamed up my nose and down my throat. *How deep am I? How long have I gone without breathing? Something's wrong.* Panic setting in, I thrashed frantically upward, water surging through the corners of my mouth each time I fought to suppress a breath. When, finally, the wave lost interest, I burst into the sunlight and took shallow, rapid breaths. My neck was sore with whiplash, my tonsils swollen from salt.

Matt, who'd managed to duck under the lip that threw me, caught a wave and rode it toward shore. I paddled over, relieved to see him. But he looked, if anything, even more shaken than I was.

"You gotta hang on to your board," he said. "That was really close back there."

I didn't know what to say. I'd tried to grip the rails, but I hadn't been strong enough. I'd ditched. And Matt had been sprint-paddling right behind me. If he'd been just a few inches closer, or my board had flown backward at a slightly different angle, it could have knocked his teeth out, or knocked him out, or both.

We'd faced hundreds of waves together, maybe thousands. On the most consequential one yet, I'd been nothing more than a liability.

Matt kept his distance for the rest of the session. He did the same the following day, our last in Europe. That night we shared a room at an airport hotel in Bilbao—he somehow found Spanish Nickelodeon—and when we parted ways the next day it was with a fist bump rather than a hug.

A few days after returning to New Jersey, I tried my usual spot at Loch Arbour and, when a waist-high right arrived, couldn't go. I felt like one of those too-smart cars that automatically slams on the brakes when it detects even a hint of an impending collision. Something deep inside me never wanted to be trapped underwater, for any length of time, ever again. For the rest of October, unless conditions were perfect, and they mostly weren't, I stopped paddling out. I told myself I was saving strength for the North Shore. In truth, my stoke was gone.

Matt told me he wasn't surfing much, either. That seemed suspicious. *Maybe he's surfing, just not with me*, I thought.

If that was the case, I honestly didn't mind. Spain was supposed to cement our foundation. Instead, it had revealed new cracks. I'd thought twelve months of surfing together would render our differences irrelevant, but the divide between us now seemed less bridgeable than ever. Even when sharing a brand-new experience, as we had in Europe, we lived in polar-opposite worlds. No matter how much time we spent together, how many waves we caught or didn't, that wasn't going to change.

I never considered canceling our Hawaii trip. I wasn't looking forward to it, though. I hadn't been this terrified of consequential waves in months. I hadn't been this tense about spending time with my brother-in-law ever. Whenever I opened my Google Calendar, I counted down the days to our November 4 flight grimly. Before I knew it, Matt and I were headed to Newark once again.

I wouldn't describe the atmosphere between us in the airport as frosty. It was formal, though, as if we were divorced parents on their best behavior at a wedding. Embarking on what should have been the trip of a lifetime, we spoke only of logistics: gate numbers, security lines, the difficulty of checking oversized luggage. On the eleven-hour flight, his eyes remained glued to his Nintendo Switch. Mine remained glued to my computer. Neither of us tried making conversation.

"I got us a minivan!" I announced in Honolulu. It was nearly identical to our surfmobile from Santa Cruz, and I presented it as a goodwill gesture, a tribute to our shared past.

"Okay," Matt said flatly. We loaded our bags and headed north.

As is the case with most Pacific islands, the wind on Oahu—and thus the rain—comes from one direction only, leaving the east side

lush and the west side dry in an ecological mullet. The road running from the Honolulu airport to the North Shore slices through
the close-cropped end, and after a right turn near Pearl Harbor,
we drove between the shoulders of dead volcanoes into pineapple
plantations and the scrubby remnants of old sugarcane fields.

Then, as though our minivan were a roller coaster approaching
its first drop, we crested a hill and saw it. Line after line of perfect, breaking waves. Birthed from storms in the distant Aleutian
Islands, they, too, had traveled a long way to reach Hawaii. Now, as
we wound down the mountainside toward the town of Haleiwa, we
watched them charge toward shore, trip, and fall like crashing sumo
wrestlers over tendrils of hardened lava.

As the sun began to dip, we reached the North Shore itself. We
rounded Waimea Bay, home to the planet's most prestigious big-wave
competition, then passed the Foodland shopping plaza that serves
as the Seven-Mile Miracle's unofficial town square. Minutes later, we
reached the parking lot for Pipeline. This small stretch of sand, and
the wave that breaks beyond it, is to surfers what Notre Dame is to
cathedral enthusiasts. People spend their whole lives dreaming about
standing just a few dozen yards from where we were now.

"Want to stop, just to see it?" I asked Matt.

"That's okay," he said.

Our rented apartment, a few miles down the road, had stunning
views. You could even see a corner of Sunset Beach from our porch.
But the place seemed designed to answer the question "How can
an Airbnb with a location this good be so affordable?" and it did
nothing to improve Matt's mood. The screen doors were busted. A
cheerful note on the table informed us that "friendly critters" would

arrive if we forgot to take out the trash. The refrigerator was set to room temperature.

"Who wired this place?" Matt wondered aloud, flicking switches.

"Maybe you'll need to move here and fix it," I joked.

"Nah," he said. "I'm never leaving New Jersey."

I lay awake in thought that night, trying to figure out why he was so cranky. The North Shore is home to roving packs of wild chickens, and because these chickens greet the dawn not with *cock-a-doodle-doo*s but with bloodcurdling screams, I lay awake in thought that morning, too. It was futile, though. His sour mood remained a mystery to me. By the time I cracked open my morning Celsius, I'd reached a new conclusion.

Who cares if he's cranky? This is your big trip. You've got surfing to do.

~~~~~~~~~

"I think Lani's is the move," Matt said later that morning. He was sitting at a small table by the window, his own empty Celsius and a plate of toast crumbs in front of him, scrolling through Instagram.

"Fine by me," I replied. I'd read that the break, whose name is short for Laniakea and which sits on the Haleiwa side of Waimea Bay, was popular among longboarders and surf schools. It seemed like a low-pressure way to start. We drove down the two-lane Kamehameha Highway and parked the minivan on the shoulder of the road beside a horse farm. Matt grabbed his Pyzel. I'd left surfboard Stewart in New Jersey—I felt it was too big to travel with—but had rented a locally shaped board of similar length.

We followed a dirt path that ran along the road and wound

beneath a gnarled pine. It felt strangely claustrophobic. Then we stepped into the light and saw open ocean. The landscape was pure paradise, with green volcanic spines slicing into turquoise water. But it was a threatening beauty, like one of those skeletal fashion models whose runway glare is full of wrath. Coarse, sticky sand clung to my feet. The beach smelled sulfuric, as though someone had buried eggs there. Powerful currents crisscrossed; many ran for miles out to sea.

Most menacing of all, the waves broke so far from us they resembled children's drawings of waves rather than the real things. I'd never been more than a hundred yards from shore on a surfboard. Lani's was at least three times that distance. I watched a trio of fit, confident-looking older women stride into the water. They allowed an undersea current to sweep them north and west, changed trains at an invisible station, and rode a new current east to the lineup.

"Let's get after it," I said to Matt. I'd hoped to sound brave, but my voice lacked enthusiasm, and I waited until he was a distant figure before hopping on my board to follow.

Almost at once, my throat tightened as adrenaline surged. I'd paddled out in rips before, but this one was different. It felt like being vacuumed. When, after a minute, I looked back over my shoulder, the people on the beach were the children's drawings. I lurched free from the channel and paddled in search of Matt, heart racing even more from terror than from exertion.

The Lani's lineup couldn't have been less like that of a crowded day in Jersey. There were no foamies in sight. Every surfer had the quiet, firm confidence of those who take their competence for granted. They skewed male, but only barely. Also, there were older people in the water. I couldn't figure out their exact ages. Lives spent outdoors had given them the bright eyes of teenagers and the skin of mummies. But despite their years, or because of them, they surfed longboards stylishly, aggressively, with quick pivots off the lip.

The waves bore no resemblance to Jersey, either. Nearly all big swells bump into something—an island, a continental shelf—that slows their momentum as they travel from their stormy origins toward shore. But on the more than one-thousand-mile journey between the Aleutians and the North Shore, there are no speed bumps. The first thing a wave hits, at full momentum, is the reef. The second thing it hits is you. Without even trying a takeoff, I could see the difference in power between a chest-high peak at Loch Arbour and one at Lani's. It was the difference between being bull-rushed by a person and being bull-rushed by a bull.

That morning, listening to the chickens howl, I'd been determined to recover my wavering courage. Now, adrift, I seized up. All the mantras I'd learned—*focus on paddling when you're paddling; lift your chest; get your shoulders down the line; fully commit*—felt puny and ridiculous in Hawaii, the way Nerf arrows might if you brought them to a war. I kerplopped over the rail. I windmilled backward into the sea. I got tangled in my leash as I popped up. It was like surfing on my Wavestorm all over again. Then there were the hold-downs. They weren't the longest or most violent I'd ever experienced, but they were more than long and violent enough, and after Spain I could feel myself start to panic each time I plunged underwater.

Matt and I didn't get too close. Occasionally, though, I spotted him, and I could see he was struggling, too. Better surfers frequently beat him to the peak. When he did catch a wave, its outsized power seemed to flummox him. He puzzled his way along the face, as if trying to open a lock whose combination he'd forgotten.

After each wipeout, I was supposed to tell myself, *Good job! You're a better surfer than you were before.* Instead, I had a very different thought:

If this is the North Shore definition of a beginner break, what on earth is overhead Sunset going to be?

Neither of us was ready to find out. In the afternoon, we took our minivan to Chun's Reef, which is one break to the east of Lani's and regarded as an even friendlier spot. It made no difference. The paddle-out was just as brutal. I got whomped just as hard.

On countless occasions since I'd picked up a surfboard, it had felt like the ocean was trying to kill me. Now, after less than three hours of surfing the North Shore, I finally knew the truth. The ocean didn't care. The waves could snap my leash, beat my head against a reef, deposit my unconscious body in a deep-sea trench for sharks to feast on, and continue on their way as though nothing whatsoever had occured. It's the most violent and oppressive form of power: the ability to hurt someone without even noticing them.

This realization did not exactly help my surfing. "It's like when a pitcher gets the yips and can't find the strike zone," I explained to Matt, during a rare moment when we found ourselves next to each other.

"Uh-huh," he replied, not really listening.

Too late, I realized why. The first wave of a cleanup set broke directly on top of me, flipping my board like a Prohibition-era gangster flicking a toothpick into the trash. Fighting against the underwater current, I felt pain slice from heel to toe as one of my fins hit my right foot. My mouth filled with salt as I yelped underwater. When I resurfaced, I realized Matt had been taken out by the wave as well. I turned toward him, yanking my ankle parallel to my head.

"Am I bleeding?" I yelled.

"This is no time to think about bleeding!"

I hoped I'd severed an artery—that would show him—but I barely had a bruise. That night, by way of apology for my lack of toughness, I drove alone to Foodland and offered to buy Matt a frozen pizza. He told me he'd stocked up on chicken tenders and didn't need anything else. When I returned to the apartment, he was sitting on the couch, flipping between YouTube videos of Joe Rogan podcasts. I went straight to bed.

The next morning we met up with Zach, a local guide with the sweeping hair and equal-opportunity enthusiasm of a Disney Channel heartthrob.

"This," he said at our first stop, "is Sunset Beach."

It was a strangely low-key introduction. But still: I was standing in the spot I'd pictured most often when I'd pictured the North Shore, staring at the break Josh from Costa Rica and Lenny from Waco said I might, just might, be able to ride. To my right, a mile of sand swept up a peninsula before narrowing to a jagged point. To my left, a deep, flat channel stretched to the horizon. Together, they formed the walls of a gigantic, U-shaped arena, a coliseum of consequential surf. The waves were even farther from shore than those at Lani's, but their deadly seriousness was obvious from where we stood. Surfers paddled toward them cautiously, respectfully, like subjects approaching a throne.

Is today the day? I wondered.

"Swell's not great for Sunset," said Zach. "Let's check some other spots."

"Sounds good," I said, barely able to hide my relief.

On the Surfline map, the wave we tried next had been dubbed Chambers, but its original name was Gas Chambers, and that's what everyone calls it. I could tell right away we wouldn't surf there. The waves were tricky, pitchy and unpredictable, and they broke so close to shore that riders dodged stalagmites of exposed rock. Still, Gas Chambers is one of the most famous breaks along the Seven-Mile Miracle, and Zach was a local expert, so I peppered him with questions about the area. Matt sat on the hull of a beached catamaran, bouncing with impatience. By the time we headed back to the car he seemed ready to shed his skin.

"We know a lot more than we did when we started!" I said brightly.

"Yeah, well," Matt said, "nothing's worse than knowing too much."

We ended up back at Lani's. I was feeling less panicked, ready to snag a ride good enough to snap me from my slump. But I couldn't get one. Occasionally, the lip shoved me into the pounding whitewater. More often, I missed the wave altogether.

"You've got to relax," said Zach, which is the kind of advice helpful only to someone who doesn't need it.

That afternoon, I lay on the mildewed futon in our tiny living room and felt sorry for myself. Matt sat down on the couch across from me and turned on the TV. I was hoping he might make a peace offering of his own. *Seinfeld* would have been nice. Instead, he opened the YouTube app and slowly, deliberately, scrolled through videos of Joe Rogan again before settling on an interview with Tucker Carlson.

Around four o'clock, we agreed it was finally time to try surfing the Seven-Mile Miracle. The peaks were forecast to be only chest-high, so there was no chance this would be the day I encountered the overhead wave I'd been working toward. Nonetheless, my mouth was dry as we stood by the minivan, talking about where to go. Matt suggested a break called Kammieland—Kammie's, for short—that shared the same deepwater channel as Sunset.

"You sure?" I asked. "When Zach pointed it out, he said Kammie's looked pretty gnarly."

"Yeah, but it was empty. We'll just be careful."

"Here's the thing, Matt. Not to be rude, but I've never really associated you with 'careful.'"

He stopped in his tracks. His expression turned deadly serious. I'd never seen this look on his face before. He didn't seem angry. He seemed hurt.

"I'm super careful out there," he said. "If I get injured doing something that's not on the job, I don't get workers' comp."

Is that why he's been acting so strangely? I wondered. *Did I think he was being cranky, when in fact he's . . .*

It had never crossed my mind that, where surfing was concerned, Matt was even capable of feeling afraid. Nor had I appreciated how much he had to fear. "You don't have anything to worry about," he'd told me the first day we'd surfed together. "You can break your body and still do your job." I'd thought of his remark as another example of how little we understood each other. Now, I realized I'd been at least half right. I hadn't understood him at all.

As we walked down the path toward Kammie's, Matt didn't say much. I didn't blame him. I felt foolish and ashamed the whole way to the beach, and even more so once we saw the water. For a man who distrusted all forms of bigness, surfing was a way to distill the world. At Deal or the dog beach, my brother-in-law could reduce the universe to him and a single wave. He was master of his fate. But on the North Shore, you don't surf a single wave. You surf the ocean. What could be bigger, more terrifying, than that?

With new respect, I watched him paddle out, his board an alabaster leaf against the midnight-blue channel. He wasn't charging ahead because he was fearless. He was harnessing his fear.

As Matt had predicted, the place was practically empty, just a pair of teenaged redheads and a silver-haired man in long sleeves. But rather than go right for a wave, Matt sat on the shoulder of the takeoff zone, observing.

"What do you think?" I asked him.

"Looks good," he said. Then he nodded in the direction of the three surfers already out there. "I just don't want to get in their way."

I hesitated a moment, wondering if I should even bother trying another peace offering. Then I opened my mouth, and spoke in my best French accent.

"What are you," I asked, "*le snake*?"

The nose of his board still facing the wave, Matt turned his head toward me. I could tell I was not fully forgiven. But he couldn't help himself. He laughed.

~~~~~~

Kammie's was by far the trickiest wave I'd ever surfed. While the peak was double-black-diamond steep, the shoulder beside it was bunny-slope flat. Paddle more than a surfboard's width to the right of the pocket and I'd miss the wave entirely; paddle an inch too far left and I'd fall down an elevator shaft.

In our five-person lineup, the silver-haired guy and one of the teens made riding the wave look easy. The other teen and I made it look hard. This left Matt in a position I'd never seen him occupy before. Average. For the first few minutes, he stared at the breaking lip, perplexed. When the teens paddled in, giving him more space, he seemed relieved.

The real change came after he took off on a few waves, gauged the depth of the water, and realized the reef was a safe distance below the surface. No longer afraid of hitting the bottom, he surfed like himself again. Instead of seeking the sweet spot next to the cracking lip, he muscled his way over the ledge, nailed the elevator drop, and leaned into the wave as it broke against him. His technique wasn't elegant, but it worked. Once on the face, he turned up and down the wave for hundreds of yards.

"*That* was pretty awesome," he said after he got back.

"It *looked* awesome," I replied.

There was a lull, so we kept chatting. It was the first time we'd made small talk in weeks. I hadn't realized how much I'd missed it.

The subject turned, perhaps inevitably for men of our age, to hair loss. "Finasteride is the cream one, right?" Matt asked.

"No, finasteride is Propecia."

"I thought they were different."

I paddled until our boards were nearly touching, so I could hear him over the trade winds.

"Finasteride's the name of the drug! Propecia is the brand name!"

"Oh. What's the other one, Oxanyl?"

"Minoxidil! Rogaine!"

"Oh yeah, Rogaine!"

A pulse of swell took us both by surprise. I glanced at Matt. *You want this one?* His look in reply was both offer and order: *All yours.*

I turned my board, trying to pick the perfect mantra. Instead, all I could think was, *Oh shit.*

And then I was up. Maybe the mantras were part of me now. Maybe sometimes good things happen for no reason. Whatever the case, I was riding. Not well, mind you—the lip jolted me and I bent at the waist, flailing my arms—but I regained my balance, felt the grip of wax against my feet, and soared down the line. The face opened before me, a clean slate, a blank canvas, wondering what we might create together. I answered by cruising toward the breaking lip, leaning back down the face, and letting thousands of miles of ocean push me back into the pocket. Then I turned down the line and did it again. By the time the ride was over, I was nearly at the beach.

"*That* was pretty awesome," I said to Matt when I finally returned to the lineup.

"*Looked* awesome," he replied.

That evening, Matt chose a Joe Rogan episode involving mixed martial arts rather than politics, and in exchange I didn't totally tune it out. It was Election Day in New Jersey, though, so I scrolled through my phone as results came in.

"Whoa!" I announced to Matt, who had gotten up to wash dishes in the sink. "A Democrat won the mayor's race in Brick."

"I don't think it really matters," he said, moving a plate to the drying rack. "I don't think my life is gonna be different depending on who gets elected."

"What about health care? Or school districts? Or climate change?"

"Nah," he replied. "I think everything in my life is really just because of my own decisions. I think I'd live in the same house, make the same amount of money, same everything."

I tried again. "What about tax rates? Those affect how much money you make, and they depend on who's elected." Matt listened with the polite smile of someone who already knows what he's going to say.

"Yeah, I don't think you convinced me to vote."

Matt finished the dishes and, to my relief, put on *Seinfeld*. We watched together in silence, each splitting our attention between the TV and our phones. Then he looked up. He must have seen something on his Instagram feed, because he had a concerned expression on his face.

"Hamas is the group that wants to kill all the Jews, right?"

He'd never before asked me about a subject this sensitive, and I answered carefully. "At the moment," I said, "they're primarily trying to kill Israelis. But I don't think they'd like me much, either."

Matt thought about this for a while, taking several deep breaths.

"Well," he said finally. "You could always try to find common ground with them by taking them surfing."

We both laughed darkly. But the next morning, shortly after sunrise, I stared at the ceiling and frowned. Matt's joke had contained a kernel of truth—and it was one of those kernels that gets stuck in your teeth and won't stop irritating you, no matter how much you worry it with your tongue. I *had* hoped the two of us would find common ground through surfing. I didn't think we'd end up seeing eye-to-eye on everything. But I'd imagined that on big, consequential, divisive issues, we would find ways to agree.

That hadn't happened. Not on voting, not on Joe Rogan, not on "The Vid," not on the link between soy and testosterone or the urgency of fighting climate change or the fundamental question of whether it's better to solve problems together or alone. We surfed. We disliked the same Capitola burrito joint. Each of us was, in our way, frightened by the bigness of the world. But when it came to the culture war into which we'd been drafted, the divide that defined us, nothing had changed.

Not all of our disagreements were matters of opinion. In some cases, one of us was objectively right. And usually, it was me. But this was cold comfort at 5 a.m., staring at a busted ceiling fan and wondering where we'd gone wrong.

I tried to distract myself by reading the news, then by scrolling social media, and then, when those things didn't work, by opening Surfline.

The moment I saw the forecast for Sunset, I knew I wouldn't be falling back asleep.

Head-high to a bit overhead. Good swell direction. Mild winds.

It was time.

CHAPTER SEVENTEEN

Between Us

SUNSET WOULD BE BEST in the early afternoon. That meant several hours of anxious waiting before we could paddle out. Matt read, scrolled through his phone, and watched TV. I stepped onto the porch and listened to a podcast while waxing and rewaxing my board. Sometime around the sixth or seventh coat, one of my tiny black earbuds slipped loose and tumbled over the balcony onto the lava rock below. I peered over the railing but couldn't spot it. I turned up the volume on the podcast but couldn't hear it. I was staring at the ground, brow furrowed, when I had an idea. I poked my head through the broken screen door.

"Hey, Matt," I asked, "could you recommend some heavy metal?"

"What kind?"

"Doesn't matter. Just needs to be loud."

He thought for a moment.

"Austrian Death Machine's pretty good."

A few seconds later, an unholy hiss echoed from beneath a rock. My earbud was soon back in hand. I went inside to make breakfast, and a few minutes later, as Matt and I each sipped a Celsius, we picked up our hair-loss discussion from the day before.

"My friend John's our age," he said. "Completely bald."

"You've got to look at his mom's dad. That's where baldness comes from."

"Actually, I don't think that's true," Matt replied carefully. "I think that's an old wives' tale."

"No, I definitely remember this from biology class," I said. But just to be sure, I googled it, and he was right.

By the time we were in the minivan for the two-minute drive to Sunset Beach, I was in shock. I'd spent the morning listening to death metal and accidentally sharing misinformation. He'd spent the morning carefully deciding how far to go in correcting his brother-in-law. I had half a mind to check my body for tattoos.

In the parking lot, we met up with a photographer friend of Zach's, a big-wave surfer named Saul I'd hired for the afternoon. With his mop of brown-blond curls and giant, hairy feet, Saul resembled a hobbit stretched to six foot three. When he spoke, his lips went into slow motion at the end of each sentence, as if savoring the final word.

"Lookin' *good*. We're gonna get some *shots*."

Sunset has the longest paddle-out on the North Shore, and one of the longest in the world, a full half mile. If that doesn't sound like much, imagine army crawling widthwise across Central Park. To conserve their energy before they reach the break, even experienced locals tend to ride slightly longer boards at Sunset. But Matt, contrarian as always, shot toward the point on his shortboard, leaving Saul and me behind.

Halfway to our destination, a massive peak emerged in the distance. It looked like a blue-green submarine breaching the surface parallel to shore. It rumbled toward us and I braced myself, certain I'd be demolished, but the wave bulged over the reef without breaking and sank back into the water. "On a really big day, that's where it's firing," said Saul. "The *bowl*. Really nice right. Don't go left, though, that's super dangerous. Anyway, it's too small for the bowl today. We're going to the *point*."

"Do you think it's head-high right now?" I asked, trying to sound casual.

"I don't think about that stuff, man. All I know is, this is *nice*."

We reached a second channel, not far from the point. While Saul readied his camera in its waterproof housing, I got my first up-close look at the wave.

Big peaks at Deal or Zurriola came out of nowhere. Sunset was the opposite. Each wall of water began building on the furthest edge of the horizon. It was like watching a time-lapse video of a sprouting plant. The wall grew and grew, and then it did something unusual. It stopped growing but didn't break. Instead, it charged forward at full strength, as unyielding as an oncoming locomotive, until it drew close enough to blot out the afternoon sun. At the very last second, the peak jacked up, gained a final burst of height, and went supernova against the reef.

In college, I took Chinese classes with a sophomore named Ken who played offensive line on the football team. He was a nice guy. Also, I heard through the grapevine that whenever he drank too much, which was often, he walked around knocking people out. It wasn't personal. For drunken Ken, leaving a trail of unconscious bros at a frat party was like turning off the light switches in a house. Violence was in his nature.

Ken was who I thought of as I looked at Sunset now.

As usual, Matt had leapt into action while I was thinking. By the time Saul had set up his camera, he was already halfway to the crowded lineup on his Pyzel. "*Dude*," Saul yelled after him. But it was as though the photographer and I were the parents of a teenager. Matt cruised toward the cool kids in the lineup, pretending we didn't exist.

"This isn't a typical break," Saul said to me, shaking his head. "I've been surfing here thirteen years. I could help him out."

"He doesn't really believe in experts," I explained.

"Okay, well, I'll tell *you*," Saul replied. "Don't go where the other guys are. If you stay inside and a little right, you'll have to wait a little longer, but you'll get the swells coming from the west. Those have more juice than the ones from the north."

I did as I was told. From my new vantage point, I could see Matt fifty yards to my left. He took off on a wave, but was behind the peak. The lip rolled him up and dropped him in the impact zone. A minute later, a set approached me from the west. I was observing it carefully, getting a feel for my surroundings, when I heard Saul yell.

"David, *go!*" Behind me, the sun went dark. I scraped at the water. The hand of God seized the tail of my board.

I'm totally gonna make it! I thought.

And I did.

I had learned the hard way that it's never a good idea to think while riding a wave. But I had also learned that in the moments after you've felt your way through a wave, you sometimes look back and realize you got a lot of thinking done. These were my thoughts about Sunset at the end of that first ride: It was not the biggest wave

I'd ever encountered, or the most technical, or the gnarliest. It was, by far, the most self-evidently a force of nature. To stand on a board with the entire ocean behind you, water rushing up that face, is to know that you are surrounded by something incomprehensible yet undeniable. This power isn't benevolent. It might clobber you. But it also might, if you pluck the flower of fear at the perfect moment, open the door to a world you would never encounter if you didn't take the leap.

I paddled over to Saul. I could tell he was excited, because he savored twice as many words.

"Nice, dude!"

I raced back to the lineup and did it again, this time on an even bigger peak. Saul missed that one—it's a cardinal rule of surfing that your best rides are never caught on camera—but on my third wave of the day a sun-shower arrived, sending a double rainbow from break to point, and I saw his lens follow me as I swooped beneath. It was a not-so-mild miracle.

Strangely, I still wasn't sure if I'd done what I'd come to Hawaii to do. Were these waves overhead? Or just under? Asking Saul again wouldn't help. Even on video it wouldn't be easy to measure, since camera angles can play tricks. All I knew, really, was that I was having an amazing time. I surfed and surfed.

I'd lost track of my wave count when I looked up to see Matt with a blank expression on his face. Saul, floating next to him, arched his eyebrows. "Wanna paddle over to Kammieland? Your brother-in-law here is getting kind of frustrated."

"Him? Frustrated?" I replied. Matt didn't find this funny. He was clearly done with Sunset for the day, and it was useless to argue.

"Sure," I said. "Let's do it."

We turned left toward the bowl, where the blue-green submarines surfaced and descended, and headed for Kammie's. The paddle over was just as long as the paddle-out, and we'd already been surfing big waves for an hour. Saul and I took the lead, chatting amiably. Matt, exhausted from pulling a shortboard through the ocean, lagged behind.

The sets at Kammie's were smaller than those at Sunset, but not by much, and this time the break was packed with shredders. Matt nabbed one or two rides. More often, he was beaten to the peak. Once, I watched him get hung up on the lip and tossed over the falls.

"Matt's gotta paddle harder for waves," Saul told me. "If he's letting other people go, they're gonna walk all over him." I scurried over and relayed the news.

"It's not that I'm not trying," Matt panted. "I'm just tired."

He wasn't kidding. I could practically see his tongue lolling. I returned to Saul.

"Where should I sit?"

"A little inside again. You won't have to work as hard. Matt should really be there, too, you know."

"He'll be all right. He's a way better surfer than me."

"Maybe," Saul said. "You're a better listener, though."

A few waves later, I looked toward the distant shore and saw Matt hauling his Pyzel onto the beach. He disappeared through the trees, in the direction of our apartment. Saul told me he could film a little longer, so I sat inside and caught more rights. Finally, after more than two hours of hard surfing, I grew cocky, went for a peak

I knew was already breaking, and crashed down the elevator shaft into the surf.

"Good wipeout footage!" Saul laughed.

I shrugged. "Can't win 'em all."

He looked at me conspiratorially. "Seems like you're winning the *heat*, though."

I stopped short. All session, I'd suspected I was catching more waves than Matt, and coaxing longer rides from them, too. But to have it confirmed by a North Shore local who'd seen the whole thing? I felt dense with guilty pleasure, like I'd just robbed a bank.

Matt and I didn't talk much that night. Instead of Joe Rogan, he turned on an episode of *South Park*. In it, AI takes the jobs of the town's white-collar professionals, and handymen, suddenly in short supply, become billionaires competing to launch vanity rockets into space. The episode sat at the intersection of our interests—the triumph of blue-collar workers on one hand, writers mocking the vain superrich on the other—and we each enjoyed it. But we never laughed at the same things. When the show was over, he ate his chicken tenders in silence, alone at the kitchen table. I sat on the couch, watching clips Saul had sent me. Finally, I looked out the window toward the sea.

"You know," I offered magnanimously, "I don't actually think the waves were bigger than the other day."

"No," Matt said glumly from the couch. "They were definitely bigger."

I started to reply, then stopped.

"So . . . are you saying . . . I surfed an overhead wave at Sunset?"

"Yeah," he said. "I believe so."

~~~~~~~~~~~~~

I slept like a baby despite the screaming chickens. At six the next morning, I sprang out of bed beaming, and I continued beaming as I strutted to the kitchen and put bread in the toaster. Eighteen months ago, at the advanced age of thirty-five, I'd canceled my first surf lesson out of terror. Now, I'd ridden overhead Sunset Beach.

And not only that. On the very same day, on the very same waves, I'd outsurfed my brother-in-law.

Matt strolled groggily from his room. For the past year I'd assumed his approach to life, as reflected in his surfing, meant he would always surf better than me. Not so. On one hundred percent of the days we'd paddled out at one of the world's most hallowed breaks, I'd trusted the experts, and he'd ignored them, and I'd triumphed. I buttered my toast proudly, haughtily, a lord of breakfast. Matt ate his own toast in silence. Then he said:

"Want to do Sunset again?"

He tried to sound casual. But I knew him too well. *He wants a second chance*, I smirked. *I'm on top of the leaderboard and he knows it.*

Then something very annoying happened. I began to feel bad for him. I didn't regret winning the heat. I didn't wonder if I should have backed off to preserve his ego. It was simpler than that. He'd had a rough day, and I wished he hadn't. As triumphant as I felt, I knew now that I would have much preferred to triumph with him rather than over him. Imagine if, on the day I'd caught my overhead wave, he'd caught a double-overhead one. *That* would have been special.

We washed dishes side by side, and I searched my sympathy for deeper meaning. If the best surfing days of our lives had coincided, would that have brought us closer together? Might a pair of epic waves have finally bridged our cultural divide? I thought about these questions for a long time, well after the plates were dry, and concluded, somewhat to my horror, that the answer was no.

I cared about him. That was all.

Sunset was even larger than it had been the day before, and we were both more tired, but Matt had finally agreed to borrow my backup mid-length board. On our way to the break, we resembled two ends of an inchworm. He raced out ahead of me, stopped to let me catch up, then sprang forward again. While we were rarely by each other's side, it was our first paddle-out I could remember in which he coordinated his movements with mine.

Matt had just reached the safety of the small, secondary channel when I looked over my shoulder and said, softly, to myself, "Oh no." It was as if King Kong had chucked a shipping crate in my direction. The block of water charging toward me in the bowl was the same height as the wave that threw me off the lip in Zurriola—easily head-and-a-half, maybe more—but supercharged by Sunset's open-ocean force. Every neuron in my body joined the same screaming chorus. *Sprint! Outside! Over the peak! To safety!* But I knew, without thinking, that I was going for it.

I popped up, and for a moment I had a sense of déjà vu. I was back at Deal. It was the first day Matt and I had ever surfed together. I was standing atop an open face and looking out at the world. But there were two big differences. That wave was the height of a kitchen counter; this was the height of a kitchen. Also, this time, I wasn't about to bail. I leaned into the face, hoping to gather speed. I felt myself slipping and fought with every muscle to stay on my feet.

Just before making it onto the shoulder, my front foot slid out of position and couldn't recover. My head cracked against the breaking lip, which grabbed me by the neck and plunged me underwater. Deep-sea rivers played catch with my body long after my lungs clamored for air.

When I washed to the surface, though, I was more stoked than ever. I hadn't caught the wave. I hadn't ridden it. I'd barely even taken off. But I'd gone for it, and wiped out hard, and waited out the hold-down without panicking.

Not just that. I was ready for more.

Maybe that explained why, twenty-four hours after surfing my first overhead wave at Sunset, I hadn't been seized by a crushing letdown. That's what I'd assumed would happen. It had always happened before. Writing my first speech for the president; publishing my first book; buying our first house. These accomplishments had felt amazing, at first. But the sense of satisfaction was soon swallowed by a chomping Pac-Man of emptiness. I'd imagined achievement would transform me, then been shaken to find myself untransformed.

This felt different. Or rather, I did. I was proud of what I'd done. But I was me before I rode the wave I'd been working toward, and I was still me after, and that was fine. The reward for having done it was to keep doing it. If I wanted to set my sights on a new, scarier peak, I could. If I wanted to surf simply because I enjoyed it, I could as well. While it had taken a few decades, at last I had realized: milestones tell you where you are, not who you are.

Back on my board, as I reached the point, I noticed that Matt was sitting inside, just as Saul had recommended the day before.

The first time I saw him take off, he stuck to the face and flew over the nose. Over the next half hour, though, he dialed it in. He began paddling for waves more frequently, riding them more assertively. He outsurfed me by miles. I was happy for him.

Then we both took a break to watch a maniac do something crazy.

He was, I think, in his mid-fifties, with tanned and leathery skin. He looked strong but not fit, and compensated for his receding hairline with three strands running nape-to-forehead along his scalp. One of his front teeth was missing. His board, decorated with a lightning bolt, was built for speed instead of turning. I could tell he was nuts, because he paddled to a spot guaranteed to put him behind the gnarly rights breaking in the bowl. Then I realized he was even more nuts than I thought. He was going left.

The wave I'd wiped out on earlier was the largest I'd ever seen. The wave he took off on was much, much larger than that. He rose to his feet, wobbling slightly before straightening out. White-blue water streamed from the tail of his bright red board as he hurtled down the face. It was like watching a comet blaze toward earth. When the wave finally spat him into the channel, just a few feet from Matt and me, his eyes were as wide as cue balls. He looked like a man who had not just seen the face of God but done cocaine with him.

"*Whaaaa!*" he yelled. "Wow!" Realizing he had an audience, he turned to us. "I'm gonna need a bomber jacket after that one, huh?" He paddled back to his mad, magic spot, his giant smile showing off his missing tooth.

Matt and I floated in shock. In some ways, now that he was surfing better than I was, the universe had restored itself. But we knew, in that moment, that neither of us had what it takes to be the nutjob on the lightning-bolt board. There were promised lands we would never see, mysteries of the universe that would forever go unsolved. For a moment we sat there, a two-person audience, floored and humbled and united by all we'd never know.

I gave him a look that said, *I'm not sure I would have believed this if you weren't here to witness it.* And while I'd never ask him to admit it, he gave me the same look back.

I thought back to Matt's quip from two nights ago. It was true. My brother-in-law and I had uncovered far less common ground than I'd expected. But we'd found far more neutral ground than I ever could have imagined. I'd spent a year thinking of these experiences—the waves and paddle-outs, car rides and grocery runs, tiffs with obnoxious locals and small talk in the water—as a means to an end. But this neutral ground mattered no matter what it led to. As Josh from Costa Rica certainly would not have put it, its value was intrinsic.

So no, we hadn't changed each other's minds. But we had changed each other. He'd made me more courageous at an age when most people start becoming more afraid. He'd made me more optimistic in a pessimistic era. He'd introduced me to things I'd never before encountered. To a really interesting interview with Kelly Slater. To the way waves open when you square your shoulders. To first light.

He also taught me how foolish it was to presume to know what he was thinking. Which is why, while I believe I changed him for the better, too, I'll leave it to him to decide whether that's the case, and if so, how to describe it.

Where I feel confident speaking for both of us is in saying we experienced so much more together than we ever would have apart. Two years earlier, keeping someone like Matt at arm's length had been a matter of principle. I felt a civic responsibility, if not to shun him, then at least to be unwelcoming until his worldview matched mine. It's hard to list all I would have missed out on—all *we* would have missed out on—if I hadn't betrayed my principles before it was too late.

That didn't mean everything turned out perfectly. Would I have preferred it if Matt had tried the local Hawaiian delicacies instead of the chicken tenders, abandoned his fundamentalist individualism for a spirit of solidarity, and given up Joe Rogan for NPR? Yes. Absolutely. Finding our piece of neutral ground was not perfect, or complete, or sufficient. But in a world on fire, few things are.

I didn't know it, but my time at Sunset was almost up. A few minutes after the man with the missing tooth came flying down the face, I felt a shard of fiberglass slice against my thigh. My big wipeout in the bowl had cracked my board across the middle like a fractured rib, rendering it unrideable. Matt offered to paddle in with me, but I told him he should stay out and surf. I had a feeling he wanted some time to himself, and, after chaperoning me for several days, it seemed only fair that he got it.

At a surf shop back in Haleiwa, I tried to sound chill, even when the guy behind the counter informed me my board was so badly buckled it couldn't be repaired.

"What do you think did it?" I asked, hoping, as we all do, that everything happens for a reason.

He shrugged.

"It's the North Shore," he said. Which felt like reason enough.

There was one more big item I wanted to take care of before we returned home. Technically it could have waited. While the first chapter of my surfing life was over, I knew there were plenty of family cookouts and Jersey summers and hurricane swells and 5/4 seasons and rented minivans in our future. But I also knew there's never a right time. You just have to go over the ledge.

"So, Matt," I said that night, as he watched Joe Rogan, "did you ever end up getting vaccinated?"

"Neh," he replied.

"Why not?" I asked.

I don't know when I first picked up the idea that talking about difficult issues resolves them. I was under no such illusion anymore. I didn't raise the issue of vaccines thinking I'd persuade Matt, and I doubted his reasoning would make sense to me, and I was right on both counts. And that was okay. What mattered about our conversation was not its contents, but the fact that we'd reached the point where it could take place.

So while "Why not?" wasn't the end of our discussion, it's the last part I'll describe. The rest is between us.

~~~~~~~~~

The next morning, the final one of our trip, I was watching waves out the window when Matt came over and stood next to me, Celsius in hand.

"You know," he said, "if I don't go and get walloped by big Sunset today, I won't regret it."

"You know," I replied, "neither will I."

We went back to Lani's, which despite everything was the break we knew best. As we rounded Waimea Bay, Matt sighed thoughtfully.

"Hawaii's tough," he said. "I feel really accomplished to have surfed here. But it wasn't fun. I'm always thinking about how I could have done better. Like, it's almost depressing."

"Matt," I said, soaking in the moment, "now you know how I feel literally every time we surf."

Lani's did not require a bomber jacket. Still, the waves were heavy, especially on the outer reef, where the sets were easily overhead. I stuck to the inside, feeling I'd earned the right to enjoy myself. I took off on manageable, chest-high waves and floated smoothly down the line. Sometimes I took a break from my own surfing and watched Matt. He'd become far more comfortable with open-ocean power, and he blasted out of turns with jet-pack speed, even as he danced with the wave. I could tell he was happy. Not New Jersey happy. Nothing could make him New Jersey happy. But close.

Finally, he paddled up to me. He looked oddly serene. "I've done everything I came to do," he announced. "I'm going in."

"Okay," I said. "I'll stay out just a little longer."

He nodded, caught a wave, then stood on the beach. I thought about sticking to the manageable inside peaks. Then I inched toward the big ones.

It is silly to tell yourself the last wave of a trip will be your biggest or steepest or scariest. But I'd long ago learned that there's no room for realism in surfing. As Matt waited patiently, I told myself it was time to ride the biggest wave of my life. A set came. It was massive. Two surfers to my right backed off, giving me priority on the peak. I paddled toward the point where I knew the wave would start to break, and leapt to my feet.

My hands flew skyward as my board fell out from under me. As always, time slowed. *I'm falling*, I thought. *I need to stop thinking*, I thought. And then I thought, *I refuse to fall on this one*. Instead of leaning back, I brought my weight forward, meeting the steepness of the face. I pressed my bare feet into the deck, gripping with strength I didn't know I had. There was an impact as I hit the flats, then an explosion of water behind me. The takeoff was far from perfect. But I was up. I was riding.

I was done.

It took me a few minutes to get back to the beach. When I hauled myself onto the sand, Matt was standing by the lifeguard tower, still staring out to sea. At first I thought he was looking for me. Then I realized he was just looking.

"So, what do you think?" I asked.

"It's pretty great," he said.

Was he talking about the break, the trip, the past year, everything? As usual with my brother-in-law, I couldn't tell.

"What do *you* think?" he asked.

I didn't answer right away. I wanted to do justice to his question. How did it feel to stand on sticky sand in a perilous paradise, plenty of life behind me but so much yet to come? How did it feel to have the opportunity of a lifetime, the opportunity to *have* a lifetime: to get better, to be part of things, to see rainbows across a broken world and smile, to commit without full knowledge, to relish a wipeout, to try although trying is not enough, to start, to start over, to start again?

I looked my friend in the eye and spoke honestly.

"Yeah," I said. "It's pretty great."

ACKNOWLEDGMENTS

UNLESS YOU HAVE A STRANGE FONDNESS for reading the acknowledgments first, you will not be surprised to learn that for the past several years, whenever Jacqui asked me how book writing had gone that day, my answer would often begin, "It's like taking off on a wave." There's a long list of similarities—enough, in my experience, to test even the most tolerant spouse's patience—but there's also one big difference. To write a book, you need people willing to go over the ledge with you.

With that in mind, I want to thank everyone who believed without evidence in *It's Only Drowning*, embracing a germ of an idea and refusing to give up on it until, finally, it became what I think it was supposed to be. I'm sure I'm forgetting some names, and I apologize in advance for that, but I wanted to express particular appreciation to:

My agent, Dan Greenberg, for being the first to encourage me to pursue this book, and for helping me begin to understand what it might become.

My editor, Max Meltzer. From the beginning, we spoke often about forming a true partnership, and to be honest I assumed that would mostly turn out to be empty talk. But it didn't. You put so much of yourself into this work, you were always there for me

Acknowledgments

(except when you were on paternity leave, which is pretty understandable), and I can't tell you how grateful I am.

Everyone at Gallery Books, starting with Jen Bergstrom, Aimée Bell, and Sally Marvin, who embraced *It's Only Drowning*, and me as a writer, from day one. And Lauren Carr, Sierra Fang-Horvath, Mackenzie Hickey, Jamie Selzer, Lloyd Davis, Jaime Putorti, and Brigid Black, who helped me polish this book, made it look great, and figured out how to get you to read it. So many authors have an endless supply of horror stories about their publishers; I'm thankful for my total lack of material.

Danny Germino-Watnick, whose job title was (I think) "assistant," but whose work went far beyond that. He was an ever-reliable sounding board as I tried to figure out how to tell this story, and a tough but fair critic who made me question my assumptions. His research, ideas, and proofreading are evident on every page.

Caroleine James and Omar Zakaria, who read early not-so-great drafts, provided thoughts that made them better, and, despite their youth, only occasionally referred to me as "middle-aged."

Everyone at Glide. Especially "Katie," who, while no longer my surf coach, is exceedingly patient each time I come into the shop, examine every surfboard on display, ask the same dozen gear-related questions I asked the last time I came in, and then leave with a single bar of wax.

Catherine Burns, for what is now frighteningly close to a decade of friendship and storytelling wisdom.

Stewart, my now-former therapist, for more than earning his retirement.

My mom, my dad, and my entire family, who are always there

for me—even when I do things they don't understand, like start surfing.

Jacqui, who, in addition to just generally being great, puts up with being married to a writer with shocking amounts of grace. I'm not quite sure how authors who aren't married to you manage, and I plan on not finding out.

And finally, Matt, for being cool with me writing this book and trusting me with what is your story, too. For reasons I will never fully understand, you said you didn't want to see an early copy and would wait until after the book was published to read it. I hope you liked it.